Politics and the Media in Britain

Raymond Kuhn

First published 2007 by
PALGRAVE MACMILLAN
Houndmills, Basingstoke, Hampshire RG21 6XS and
175 Fifth Avenue, New York, N.Y. 10010
Companies and representatives throughout the world

PALGRAVE MACMILLAN is the global academic imprint of the Palgrave
Macmillan division of St. Martin's Press, LLC and of Palgrave Macmillan
Ltd. Macmillan® is a registered trademark in the United States, United
Kingdom and other countries. Palgrave is a registered trademark in the
European Union and other countries.

ISBN 13: 978–0–333–92689–5 hardback
ISBN 10: 0–333–92689–7   hardback
ISBN 13: 978–0–333–92690–1 paperback
ISBN 10: 0–333–92690–0   paperback

This book is printed on paper suitable for recycling and made from
fully managed and sustained forest sources. Logging, pulping and
manufacturing processes are expected to conform to the
environmental regulations of the country of origin.

A catalogue record for this book is available from the British Library.

A catalog record for this book is available from the Library of Congress.

10   9   8   7   6   5   4   3   2   1
16   15   14   13   12   11   10   09   08   07

Printed in China

In memory of my sister
Kathleen
1949–1994

Contents

List of Tables

List of Abbreviations

AOL	America OnLine
BBC	British Broadcasting Corporation
BIB	British Interactive Broadcasting
BMA	British Medical Association
BMIG	British Media Industry Group
CBI	Confederation of British Industry
CCO	Conservative Central Office
CLEAR	Campaign for Lead-free Air
CND	Campaign for Nuclear Disarmament
DCMS	Department of Culture, Media and Sport
DTI	Department of Trade and Industry
DTT	digital terrestrial television
EC	European Commission
EPG	electronic programme guide
ERM	Exchange Rate Mechanism
EU	European Union
FAC	Foreign Affairs Committee
FOI	Freedom of Information
GUMG	Glasgow University Media Group
IBA	Independent Broadcasting Authority
IRA	Irish Republican Army
ITA	Independent Television Authority
ITC	Independent Television Commission
ITV	Independent Television
LWT	London Weekend Television
MMC	Monopolies and Mergers Commission
Ofcom	Office of Communications
Oftel	Office of Telecommunications
PEB	party election broadcast
PCC	Press Complaints Commission
TUC	Trades Union Congress
TVWF	Television Without Frontiers
UK	United Kingdom
US	United States

Acknowledgements

My thanks to various people who, sometimes unbeknown to themselves, helped me in the writing of this book. They include John Benyon, Ralph Negrine, Erik Neveu, Paul Smith, James Stanyer, Jeanette Steemers, Thierry Vedel, Mark Wheeler and Dominic Wring among others. I am grateful to all my colleagues in the Department of Politics at Queen Mary, University of London, for providing an atmosphere supportive of research and to those many students over the years who have contributed to seminar discussions on the politics of the media. I owe a particular debt of gratitude to Steven Kennedy at Palgrave for his encouragement and patience. Keith Povey and Marilyn Hamshere did an excellent job on the copy-editing. Above all, I should like to thank my wife, Shirley, for all her love and support.

This book is dedicated to my sister, Kathleen, who died of cancer at the age of 45 after a long illness.

RAYMOND KUHN

This book draws in places on earlier work published by the author. I should like to thank Routledge, Palgrave Macmillan and Cambridge University Press respectively for permission to include material reproduced or adapted from the following works: 'The First Blair Government and Political Journalism' in R. Kuhn and E. Neveu (eds), *Political Journalism: New Challenges, New Practices*, p. 52 (pp. 184–5 of this work), London, Routledge, 2002; 'The Media and Politics' in P. Dunleavy, A. Gamble, R. Heffernan and G. Peele (eds), *Developments in British Politics 7*, p. 149 & p. 150 (pp. 192 & 188 of this work) Basingstoke, Palgrave Macmillan, 2003; and 'Media Management' in A. Seldon and D. Kavanagh (eds), *The Blair Effect 2001–5*, pp. 95–110 (pp. 190–201 of this work) Cambridge, Cambridge University Press, 2005, © Cambridge University Press.

Introduction

The relationship between politics and the media in contemporary Britain is endlessly fascinating, generating questions which are of interest to practitioners, students and citizens alike. Do media proprietors exercise too much political power? Should we be worried about the 'spinning' activities of government? How is political journalism changing in the digital age? Are the media responsible for the 'dumbing down' of political communication?

This book seeks to address these and other questions at a time of significant change in the spheres of both media and politics in Britain. New technologies, outlets and genres now compete for audiences and revenue with traditional sources of media content, while audience consumption habits adjust to an era of digital supply and internet proliferation. This expansion of media has called into question some long-standing features of government policy, notably in the area of media regulation, as well as altering practices of public communication by a wide range of political actors. In politics, the Blair premiership was renowned – and in some quarters vilified – for the central importance it attached to political communication, from top–down management of the news agenda to the selection of appealing soundbites. The end of the Blair era draws a line under a particular example of communicative leadership. Yet his successors still have to deal with the demands of a 24/7 news culture, the need for image projection via the media and the constant critical scrutiny of political journalists. No political leader can simply afford to ignore the significance of public communication in an age of mediatized politics.

The book begins by addressing two fundamental questions: (1) What are the principal news media in Britain? (2) What are the key political functions they perform? Chapter 1 examines some of the main structural and operational features of the political news media of press, broadcasting and the internet over the past twenty-five years and then considers some of their important political functions such as information provision, agenda-setting and public watchdog.

Chapters 2–5 deal with aspects related to media policy. Chapter 2 focuses on the way in which values have helped to inform policy debates. For most of the twentieth century different sets of values underpinned the functioning of the two main news media in Britain: freedom (of the press) and public service (for broadcasting). This chapter examines the policy framing impact of these two values. It then considers the main terms of the debate between those arguing for greater media freedom and consumer sovereignty on the one hand and those defending a modernized version of public service appropriate for the digital age of communications on the other.

Chapter 3 concentrates on selected features of the media policy-making process. It begins by examining two developments which have been particularly influential in shaping the context of policy-making in recent years, notably technological convergence and transnationalization. The chapter then goes on to look at the input of the main actors in the media policy community, including central government, the big media companies and the European Union. The final section provides an evaluation of the coherence of the media policy-making process in Britain.

Chapters 4 and 5 have a regulatory focus. Chapter 4 analyzes developments in media ownership and in particular the extent of ownership concentration both within and across different media sectors. The chapter then examines some of the central themes informing the regulatory debate on media ownership, from broad issues of principle to more detailed questions of formulation and implementation. Chapter 5 examines the political and policy debates on media content regulation. Such regulation has long been sector-specific, with the press and broadcasting subject to separate and distinct regulatory regimes. While some of this sector-specificity is breaking down as a result of digital convergence, different regulatory obligations still apply across the news media, as do distinct modes of regulation, including statutory regulation and self-regulation by the industry.

Chapters 6–9 focus on issues related to political communication. Chapter 6 is devoted to news. It begins by looking at the different variables – economic, organizational, cultural and source-related – that influence the process of news production, notably the selection and construction of news stories. The chapter then looks at news content, and in particular at the thorny issues of bias and impartiality. It concludes with an examination of key features of the news environment in the digital age.

Chapter 7 analyzes and evaluates the news management activities of the government. These include censorship, restrictive legislation, on-the-record briefings and overt promotion, as well as behind-the-scenes leaks and the provision of information to journalists on an off-the-record basis. The government has to work hard in its attempts to drive and dominate the news agenda. This involves trying to determine what issues do – and just as importantly which do not – feature in media coverage and how these issues are framed. This chapter uses illustrative material from the premierships of Thatcher, Major and Blair, with a long section on news managment by the New Labour government.

Chapter 8 focuses on the interrelationship between the news media and two sets of political actors: parties and pressure groups. With regard to the former, the chapter analyzes the professionalization of parties' political communication activities and also examines the changing nature of national newspaper partisanship. With reference to pressure groups, the chapter analyzes the factors which may influence the process whereby a pressure group secures media access and considers whether there is any correlation between a pressure group's media profile and its political influence.

Chapter 9 concentrates on the media and elections. General election campaigns are heavily mediatized events involving three sets of political communication actors: political parties, the news media and the public. This chapter first considers the impact of the media on the process of campaigning: campaign effects; and then examines the influence of the media on the electorate: voter effects. It is clear that the news media have significantly altered the nature of election campaigns in contemporary Britain. Their impact on the electorate, however, is more open to debate, especially with regard to media effects on voters' partisan preferences.

The concluding chapter (Chapter 10) examines some of the main debates concerning the role of the media in a democratic society. It looks first at media performance and in particular examines whether a combination of factors has resulted in an ongoing crisis of public communication in Britain. It then asks how the media ought to be organized and regulated to enable them to function as an effective public sphere. These two issues are closely interlinked. Empirical research on political communication is often laden with normative assumptions, sometimes more implicit than explicit, as to how the media ought to perform. Similarly, normative-based theories on the desired contribution of the media to fostering a healthy democratic polity frequently derive from a critique of the perceived defects of existing practices.

The media are now integral to the functioning of politics in Britain in so many ways. It is important, therefore, that in our varied roles of media users, cultural consumers, voters and citizens, we understand as much as possible about the multi-faceted interrelationship of the different actors involved in media policy and political communication. This book represents a small contribution to the achievement of that objective.

1

The Media in Britain

Contemporary Britain is a media-rich and media-dependent society. The tastes and interests of every section of the adult population – differentiated by geographic location, social class, age, gender, ethnic origin and sexual orientation – are well catered for by a wide range of media outlets and content, ranging from national newspapers with a long history of publication to the latest internet websites. This impressive variety in supply is matched by a high and extensive level of demand, demonstrated by the popularity of many newspapers and magazines, radio stations, television channels and online services. As both citizens and consumers, British adults rely on the mass media for most of their information, entertainment and cultural provision.

Britain also has a highly developed media economy. Various media and communications companies make an important contribution to the national balance sheet, either directly as a source of employment or indirectly as a conduit for advertising to stimulate the market for goods and services. At the end of the twentieth century, for example, UK creative industries employed around one and a half million people; just under 4 per cent of consumer spending went on telecommunications, television and other communication services; and the media and communications industries were growing faster than any other part of the UK economy. In particular, Britain had 'major industrial strengths in many areas of the communications revolution, such as network infrastructure, opto-electronics, software, mobile technology and creative content production' (DTI/DCMS, 2000: 9). By 2005 the UK was spending more on its television market as a share of GDP than any other country: nearly 1 per cent (DCMS, 2005: 48).

In the light of the media's social and economic importance, it is not surprising that to a significant extent British politics has also become 'mediatized'. Yet while the concept of 'the media' embraces a wide range of means of communication and technologies of distribution, including books, film and recorded music (McQuail, 2000: 16–34),

1

not all of these are systematically of interest to practitioners and students of politics. The first section of this chapter, therefore, maps out the field of those media that are generally held to be most important for the purposes of political communication: the press, broadcasting and the internet. The objective is to provide an introductory overview of selected structural and operational features of these news media, with an emphasis on key developments over the past twenty-five years. The second section concentrates on some of the key political functions the news media perform. The aim here is to foreground some important features of their contribution to the conduct of politics in contemporary Britain.

The news media

This section focuses on those media that routinely have as one of their principal functions the provision of political information and that also aspire to reach audiences of a significant size. In historical order of appearance on the political communication landscape these news media consist of the press, broadcasting and the internet.

The press

The press in Britain is characterized by the following key features:

- The market dominance of national newspapers rather than local, regional or city titles
- A stratified national market with 'quality' newspapers at one end ('broadsheets/compacts'), popular tabloids at the other ('red tops') and mid-market papers in between ('black tops')
- Some evidence of the blurring of the boundaries between these different strata in recent years, in terms of both content and format
- A considerable degree of stability over the past half century in the total number of individual titles in the national daily and Sunday newspaper markets
- A continuing slow decline in the total circulation of national newspapers since the late 1950s
- Strong competition between individual national titles in their respective market segments
- A minimal level of state-imposed regulation compared to the broadcasting sector

- A significant extent of ownership concentration in the national newspaper industry.

The national newspaper industry

In terms of both market reach and political clout the most important press outlets across Britain as a whole are the national daily and Sunday newspapers, several of which have nationwide circulations of over a million (see Tables 1.1 and 1.2). National newspaper provision is stratified to cater for specific market segments. Among daily newspapers, for example, there are 'quality' titles (*The Daily Telegraph*, the *Financial Times*, *The Guardian*, *The Independent* and *The Times*), middle market papers (the *Daily Express* and *Daily Mail*) and popular tabloids (the *Daily Star*, the *Daily Mirror* and *The Sun*). Most of these titles have a Sunday equivalent.

The supremacy of national titles in the British newspaper market stands in marked contrast to the situation in the United States and many continental European countries, where local, regional and city newspapers dominate supply. British readers, however, tend to use local and regional papers as a supplement to – rather than a substitute

Table 1.1   National daily newspaper circulation in 2006* (in thousands)

Quality broadsheets and compacts	
The Daily Telegraph	817
Financial Times	401
The Guardian	350
The Independent	200
The Times	586
Middle market tabloids	
Daily Express	774
Daily Mail	2,203
Mass market tabloids	
The Sun	3,029
Daily Mirror	1,541**
Daily Star	750

Notes: *All figures refer to December 2006 and exclude bulk sales.
** This figure excludes the 404 thousand circulation of the *Daily Record*, the sister paper of the *Daily Mirror* in Scotland.
Source: Data from original figures accessed from http://media.guardian.co.uk/presspublishing/table/0,,1991715,00html on 2 February 2007.

Table 1.2   National Sunday newspaper circulation in 2006* (in thousands)

Quality broadsheets and compacts	
The Sunday Times	1,192
The Sunday Telegraph	591
The Observer	407
Independent on Sunday	161
Middle market tabloids	
The Mail on Sunday	2,156
Sunday Express	759
Mass market tabloids	
News of the World	3,381
The People	767
Sunday Mirror	1,323*
Daily Star Sunday	355

Notes: *All figures refer to December 2006 and exclude bulk sales.
** This figure excludes the 499 thousand circulation of the *Sunday Mail*, the sister paper of the *Sunday Mirror* in Scotland.
Source: Data from original figures accessed from http://media.guardian.co.uk/presspublishing/table/0,,1991728,00.html on 2 February 2007.

for – reading a national title, while most city newspapers are published as evening titles so as not to compete directly with the morning national dailies (Tunstall, 1996: 60–75). The UK thus has 'by far the largest national newspaper press in Europe' (Deacon, 2004: 10).

This should not be taken to imply that non-national newspapers have no political significance. The range of local/regional/city titles and the substantial circulation figures they achieve ensure that they fulfil important publicity and information functions in their respective sub-national markets (Franklin and Murphy, 1991: 3–10; Hetherington, 1989). Moreover, even on national issues the local press may be politically influential, as was the case with the introduction of the 'poll tax' during the last years of the Thatcher premiership, when local newspapers acted as a channel for the expression of popular and elite dissent (Deacon and Golding, 1994). In addition, certain parts of the UK such as Northern Ireland and Scotland have their own distinctive newspapers. Scotland, for example, is home to the mass circulation *Daily Record* (the stablemate of the *Daily Mirror*) and quality broadsheets such as *The Herald*, *The Scotsman* and *Scotland on Sunday*, which cover the agenda of Scottish politics from a predominantly Scottish (though by no means necessarily Nationalist) perspective (MacInnes, 1992; Schlesinger, 1998). Nonetheless, in general across the UK as a whole it is the national (i.e. London-based) dailies which dominate the market and provide the primary print-based source of political information on national and international issues and events.

Nor are news magazines and periodicals as politically important in Britain as in some other advanced democracies. *The Economist, New Statesman and Society*, the *Spectator*, *Private Eye* and *Prospect* among others cover political issues for either elites or small sections of the mass readership. Even what at first sight might appear to be non-political periodicals, such as women's magazines, may well pay attention to social and political topics: not just classic 'women's issues' such as abortion, nursery school provision and child benefits, but also wider themes including health, education and the environment (Anderson, 1997: 55). However, largely because of the market presence of broadsheet Sunday newspapers, there is a lack of high-selling news magazines in Britain along the lines of *Newsweek* and *Time* in the United States, *Der Spiegel* in Germany and *L'Express* and *Le Nouvel Observateur* in France.

While the number of local and regional newspaper titles (excluding free papers) has dropped considerably since the late 1940s (Seymour-Ure, 1996: 45–58), the overall total of national titles has remained reasonably stable (see Table 1.3). This is despite a significant turnover in individual titles as a result of launches, closures, relaunches and changes of status (ibid.: 21–44). New papers have come on to the market (for instance, *The Independent*, *The Independent on Sunday* and *The Business*); some titles have closed down (such as the *News Chronicle* and the *Daily Herald*); papers have re-launched themselves with a different format and sometimes under a new owner (for example, *The Sun*); and newspapers have both

Table 1.3   Number of national newspaper titles 1948–2006

	1948	1961	1976	1988	2006
Daily titles	11	10	9	12	10
Sunday titles	10	8	7	9	10

Sources: Data from Curran and Seaton, 1997: 291 and author's own figures.

entered and left the market (including *Today*) in some cases after only a very brief existence (for instance, *News on Sunday* and *The Sunday Correspondent*).

The introduction of new technology

The technologically driven changes in newspaper production in the 1980s did not lead to a significant and sustained increase in the number of national titles or indeed to greater diversity in national newspaper ownership (Leapman, 1999). This may seem surprising since developments in print technology seemed to offer the prospect of opening up the newspaper market to new entrants at a time when the media advertising budget was healthy and the general economy buoyant (Whittam Smith, 1989: 19–20). Yet while several major launch attempts were made from the late 1980s onwards, most soon collapsed (Greenslade, 2004: 469–97). Only two national daily titles succeeded in establishing an apparently secure market position, *Today* and *The Independent*. Yet even they experienced difficulties in maintaining a sustained and vibrant challenge in their respective market segments. The *Independent* was absorbed by the Mirror Group in 1994, only to be sold off four years later, while *Today* was closed down as part of a cost-saving exercise by its new owners, News International, in 1995.

The closure of *Today* emphasized the limited impact of technological change on both the conditions of entry into the national newspaper sector and subsequent market survival. The newspaper was losing money at a time when the Murdoch group had engaged in a price war in both the broadsheet and tabloid sectors. The huge rise in newsprint costs in 1995, which helped bring the price war to an end, also contributed to the decision to kill off *Today*. Despite an attempt by its editor to reposition the newspaper in support of the Labour party and therefore distinguish its political stance from its middle market rivals, the *Daily Mail* and *Daily Express*, the circulation of *Today* remained disappointing and, more importantly, the paper was making substantial losses. In the end, it was a newspaper which the Murdoch group could allow to go under.

New technology certainly had a huge impact on labour relations in the newspaper industry. In particular, its introduction challenged the power of the print workers and revolutionized the professional practices of journalists. Not surprisingly, management attempts to modernize the printing process were fiercely resisted by workers, who sought to protect staff levels and conditions of service. This led to scenes of industrial conflict, first at Eddy Shah's plant in Warrington and then most memorably at Wapping, where Rupert Murdoch's News International had moved in a spectacular entrepreneurial coup in 1986. Backed by the Conservative government's anti-trade union legislation, Murdoch defeated the print workers after a prolonged and sometimes violent dispute (McNair, 1996: 142–57; Neil, 1997: 82–196). For staff in the newspaper industry the situation in the early 1990s contrasted sharply with that of fifteen years previously, as what had been some of the most powerful trade unions in Britain painfully came to terms with the consequences of a combination of political, technological and industrial change.

The introduction of new technology, however, did not have a major influence in reducing the costs of entry into the newspaper market. These remained extremely high, especially for a national paper. Moreover, the general economic climate of the 1990s was much less favourable to newspaper launches than that of the late 1980s:

> Cheaper pre-press production costs were illusory: distribution costs had increased; newsprint prices were rising, competition for advertising was cut-throat, finding print capacity at a reasonable rate was getting more difficult and the requirement to publish in colour was a heavy additional expense. A start-up still required huge funds. (Greenslade, 2004: 496–7)

In fact, between 1945 and 1995 the only long-term entry to the group of dominant newspaper companies, News International, took place well before the era of new technology when the industry was still dominated by powerful print unions (Sparks, 1995: 189).

Declining circulations

Circulation figures for national newspapers, especially for the Sunday titles, have been in an apparently remorseless decline since the high-point of the 1950s, despite a significant growth in population and a huge increase in formal education over the past half century (see Table 1.4). The total circulation of the popular and middle market newspapers has decreased, especially among the Sunday titles. In contrast, the 'quality' segment has performed reasonably well, whether measured by circulation figures or market share (see Tables 1.5 and 1.6). Yet despite this, *The Sun* on its own still sells more copies than all the upmarket 'quality' dailies combined.

A variety of reasons for falling newspaper circulation have been put forward. Franklin cites television, unemployment, increases in the cover price above the general rate of inflation, a lack of literacy skills

Table 1.4   Total national newspaper circulation figures 1945–2005
(in millions)

Year	Daily	Sunday	Total
1945	12.35	19.76	32.11
1955	16.22	30.22	46.44
1965	15.59	23.98	39.57
1975	14.11	20.50	34.61
1985	14.73	17.83	32.56
1995	13.75	15.47	29.22
2005	11.20	12.20	23.40

Note: While the basis for calculating the figures may not be exactly comparable, the general downward trend in circulation figures since the 1950s is
clearly discernible.
Sources: Data from Seymour-Ure, 1996: 17; Peak and Fisher, 1995: 30;
MediaGuardian, 12 December 2005.

Table 1.5   Market segmentation of national daily newspaper circulation figures 1945–2005 (in thousands and percentage
market share)

Year	Quality	Middle market	Mass market
1945	1,017 (8%)	8,445 (68%)	2,883 (23%)
1955	1,277 (8%)	9,116 (57%)	5,675 (35%)
1965	2,007 (13%)	7,724 (49%)	5,863 (38%)
1975	2,150 (15%)	4,548 (32%)	7,414 (53%)
1985	2,401 (16%)	3,717 (25%)	8,613 (58%)
1994	2,560 (19%)	3,709 (27%)	7,316 (54%)
2005	2,500 (22%)	3,037 (27%)	5,660 (51%)

Note: While the basis for calculating the figures may not be exactly compa-
rable, the general trends in market breakdown are clearly discernible.
Sources: Data from Seymour-Ure, 1996: 28–29; *MediaGuardian*, 12
December 2005.

especially among young people and the unattractiveness of much
newspaper content (Franklin, 1994: 31–2). One might also add that
newspapers have to compete with a host of other leisure pursuits, as
well as specialist magazines and the internet, for people's time and
attention. Reading a newspaper is for many still part of a well-
ingrained daily ritual, which is why the impact of television and electronic media has been gradual rather than sudden. Yet the

Table 1.6   Market segmentation of national Sunday newspaper circulation figures 1945–2005 (in thousands and percentage market share)

Year	Quality	Middle market	Mass market
1945	759 (4%)	5,216 (26%)	13,785 (70%)
1955	1,170 (4%)	7,193 (24%)	21,854 (72%)
1965	2,764 (12%)	4,423 (18%)	16,796 (70%)
1975	2,862 (14%)	3,715 (18%)	13,918 (68%)
1985	2,673 (15%)	4,080 (23%)	11,074 (62%)
1994	2,703 (17%)	3,470 (22%)	9,672 (61%)
2005	2,659 (21%)	3,130 (26%)	6,420 (53%)

Note: While the basis for calculating the figures may not be exactly comparable, the general trends in market breakdown are clearly discernible.
Sources: Data from Seymour-Ure, 1996: 30–1; *MediaGuardian*, 12 December 2005.

performance of rituals may change over time as lifestyles adapt to new technology and socio-economic change. The concern among press owners and journalists is that young people may not acquire the habit of newspaper reading even as they grow older. With the routinization of multi-channel television and the internet in households, total newspaper circulation will almost certainly continue to decline. Increasingly many people will prefer to obtain much of their information from broadcasting and electronic sources rather than the printed page. It is, therefore, against a background of declining circulations that British newspapers need to adapt to the new world of information provision and distribution. Nonetheless, it is still the case that in comparison with several other member states of the European Union – including France, Ireland, Italy and Spain among others – newspaper circulation figures *per capita* in Britain remain high.

A competitive market

The press is a highly competitive commercial industry. In a declining market for their product, newspaper titles battle against each other for audiences and advertising revenue in their respective market segments, while the press as a whole is engaged in competition with other media sectors. The adaptation of newspapers to increased competition has been particularly evident in three areas: ownership strategies, format and content. First, several press groups have tried to acquire a stake in broadcasting and some have sought to establish close business relationships with internet companies in an attempt to protect their market position (see Chapter 4). Second, newspapers have expanded both in terms of pagination and sections, as they try to win readers through an emphasis on lifestyle issues such as health, fashion, cookery, travel and finance. Upmarket papers also have frequent inserts specially targeted at particular professional occupations (for example, education, the legal profession and executive management). In 2004 *The Times* emulated the successful switch by *The Independent* to a tabloid-size format ('the compact') in a bid to boost sales, while in 2005 *The Guardian* adopted the 'large compact' Berliner format used by several continental dailies, including *Le Monde*. Finally, the success of many niche-oriented magazines in attracting readers suggests that the print medium still has a role to play in providing entertainment, features and commentary, even if the public has become less reliant on generalist newspapers as their primary source of news. Features journalism in newspapers has hugely expanded, as has sports coverage (Tunstall, 1996). In addition, upmarket papers provide considerable analysis and commentary in addition to news reportage, while tabloids have a liberal dose of stories covering the lives of stars and celebrities from the worlds of television, entertainment and sport.

Various factors contribute to keeping a paper competitive. Content and brand image are both important, as *The Sun* showed in the 1980s in winning readers among the aspirant working class and the *Daily Mail* in the 1990s in courting a new generation of women readers. In the circulation war among the popular tabloids the *Daily Mirror* has lost out as market leader to *The Sun*, while *The Times* won over readers from its competitors, especially *The Daily Telegraph* and *The Independent*, in the early 1990s thanks in large part to a cut in its cover price. The price war underlined the extent to which newspaper market share and even survival could not be taken for granted. It also showed that the readerships of some newspapers were capable of being attracted to other titles purely on the basis of cover price – consumer loyalty to newspaper brands was not as secure as many in the industry had previously imagined. Most worryingly for some observers, Murdoch's tactics illustrated his capacity to transfer resources across his global multi-media empire and to cross-subsidize newspaper losses in the short term as part of a long term strategy for control of a market which, though in decline, still remained commercially and politically important to his company's interests.

Broadcasting

Broadcasting in Britain has displayed the following main characteristics:

- A relatively recent expansion in supply of radio and television services, driven by technological change and a more liberal public policy approach, following many years of highly restricted provision
- The dominance of a few free-to-air terrestrial broadcasters up until the last decade of the twentieth century
- The comparatively modest impact of cable as a distribution system for programming
- Strong competition to terrestrial networks from satellite distribution from the late 1980s onwards
- The roll-out and popular take-up of digital services on terrestrial, satellite and cable platforms in the early years of the twenty-first century
- High popularity of radio listening and television viewing among audiences
- Historically a highly regulated system underpinned by public service values
- Significant marketization and lighter touch regulation of broadcasting since the late 1980s.

A long, slow growth in broadcast supply

For much of its history one of the key features of British broadcasting was the restricted nature of its supply. For example, in 1980 there were only three television channels available in the UK; by 2005 this figure had shot up to over 400. In 1980 viewers could select from only 300 hours of television programming a week, while at the turn of the millennium this figure had increased to 40,000 (DTI/DCMS, 2000: 7).

In the radio sector the BBC enjoyed a monopoly in national provision until as recently as 1990, running four networks with clearly differentiated output (pop music, easy listening, classical music and news/features/drama) from the late 1960s onwards. Local radio stations, managed by either the BBC or Independent Local Radio, were established only in the 1970s. When television began to develop as a mass medium after the end of the Second World War, the BBC as a matter of course was given sole responsibility for running the new service. The Corporation's reputation had been enhanced by its role during the conflict, its professionalism in broadcasting was unrivalled in Britain and its relationship with the state had been consolidated over the preceding twenty years. The British television audience of the first postwar decade was confined to the scheduled output of just one BBC channel.

The BBC's monopoly in television was brought to an end with the establishment of a second nationwide television network, Independent Television, in 1955. The BBC's approach to television broadcasting had not met with universal approval. The Corporation was open to the charge of not providing enough popular fare and failing to meet the new expectations of postwar British audiences. A group of Conservative MPs lobbied for change, arguing that another television service would increase demand for television sets, extend viewer choice and provide advertisers with a new medium to boost economic consumption (Sales, 1986: 54–62; Wilson, 1961).

The newcomer was different from the BBC in several respects: the ITV franchise holders had a more commercial approach to programming; the new service was financed from advertising rather than an annual licence fee levied on each household possessing a television set; and the network consisted of a federal system of several companies each serving a specific geographical region in contrast to the predominantly national network of the BBC (though in practice regional differentiation in ITV programming was significantly offset by national networking agreements). The creation of the BBC/ITV duopoly resulted in what came to be regarded by the system's defenders as a key component of its success: competion between the two services for audiences but not for revenue (see Chapter 2).

Following the establishment of ITV the duopoly grew incrementally, with only two additional terrestrial channels coming on stream during the following forty years: BBC2 in 1964 and Channel 4 in 1982. BBC2 was designed to complement the mass audience approach of BBC1 and to help BBC television counter the audience pull of ITV (Seymour-Ure, 1996: 103–4). Channel 4 was intended to be an innovative service in terms of its programme remit and production approach. Proponents of the new channel in the 1970s argued that much of the mainstream in-house production output of the BBC/ITV duopoly did not sufficiently reflect the pluralism of British society, while it also excluded much independent production talent from access to the television screens (Blanchard and Morley, 1982; Isaacs, 1989; Lambert, 1982). Britain, it was argued, was now a more multi-ethnic and multicultural society than ever before, youth culture had become more important after the pop music explosion of the 1960s, traditional gender roles were being questioned and alternative sexual orientations were becoming more socially acceptable. Therefore, when Channel 4 was set up, legislation prescribed a programme remit to ensure that in its range and diversity the channel's programming would cater for the tastes and interests of minority audiences across society (Goodwin, 1998: 20–34). These were defined not just as specific social groups such as ethnic communities, but also all those with minority cultural or special interest tastes, from jazz fans to cycling enthusiasts.

After a prolonged period of slow incremental growth the supply of broadcasting grew considerably in the final years of the pre-digital era. In particular, during the last decade of the twentieth century the number of radio stations and television channels increased as a result of technological change and a more liberal regulatory environment. In the national radio sector the BBC added a fifth station, while three new commercial networks (Classic FM, Virgin 1215 and Talk Radio UK) were also established. In local radio, stations catering for niche audiences were set up to supplement more generalist local services. Between 1992 and 1996 the number of Independent Local Radio stations alone increased from 120 to 218 (Franklin, 1997: 14), a powerful indicator of the growth in radio provision as a whole. By 2005 there were 325 radio stations broadcasting in the UK, an increase of well over a hundred in a ten-year period, while at the start of the twenty-first century half of all radio listening was to commercial stations (DTI/DCMS, 2000: 48). In television a fifth analogue terrestrial channel, Channel 5, came on stream in 1997 with an audience reach covering about 70 per cent of the country by the end of the century.

The 'new media' of cable and satellite

More importantly, the traditional mixed-scheduling television networks funded either from the licence fee or commercial advertising were joined by entertainment and thematic channels, financed principally by viewer subscription and transmitted via cable and satellite delivery systems. During the final years of the twentieth century these distribution systems began to make inroads into the dominance of the BBC/ITV duopoly. The process of expansion started quite slowly in the 1980s and then became more marked in the following decade as the so-called 'new media' of cable and satellite were taken up by an increasing number of households.

At the start of the 1980s it seemed that cable (rather than satellite) would be the technology that would bring about significant change (Goodwin, 1998: 54–68). Cable was not strictly speaking a new technology, since it had previously been employed as a means of

programme distribution by broadcasters in areas where off-air reception was poor. At the start of the 1980s, however, it was widely regarded
as a technology that could have radical implications not just for broadcasting but for communications generally. Not only could cable deliver
multi-channel television to households, but more importantly the
combination of fibre optics and star switched networks opened up the
way for the construction of a sophisticated national communication
system which would carry a wide range of interactive services.

Perhaps surprisingly, given the enthusiasm of official policy statements in the early 1980s, cable was in fact rather slow to make much
impact. In 1981 the report of the Information Technology Advisory
Panel had recommended to the Conservative government that an
active policy of cabling Britain should be pursued without delay, so
that the industrial and economic potential of the new technology
could be fully exploited (Hollins, 1984: 54–60). However, in contrast
to some other European countries, such as Germany, where public
investment allowed cable to make spectacular market growth, the
Thatcher administration steadfastly refused to invest any public
money in the construction of cable networks (Katz, 2000).

In the absence of financial backing, the incentive for companies to
persist with cable came through the regulatory regime. In 1983 the
government-commissioned Hunt Report recommended a light touch
regulatory approach to foster cable's rapid development. Accepting
the thrust of Hunt's recommendations, the 1984 Cable and
Broadcasting Act imposed less stringent regulations on cable (and
satellite) programming than those that governed the output of the
terrestrial broadcasters. A new regulatory agency, the Cable
Authority, was established to oversee programme output, though in
fact the authority quickly came to regard its principal function as
representing the interests of network operators and promoting audience take-up of cable. The most significant government initiative,
however, was the decision to allow cable operators to offer voice telephony and telecommunication services to subscribers in addition to
television programming. This regulatory initiative encouraged
telecommunication companies, notably from North America, to enter
the sector as network operators during the 1990s.

Nonetheless, the cabling of Britain still proceeded much more
slowly than had been anticipated in the early 1980s and growth in audience take-up of available services was patchy. By the end of the twentieth century cable was available to approximately half of Britain's
households. However, of the twelve and a half million households that

could receive the technology, only four and half million were actually connected, of which just over three million subscribed to cable television. As a result, at the dawn of the digital era cable was not as big a player in the roll-out of digital services as might have been anticipated twenty years previously when its potential contribution to the 'wired society' was being much trumpeted by government and industry alike.

In contrast, from uncertain beginnings satellite television became one of the major media success stories of the 1990s, thanks to the commercial foresight and political skills of the media mogul, Rupert Murdoch (Goodwin, 1998: 38–53). The major player in the supply of satellite programming to UK audiences is BSkyB, which as part of Murdoch's portfolio of British media interests has come to dominate the national pay-tv market. This dominance originated in a successful campaign waged by Murdoch's Sky service in the late 1980s with enthusiastic cross-promotion from his tabloid newspaper titles, which saw the collapse and absorption of its market rival, British Satellite Broadcasting, in 1990 (Chippindale and Franks, 1991).

BSkyB benefited from important advantages during the crucial early years of its existence. First, cable was poorly implanted and so there was a large potential market for multi-channel television delivered via direct-to-home satellite. Second, since it was regarded by the government as a non-domestic broadcaster, BSkyB effectively avoided the regulations on cross-media ownership currently in force (see Chapter 4). As a result, Murdoch did not have to choose between his newspaper and broadcasting interests; he was allowed to build up both. Third, the new satellite service was less highly regulated with regard to programme content than its terrestrial free-to-air competitors. This allowed it to fill its output with much cheap imported programming at a time when subscriber revenue was low. Finally, by virtue of being first in the market BSkyB acquired a dominant hold over the decoding technology. As UK television geared up for the digital era at the end of the twentieth century, BSkyB (more commonly referred to simply as Sky) had over seven million subscribers, assuming an importance in British television that few would have predicted at its launch only a decade previously.

The advent of digital broadcasting

In general, consumer demand for broadcast output has always been strong: for instance, at the turn of the millennium each adult viewer devoted on average more than 25 hours per week to watching television. Yet in 2000 a large majority of British households were still dependent on the programme output of a maximum of five free-to-air analogue terrestrial channels. The slow take-up of multi-channel television during the analogue era should not therefore be taken to mean that British consumers did not enjoy television viewing, but rather that for several years many of them seemed content with the output of a very restricted number of services, all of which could be received without additional expenditure on top of the annual BBC licence fee.

This situation was to change with the arrival of digital. At the beginning of 1998 no one in the UK had digital television. Between 1998 and 2003 take-up of digital was twice as fast as that of colour television over its first five years. As a result, 50 per cent of British households had digital equipment by 2003 and this had increased to over 60 per cent only two years later, a figure that represented one of the highest rates of digital take-up in the world. In 2003 the Office of Communications (Ofcom) predicted 78 per cent digital take-up by the end of the decade, while in 2005 the government announced that the full nationwide switchover to digital would take place by 2012.

Of the three main distribution platforms – satellite, cable and terrestrial – BSkyB was initially the clear leader in delivering digital services to consumers by successfully building on its expertise in the analogue pay-tv market. The cable platform, managed by companies such as NTL and Telewest, lagged far behind. The terrestrial platform, initially owned by the ITV companies Carlton and Granada and with a much more limited channel capacity than either of its two rivals, experienced huge difficulties in attracting subscribers. ITV Digital collapsed in 2002 with massive debts, leaving BSkyB in a dominant position in the digital distribution of multi-channel premium pay-tv content such as sport and films. The terrestrial platform was taken over by the BBC in an alliance with BSkyB and renamed Freeview. While Freeview provides fewer channels than either the satellite or cable platforms, it still seemed likely that the terrestrial platform, available without subscription, would be the major driver of digital take-up in the run-up to full switchover. In 2003 Ofcom predicted that by 2010 the digital terrestrial platform would be available in 6.7 million households (3 million in 2003), BSkyB would have 8.7 million subscribers and the combined digital subscriber base of the cable operators would be 3.7 million (2.2 million in 2003).

By 2005, therefore, it seemed that the supply of digital television in Britain had divided into two broad camps: a subscription service via satellite or cable which included a substantial amount of premium content versus a one-off payment service via terrestrial or freesat (a non-premium content satellite distribution service) that provided a more limited range of product. Alongside these changes in supply, viewing patterns across all households, including those subscribing to digital services, continued to show the dominance of the traditional free-to-air channels. Their audience share, however, was in clear decline. In 2003 the five main terrestrial channels captured around 76 per cent of total viewing, compared with 87 per cent in 1998; in multi-channel households, their audience share started lower, declining from 63 per cent to 57 per cent over the same period. BBC1's average audience share fell from 29.5 per cent in 1998 to 25.6 per cent in 2003, while ITV1's plummeted from 31.7 per cent to 23.7 per cent. Thus as digital consolidated its hold in the marketplace with state-of-the-art delivery platforms and many additional channels, Britain's television system had significantly altered in terms of supply and was also changing, albeit more gradually, in terms of consumption patterns.

The internet

The internet is distinguished by the following key features (Abramson *et al.*, 1988):

● It can transmit a huge volume of information from a wide range of sources to a single access point
● It can transmit the information at great speed
● It allows for far greater user control of the information received: consumers can collate and print their own news sources
● It allows for greater targeting of audiences by distributors
● It allows for decentralization of information control: the number of sources of information has massively increased and the costs of establishing oneself as a supplier of information have substantially decreased
● It introduces interactivity to media technology, allowing citizens to debate online with politicians, journalists or other members of the public from considerable distances.

Growth of the internet

Compared with the press and broadcasting, the internet is a relative newcomer as a news medium in Britain. Yet it has already made a huge impact on the social and economic life of the country, for instance through the generation of new types of business and commercial activity in the sector of e-commerce. The internet has radically transformed information transmission, bringing interactive, online services into many households and allowing users to access these through their personal computer, television screen or telephone handset. Over the past decade the number of websites has grown enormously, while at the same time the technical quality of content provision and the speed of downloading to the user have greatly improved.

Usage of the internet is increasing at an exponential rate. In the mid-1990s only about one quarter of UK citizens had a computer in their home and only around 4 to 6 per cent used the internet (Winseck, 1998: 355). By the beginning of the twenty-first century this situation had changed quite significantly, with 28 per cent of UK households having internet access; three years later the total was between 40 and 50 per cent (Fairweather and Rogerson, 2003: 192) and at the start of 2005 it stood at 57 per cent. Broadband connections were also rising rapidly, driven by competition between suppliers. The growth in internet usage was largely a result of the pace of technological change in the computing, mobile telephony and television sectors, supported by a fall in real terms in the cost of hardware and access to internet services. It was accompanied by changing patterns of social communication, especially but not exclusively among the young, the highly educated and more affluent sections of society (Norris, 2000a).

Online news

Among online sources of political information it is general news sources which are most often consulted by the public, well ahead of party or government websites (Gibson *et al.*, 2003: 171). Almost all established media organizations have become actively involved in the provision of online services to users, consolidating a strong web presence to complement news and comment supplied by their traditional offline outlets (Coleman, 2001: 683–4). Newspapers, for example, have set up websites to ensure that they are not left behind by the internet's growing popularity. This is a substantive move to attract and retain readers, while also protecting the share of the media advertising budget attributed to the press. It is also symbolically important for newspapers to present themselves as part of the vanguard of forces embracing technological change rather than representatives of an old-fashioned communications medium.

Online versions of newspapers form only a small part of the websites of the major dailies. *The Guardian*, for example, has developed a network of special interest sites under the umbrella title of *Guardian Unlimited*, covering news, film, sport, work, education, shopping, books and money among other topics. 'The network was conceived as a way of migrating the *Guardian*'s core audience to the net, attracting like-minded readers from other newspapers and stimulating new commercial opportunities (particularly as the web threatens the newspaper's reliance on classified job ads)' (Peak and Fisher, 2000: 18). The news site, for example, has the internet newspaper edition and provides breaking news, web-exclusive comment from *Guardian* writers, an archive and subject-specific reports. Users of the news website can also listen to audio news, follow interactive graphics and interact with public figures and other users (ibid.: 18), as well as accessing online 'blogs'. In 2006 Guardian Unlimited was named as the world's best online newspaper for the second year running at the 10th annual Webby awards, regarded as the Oscars of the internet.

The BBC is another major traditional media company to invest heavily in online services. Its website is 'by far the most popular online news source' (Gibson *et al.*, 2003: 172) and has established itself as a 'central, trusted presence in the online world' (DCMS, 2005: 21). *BBC Online* has over 2 million pages of content, with 41 per cent of licence fee payers accessing it in early 2003. The site provides a wide range of services, from national and international news, to learning tools for teachers and schoolchildren and localized discussion forums.

Politics on the net

The internet has also opened up new possibilities for social and political expression. Internet websites differ from traditional media in that they allow a variety of political actors – from mainstream parties to anti-globalization protestors – the possibility of direct access to the public, bypassing the gatekeeping and filtering functions traditionally performed by journalists. For many political actors their initial internet presence might be largely explained in terms of symbolic representation – the self-perceived need to be seen as embracing a new form of communication, whatever the levels of audience access and usage. In addition, political parties may seek an online presence for the following reasons: information provision to the public and the 'old' media'; campaigning (direct e-mail, fund raising); targeting the youth audience; efficiency gains from having a virtual infrastructure; and soliciting voter/member feedback and participation (Gibson *et al.*, 2003: 168). Party political websites have thus acquired some substantive significance, though in general more for 'downward information provision' than 'upward participatory communication' (ibid.: 168–9), a situation that has not altered since the late 1990s

(Gibson and Ward, 1998: 30–1). Perhaps as a result, the impact of party websites on the general public has been low.

The New Labour government has made a huge commitment to use of the internet. Under its project UK Online it had a stated objective of making Britain a fully networked society by 2005 (http://www.ukonline.gov.uk). This involved widening public access to the internet and ensuring that as many government services as possible were available via web-based technologies. The Number 10 website was launched in February 2000 to promote the UK overseas, communicate government news and information, explain the role and history of Number 10 as a building and an institution, and demonstrate the Government's commitment to new technology (http://www.number-10.gov.uk). In 2001 the Number 10 website had over 3.2 million visitor sessions and its discussion forums proved so popular that they outgrew the site and had to be moved to the Citizens' Portal. The government's e-Democracy website provided information on how citizens may increase their participation in politics through use of the net, including electronic submission of petitions to Number 10 and the introduction of electronic voting experiments across the country (http://www.e-envoy.gov.uk).

It may be that some of this activity smacks of public relations initiatives designed to demonstrate New Labour's modernizing credentials through a high-profile symbolic presence in the use of new technology. It is certainly too early to make the wide-sweeping claim that 'one-stop, non-stop e-Government portals will revolutionise not just the way public services are delivered but government itself' (Silcock, 2001: 91). Indeed at the start of 2003 the Office of the e-Envoy was reporting that citizens had so far barely used the government's own online service offerings, ironically partly because the sheer proliferation of websites – more than 3,000 sites spawned by over 800 government bodies – had led to confusion among potential users. In the early years of the twenty-first century the vast majority of the British public remained remarkably unenthused by e-government (Coleman, 2004: 92). Yet it is also likely that at a more modest level the internet is changing how citizens interact with government departments and it is certain that the public will expect more services to be delivered online in future. At the same time, one of the major advantages of the internet for government is that 'executive websites provide new avenues for government self-publicity, allowing them to bypass hostile news media' (Chadwick, 2006: 202) and put their message across to the public without the distorting influence of journalists.

It is still difficult to evaluate the impact of the internet on political information/communication. For instance, in 2003 only 7 per cent of people used the internet on a daily basis as a source of news. This is in part because the technology has not yet reached the saturation level of television in British households, in part because the web is a 'pull' technology where consumers actively have to search out information (in contrast to television which is a 'push' technology) and in part because the internet has come into a news and information market that is already highly saturated (Ballinger, 2002: 232).

Nonetheless, the internet has undoubtedly grown in political importance over the years. First, it is an essential resource for media professionals, including political journalists, in their daily occupational routines. Second, it is a useful medium of communication for political organizations such as parties and pressure groups, helping to recruit new members, mobilize existing ones, raise money and keep activists informed about relevant events and issues. Third, online news services and other websites are used by many citizens for the purpose of acquiring political information in addition to that obtained through the more traditional offline media. In 2003, for instance, members of the public were able to access the transcripts and documents from the Hutton Inquiry into the circumstances surrounding the death of Dr David Kelly and so obtain unmediated information about the preparation and presentation by the government of its case for going to war in Iraq (http://www.the-hutton-inquiry.org.uk). Finally, in time the internet will rival and even displace traditional media outlets for at least some sections of the population. For instance, Coleman argues that for 'the younger generation, who are the most turned off by politics, the internet is already becoming *the* trusted source for political information' (Coleman, 2001: 686, emphasis in the original).

Political functions of the media

This section concentrates on five key political functions performed by the news media in Britain. These are:

● Information provision
● Agenda-setting
● Public watchdog
● Political mobilization
● Regime legitimation.

Information provision

The first and most obvious function performed by the news media is the provision of political information. The news media furnish audiences with information and comment about issues and events in local, regional, national, supranational and global arenas. They act as conduits, platforms and fora for the transmission of all sorts of political messages, providing a convenient means of communication among political elites (horizontal) and between political elites and the citizenry (vertical). This information function is mainly top-down in character: 'in political news reporting media serve as a communications channel running from the apex of a society (government, parliament, political parties, unions) to its political basis – the public, the electorate' (Cuilenburg and Slaa, 1993: 151). However, the media also serve a bottom-up information function by providing politicians with a 'source of intelligence about the mood of the country' (McQuail, 2000: 472).

There is now an unprecedented amount of political information made available to audiences via the news media: newspaper articles and editorials, radio and television news programmes, broadcast current affairs coverage, political interviews, investigative documentaries, party political broadcasts, audience access programmes, rolling news channels and a proliferation of online services. The expansion in television provision, for example, has resulted in a large increase in the amount of news output, as schedules have expanded (for example, to include breakfast news) and additional news programmes have been created by channels entering the market (for example, *Channel 4 News* in the 1980s and *5 News* in the 1990s). The volume of national news on the five main channels increased by 80 per cent between 1994 and 2003, mainly due to more daytime and weekend news. News and current affairs programmes on generalist free-to-air channels are supplemented by dedicated rolling news channels, such as Sky News and BBC News 24, and by specialist political outlets, such as BBC Parliament, all of which create voracious organizational appetites for news material.

Television has long been the most important source of political information for the majority of the population (Rossiter, 2005: 9), with the medium enjoying several distinct advantages over newspapers. First, television has the benefit of immediacy, while newspapers require time to be produced and distributed to households in their traditional format. Second, television is on tap in the household. It can be accessed by the viewer with minimal effort and in the case of free-to-air channels at no extra cost above that of the annual licence fee. Third, television is a visual medium, which gives the viewer the illusion of witnessing 'reality' at first hand. Fourth, newspapers are politically partisan in their support of a political party or policy option. This partisanship is usually (though not always) recognized by newspaper readers. Television, however, has had a regulatory responsibility to be balanced and impartial in its political coverage, at least as far as its treatment of mainstream political views is concerned. It can act as a forum for debate and a site for contestation, but in the main its political coverage eschews an overt editorial line with regard to party politics. Finally, and related to the two previous points, television has been given greater credibility than newspapers by the public. Television news stories are deemed more 'trustworthy' and 'accurate' than their newspaper equivalents, even if the proportion of the population believing that you can trust the information and analysis provided by British television news to be accurate and impartial has declined in recent years.

Faced with the overall increase in the supply of news and political information at the start of the twenty-first century, one commentator argued that the 'political public sphere . . . is larger, denser, and accessible to more people than at any previous point in Britain's cultural history, and it continues to expand' (McNair, 2000: 39). Moreover, it is not just in terms of the number of media outlets or the amount of content that the provision of political information has grown in recent years. It has also expanded in time, with a 24 hours news culture now firmly part of the mediatized political environment. This poses organizational and resource problems for political communication actors in their attempts to keep on top of – or better still anticipate – fast moving stories. In addition, the supply of information has extended in space, with the instantaneous availability of news delivered from anywhere around the globe. The events of 11 September 2001 in the United States were a perfect example of this time-space compression. Within minutes of the terrorist attacks taking place, news media organizations in Britain were taking 'live' feeds from across the Atlantic and clearing their schedules to keep audiences up to date on developments as they happened.

Though some mediated political information purports to consist of factual reporting, much contains background analysis and commentary intended to help the audience understand and interpret events and issues. In reporting and commenting, the news media are sometimes said to act as a window on the political world. The metaphor, however, is flawed in that audiences are presented with a highly selected and filtered version of 'reality'. Moreover, the range of media outlets and content available to audiences means that political coverage has to compete for space and attention in a market prone to information and entertainment saturation. In a zapping culture, both sets of political communication professionals – sources and journalists – have to compete more than ever before to gain and retain the audience's attention. In the eyes of some commentators, this may have led to a so-called 'dumbing down' or trivialization of much political coverage as part of a trend towards 'infotainment' (see Chapter 10).

On the demand side, just as there are more opportunities within the expanded media market for the politically interested citizen to obtain information, there is also greater freedom for audiences to escape from political coverage altogether. It is possible to talk, albeit rather schematically, of an information gap in British society. On the one side are those – more affluent, more educated, more interested in politics – who have access to and make selective use of a wide range of news media. On the other are those – less affluent, less educated, less interested in politics – who tend to rely overwhelmingly on television, supplemented by the uneven coverage of a tabloid newspaper. Inequalities of access to the internet have further increased this imbalance between information-rich and information-poor, creating a digital divide which risks further marginalizing already disadvantaged social groups (Silcock, 2001: 94–5).

Agenda-setting

The second political function performed by the media is that of helping to set the agenda for public debate (McCombs and Shaw, 1972). The agenda-setting hypothesis argues that the visibility of an issue in the news influences the perceived importance of that issue by the public: the more visible an issue is in the news media, the more salient it is for public opinion (Dearing and Rogers, 1996). Thus, by including some issues and marginalizing or excluding others, the news media make an important contribution to deciding what is – and what is not – a significant subject for public discussion. In practice, it may be difficult to provide unassailable evidence to support a strong causal correlation between the issue agendas of the media, public opinion and political elites respectively, since this would require a knowledge of party programmes, evidence of opinion change over time in a given section of the public, content analysis showing media attention to different issues and some evidence of relevant media use by the public concerned (McQuail, 2000: 455). Moreover, it is often difficult to establish the flow of influence in issue construction. For example, it is at least as arguable that the news media agenda reflects public concerns as much as it shapes them. Nonetheless, it seems highly plausible that the media do play a role in determining the salience of a particular issue for the public (as well as for politicians).

Media framing analysis goes further than the agenda-setting hypothesis. News framing focuses on three inter-related aspects of news content: selection, organization and emphasis. Framing analysis considers the ways in which the media select particular aspects of reality (and exclude others), organize those aspects around a central idea and so emphasize certain ways of looking at and interpreting those aspects (Semetko, de Vreese and Peter, 2000: 137). By framing an issue in a particular way, media coverage can give a story an angle or spin that directs the audience to a certain interpretation of events. During the 1984–85 coal dispute, for example, Arthur Scargill, leader of the National Union of Mineworkers, attacked much television news content for being biased against the miners and actively tried to shift the framing of the dispute away from picket line violence and towards the closure of so-called 'uneconomic pits'.

More recently, much tabloid newspaper coverage of the asylum seeker issue during the second New Labour administration (2001–05) portrayed their presence in Britain in terms of the problems caused to the host society such as financial cost, administrative overload and social disruption. Combined with the use of highly emotive language, this framing is likely to have had an impact on the public perception of asylum seekers among the readers of these papers, as well as focusing their attention on some aspects of the issue at the expense of others. In this context, the construction of the asylum issue as a social problem by sections of the media could be regarded as an example of the media's contribution to a growing propensity to present 'dramatic narratives with a strong moral content' (Thompson, 1998:7) which may help to foment a sense of 'moral panic' in society.

This is not to say that the media are able to determine the opinions of their audiences on a specific issue. Research shows that audiences use media selectively and filter the messages they receive. If, for example, personal experience of an issue clashes with the dominant media coverage, the media user may reject that coverage or at least be highly sceptical of its accuracy. Nonetheless, the media exert considerable power in helping audiences decide what constitute the important social, political and economic issues of the day. If the media cannot tell us what to think, they certainly influence what we think about and how we think about it.

The perceived importance of this agenda-setting function means that political actors are constantly trying to shape the media agenda for their own partisan purposes: a process known as agenda-building. They try to use (or exploit) the media to persuade (or manipulate) the public. Frequently, therefore, the media reflect and transmit agendas largely set by other political actors, such as political parties and pressure groups. On many political issues the media act as fora for debate or as megaphones for the messages of political elites. This is not to say that the media are neutral territories, open to all political groups with a message. This cannot be the case with a partisan press, while even public service broadcasters are more responsive to those with status, authority and resources.

Yet in helping to set the public and political agenda, the media are not just the object of lobbying by government, political parties and pressure groups. Nor do they simply reflect public opinion or the opinions of their audiences. Newspapers, radio and television may behave as political communication actors in their own right, not just observing and reporting on the political process, but actively participating in it. The media may independently seize on an issue and help bring it on to the political agenda. In the early 1990s, for instance, tabloid newspapers and television news bulletins covered in horrific detail the savaging of children and adults by so-called 'mad dogs'. On the basis of a few such stories the media created an atmosphere of public concern to which politicians felt obliged to respond. The Home Secretary promised governmental action and a bill was quickly drafted and speedily passed through Parliament. In this case a link could be established between the initial media coverage and the enactment of governmental legislation. Paradoxically, because the legislation was so badly drafted, the unintended consequence of its enforcement was that some dogs that were not a danger to the public were destroyed. This provoked outrage on the part of their owners, whose subsequent protest itself became a news story.

National newspapers are particularly important agenda-setters for British politics. First, they influence their readers directly by focusing on certain issues, even if their short-term electoral influence should not be overstated (Curtice, 1997). Second, they help set the agenda for other media such as radio and television (Tunstall, 1996), thus helping to set the terms of the debate across the news media as a whole (Hagerty, 2000: 17). Finally, they help directly to influence the terms of the political debate, as in the case of the financial press and economic policy (Parsons, 1989). A notable example of the agenda-setting power of newspapers came during the Thatcher premiership when sections of the pro-Conservative press, especially the tabloids, mounted a campaign against several Labour-controlled local authorities which were run by groups on the left of the party (Greenslade, 2004: 542–5). The behaviour of these councils was pilloried in newspapers, which fabricated stories to make the councils appear extreme. One such story was that some councils had banned the nursery rhyme 'Baa, baa, black sheep' from schools on the grounds that it was racist. Despite attempts by the councils to set the record straight, the tabloids' alliterative appellation of 'loony left' stuck. This shorthand reference was taken up by the broadcasting media, Conservative politicians and even some Labour MPs. It also helped to fuel a popular perception of these councils as extremist (Curran, Gaber and Petley, 2005). The 'loony left' campaign helped destabilize the Labour party for much of the 1980s and put the party on the defensive, contributing to the leadership's modernizing agenda of the late 1980s and 1990s. It provided material to justify the Conservative government's stance against local government and its introduction of centralizing measures. Finally, by focusing attention on the alleged ideological extremism of the Labour authorities in question, it so skewed coverage that arguably more important issues such as council inefficiency, corruption and fraud were given less attention than they may have merited.

Public watchdog

A third political function of the media is that of public watchdog, acting on behalf of citizens as a check on elite behaviour. This may take the form, for example, of a newspaper exposing ministerial duplicity or a television programme highlighting governmental incompetence. In performing their watchdog function the media can help make political actors accountable to the public, assisting in the empowerment of the latter as citizens and voters. Moreover, at times sections of the media may act more as bloodhounds than watchdogs, rooting out improper behaviour through investigative journalism.

A good example of the media's watchdog function were the revelations by *The Guardian* newspaper and Granada Television's *World in Action* programme in 1995 of the behaviour of the Conservative minister Jonathan Aitken, accused of procuring prostitutes for Arabs, allowing a shadowy Arab friend to pay his hotel bill and indulging in an improper relationship with two arms dealers (Harding, Leigh and Pallister, 1997). This account was virulently contested by Aitken, who memorably promised 'to start a fight to cut out the cancer of bent and twisted journalism in our country with the simple sword of truth and the trusty shield of British fair play'. In the end, however, the media secured a famous victory, culminating in Aitken's conviction for perjury in 1997. Aitken's political career was effectively ended by the media investigations and his injudicious public contestation of their allegations.

Does the Aitken case mean that in the exercise of its watchdog function the media exercise political power? For the careers of individual politicians the answer would appear to be a resounding 'yes'. Certain sections of the media, notably the tabloid press, frequently pursue individual politicians to expose aspects of their behaviour. Indeed, exposure and attack journalism are part and parcel of popular tabloid coverage of politics in Britain. During the Major premiership, for example, a succession of Conservative politicians, including government ministers, were shown to be engaging in adulterous relationships, and the ministerial careers of David Mellor and Timothy Yeo were brought to an end when revelations of their extra-marital affairs were revealed in the press. The New Labour Secretary of State for Wales, Ron Davies, was forced to resign from politics altogether in 2002 after tabloid stories about his sexual orientation. John Prescott may have survived the lurid stories about his affair with a civil servant in his department in 2006, but only at significant cost to his reputation. The tone of newspaper coverage in all these cases was frequently salacious.

Arguably, since the Conservative party had presented itself as the party of family values and Prime Minister had embraced a 'back to basics' philosophy, the targeting of the extra-marital sexual exploits of Conservative politicians during the Major premiership could be defended as being in the public interest. McNair argues that the public are sufficiently sophisticated in these matters to sort out the media wheat from the chaff:

> Those who argue that this knowledge is not worth knowing, or that it diverts citizens from consideration of 'serious' issues, underestimate the public's ability to judge when the human frailties exposed in sleaze journalism are relevant to sound political decision-making and when they are not. (McNair, 2000: 57)

Perhaps this is so. Certainly, some news media regard their watchdog and bloodhound functions as an integral part of their civic responsibilities. However, it is also the case that the critical coverage of a particular personality may frequently be a self-serving exercise in prurient muckraking designed to boost circulation or ratings figures. In a democracy there may be a fine line between legitimately serving the public interest and unacceptable intrusion into the private lives of public figures. The balance to be struck between public interest and the protection of privacy has not only featured prominently on the media policy agenda in recent years, but continues to remain an issue of political and legal debate, particularly with regard to tabloid newspaper coverage of leading politicians, showbusiness and sports celebrities, and members of the Royal family (see Chapter 5).

Political mobilization

Fourth, the media perform a political mobilization function. They are widely used, for example, by political parties and pressure groups for the purposes of membership recruitment. The media, especially television, have to a significant extent also replaced local political parties as agencies of electoral mobilization. Public meetings featuring party candidates, local party canvassing and constituency-based campaigning have been largely superseded by national election campaigns fought out in the media (see Chapter 9). While some old-style electoral mobilization still takes place, even this is enormously enhanced if it receives media coverage. The internet further increases the potential for political mobilization by the media. It is used, for example, by protest groups such as anti-globalization protestors to organize demonstrations and other forms of direct action.

Regime legitimation

Finally, along with other agencies of civic socialization – such as the family, peer groups, the educational system, voluntary associations and religious bodies – the media play a role in helping to shape public attitudes, values, norms and beliefs with regard to the functioning of society in general and the operation of the political process in particular. The media help to socialize citizens into acceptance of prevalent social norms and the institutions that embody them. If successful in this task, the media contribute to the legitimation of the political system. In the eyes of some critics, however, negative media coverage of the political process may turn citizens off politics and contribute to increased levels of political cynicism and voter apathy. If so, media output may have a delegitimizing and demobilizing effect for at least some of their audiences (see Chapter 10).

2

Media Values: Free Market and Public Service

For most of the twentieth century distinct and contrasting values underpinned the functioning of the two main news media in Britain. In the press sector the concept of freedom – usually interpreted in terms of a minimally regulated competitive market – had long been the guiding principle for the organization and regulation of the newspaper industry. In the broadcasting sector a contrasting set of values based on the concept of public service dominated the framing of government policy. The development of new technology and the spread of pro-market ideological views inside the Conservative government resulted in the growing influence of neo-liberal values on broadcasting policy during the Thatcher premiership. As a result, from the mid-1980s onwards debates about the future of broadcasting, and in particular the appropriate extent of its regulation, were marked by the clash of rival normative discourses, as supporters of consumer sovereignty lined up against defenders of a revised concept of public service.

The objective of this chapter is to examine the way in which these values have helped to inform debates on media policy. The chapter is divided into three sections: the first considers the principle of press freedom; the second focuses on the tradition of public service in broadcasting; the third concentrates on the emergence of the principle of consumer sovereignty in broadcasting policy and the response from the supporters of a refashioned concept of public service which they argue is appropriate for the multi-channel digital age.

Freedom of the press

The principle of a free press constrained by minimal legal restrictions and organized on the basis of a competitive market has influenced

30

policy-making in this sector of the media since the latter half of the nineteenth century. Though not wholly ruled out, state intervention tends to be justified on the grounds that in some way the market is not functioning efficiently or that, in aspects of their content, newspapers are abusing their freedom to publish. In general, therefore, with the notable exception of wartime, the presumption among the political authorities in Britain for well over a century has been that the state should intervene in the press sector as minimally as possible.

The standard defence of the free press principle tends to emphasize the following:

- There are – and should remain – few legal and technical constraints on market entry
- Market freedom allows newspapers to respond to changing consumer demands and social trends
- A segmented national market promotes the publication of a range of daily and Sunday newspapers which provide variety in terms of news content, the quality of coverage and journalistic style
- A range of different political views are reflected across the spectrum of newspaper titles: for example, among national dailies there is a spread of opinion ranging from the centre-left *Guardian* and *Independent* to the right-wing *Daily Telegraph*
- As a result, consumers are free to purchase a newspaper that conforms to their tastes and interests, as well as their political preferences.

The dominance of the free press principle

There are five main reasons for the ideological dominance of the free press principle in media policy debates. The first is the historical legacy of the struggle to liberate the press from the grip of a repressive state (Curran and Seaton, 1997: 5–108; Negrine, 1994: 39–80; Wheeler, 1997: 31–56). Up until the middle of the nineteenth century, the government sought to influence newspaper ownership and content through a combination of censorship, legal restraints on content and restrictive financial measures. The abolition of the so-called 'taxes on knowledge' in the 1850s and 1860s marked a rupture with this system of state-imposed controls.

The conventional wisdom – the Whig theory of press development – is that this led to greater political freedom for the press, helping to foster new alignments between newspapers and political

parties. At the same time, the industrialization of newspaper production and the growth of advertising as a source of revenue gave newspapers more economic and commercial freedom in the marketplace.
Meanwhile, an increase in literacy and the extension of the suffrage
provided newspapers with a growing potential readership for their
product:

> The repeal of the stamp duty in 1855, prefigured by the abolition of the tax
> on advertisements two years earlier and capped by the abolition of the
> tax on paper six years later, created a new forum for national debate by
> according newspapers a vastly enlarged readership and, consequently, an
> enhanced potential for political influence. (Koss, 1990: 1)

Radical critics such as Curran, however, have argued that political
controls were simply replaced by the control of the market, which
was actually more effective at eliminating or marginalizing alternative and radical newspapers. According to this reading of history, the
importance of advertising as a source of finance and the huge
increase in capital investment required for mass publication of newspapers resulted in either the closure of national radical papers, their
accommodation to advertising pressure by moving up-market, their
confinement to a small ghetto of readers or their acceptance of an
alternative source of institutional patronage (Curran and Seaton,
1997: 37):

> The industrialization of the press, with its accompanying rise in publish-
> ing costs, led to a progressive transfer of ownership and control of the
> popular press from the working class to wealthy businessmen, while
> dependence on advertising encouraged the absorption or elimination of
> the early radical press and stunted its subsequent development before the
> First World War. (Curran and Seaton, 1997: 41)

Whether the removal of many state controls on newspaper publishing was a genuinely liberating measure in terms of promoting ownership pluralism and content diversity in the press during the late
nineteenth and early twentieth centuries is an open question. For our
purposes the point to emphasize is that the long historical struggle for
a free press exerted a profound and continuing influence on the framing of the terms of the policy debate in this sector of the media
throughout the whole of the twentieth century and beyond (Keane,
1991: 2–10; O'Malley and Soley, 2000).

Second, in marked contrast to the frequency scarcity in broadcasting, there has been no technological barrier to market entry into the

press. As a result, apart from the exceptional circumstances of newsprint rationing during the Second World War, there has generally not been a need for the state to become involved in the allocation of resources in the press sector. In theory, anyone who wants to start up a newspaper can do so. Providing an individual or group has the financial means and can find a market for their product, there is no apparent requirement for the state to play a role in control of market entry. The assumption, therefore, has been that subject to the proviso that regulation to ensure that the market is open to competition may be required, the press is an area that can for the most part be left to the invisible hand of market forces.

Third, newspaper proprietors and editors have been keen to propagate the values of a free press. Naturally, they have emphasized its desirability on the basis of the general public good rather than particular self-interest. For example, during the twentieth century they were able to point to the disadvantages of a state-controlled press in authoritarian and totalitarian societies, where information was manipulated by political authorities, newspapers were used as transmission belts for the official ideology and the press was unable to perform any effective watchdog function through the exercise of critical judgement on behalf of citizens. During periods of cold war tension in the second half of the twentieth century the presence of a free press in Britain was referred to by newspapers as one of the distinguishing characteristics of a free society in the West.

Fourth, either out of ideological conviction or reasons of self-interest (or both) governments have been markedly reluctant to interfere in the operations of the newspaper market. Either the government felt no need to intervene on principle or it feared the negative newspaper coverage and resultant public backlash which might result if it did so. Prime Minister Thatcher, for instance, benefited from the adulatory support of an overwhelming majority of national newspapers during the 1980s. Not surprisingly, the government calculated that a system based largely on the rights of newspaper proprietors to run their newspapers as they saw fit was perfectly consonant with the Conservatives' electoral self-interest. This non-interventionist stance was given a broader ideological foundation during the Thatcher premiership through the intellectual dominance of New Right ideas which stressed the desirability of the minimalist state. Labour governments, even those generally sympathetic to state intervention in the economy such as the postwar Attlee administration, have also been influenced by the ideological dominance of the free press principle.

More pragmatically, Labour governments have been reluctant to introduce structural reform of the press or interfere in its operations for fear of the adverse newspaper publicity that would undoubtedly ensue.

Finally, the principle of a free press as an integral part of a democratic political culture has been widely accepted by public opinion. The strong emphasis in liberal democratic theory on the concept of freedom, including freedom of speech and freedom to communicate ideas, has filtered down into popular consciousness to become associated with the value of a free press. While abuses of this freedom, such as invasion of individual privacy and chequebook journalism, have frequently received widespread public condemnation, popular support for the principle itself remains strong.

Definitional dilemmas

In the past there has been no consensus on how the principle of press freedom can be defined and operationalized to guide policy-makers. For the first postwar Royal Commission on the Press the concept was couched in terms of the freedom of the market and ultimately of proprietorial control (Royal Commission on the Press, 1949: 41 and 155). The most recent Royal Commission, which reported in 1977, proposed a more sophisticated definition:

> We define freedom of the press as that degree of freedom of restraint which is essential to enable proprietors, editors and journalists to advance the public interest by publishing the facts and opinions without which a democratic electorate cannot make responsible judgements. (Royal Commission on the Press, 1977: 8–9)

This definition, however, raises as many questions as it resolves. First, it seems to assume that proprietors, editors and journalists have common interests in the production and dissemination of news and opinion. In practice, however, the interests of these different media actors are not always shared and may even be in conflict. Consequently, an increase in the freedom of one of these actors may well be a limitation on the freedom of another. Second, the definition downplays the possibility that press freedom may be inhibited not by external constraints (such as governmental interference) but by the activities of media actors themselves. For example, while newspapers will tend to portray government intervention as an illegitimate limitation on their freedom to publish, proprietors may themselves restrict the freedom of their newspapers to cover certain stories to protect and further their wider commercial interests. Third, how is the public interest to be defined? This has been a particularly complex problem, for example, with regard to newspaper coverage of the private lives of public figures.

In the absence of a written codified constitution there has been no precise equivalent in Britain of the US constitution's first amendment which formally protects freedom of speech and of the press. Consequently, in Britain 'freedom of the press remains an important cultural tradition but not the privileged legal principle it is in the United States' (Hallin and Mancini, 2004: 230). In 2000 the Human Rights Act incorporated the European Convention on Human Rights into British law. This guarantees protection, enforceable for the first time in British courts, for a wide range of fundamental civil rights. These include the right to freedom of expression, enshrined in article 10 of the Convention: 'Everyone has the right to freedom of expresssion. This right shall include freedom to hold opinions and to receive and impart information and ideas without interference by public authority and regardless of frontiers.' The full impact on press and media freedom of this new overarching legislation still remains to be fully tested in the British courts. It has been invoked both by media outlets seeking to push back the boundaries of what they regard as unwarranted infringement of their freedom to publish and by individuals trying to protect their privacy from what they regard as unacceptable media intrusion.

The belief that market competition was integral to the liberty of the press was central to the long political campaign against the imposition and enforcement of state controls on newspaper publishing during the nineteenth century and before. 'The market was viewed as an invisible, unbiased and gentle medium of circulating public opinions freely. It was regarded as an enclave of honesty, truth and integrity in a despotic world of secrecy, scheming and arrogance' (Keane, 1991: 45). In the real world of the national newspaper industry in contemporary Britain, however, the operation of the market may itself be seen as a constraint on press freedom. It has resulted, for instance, in a high degree of ownership concentration in the national newspaper industry, with both the daily and Sunday markets dominated by a small number of press groups operating in a situation of oligopolistic competition. It has also given significant power to proprietors and advertisers.

Proprietorial power

Press groups tend to be hierarchically structured and dominated by either interventionist proprietors or powerful chief executives, frequently assisted by supportive editors. Proprietors may be motivated more by commercial than political considerations, adopting a hands-off approach with regard to editorial content. For example, Wheeler contends that after the Second World War 'the domination of the old press barons declined as ownership changed and the former generation died out. Their successors were motivated more by profits and intervened less over the newspaper's editorial line.' (Wheeler, 1997: 49). In a similar vein, Hirsch and Gordon argue that newspaper proprietors of the mid-1970s were more concerned with commercial objectives than with political propaganda – 'the press lords of the present generation . . . are less interested in what their papers say than in what they pay' (Hirsch and Gordon, 1975: 39). If so, this state of affairs was soon to change as proprietors became more interventionist and more involved in the political line of their papers.

The 1980s saw increasing criticism of the willingness and capacity of newspaper proprietors such as Rupert Murdoch of News International, Victor Matthews of the Express group, Robert Maxwell of the Mirror Newspaper Group and Conrad Black of the Telegraph group to intervene in editorial decisions for political as well as commercial reasons (Curran and Seaton, 1997: 72–7). Tiny Rowland, owner of *The Observer*, interfered constantly in the running of the paper to protect the commercial concerns of his Lonrho group with its mining interests in Africa and in particular criticized the newspaper's editor, Donald Trelford, for the paper's coverage of the political situation in Zimbabwe (Hollingsworth, 1986: 8–12). The open nature of the conflict between proprietor and editor led to the former being rebuked by the paper's independent directors for improper proprietorial interference in editorial freedom.

Certainly the financial 'bottom line' always remains important. For instance, on her appointment as Trinity Mirror chief executive in 2003, Sly Bailey announced that she planned to become directly involved in the editorial direction of the *Daily Mirror*. Her announcement came after a significant drop in the already declining sales of the newspaper as a result of its campaigning anti-war stance on the conflict in Iraq under the editorship of Piers Morgan. Although Morgan had previously enjoyed a significant amount of editorial autonomy, Bailey's arrival coincided with a decision to call a halt to

Morgan's commitment to take the title upmarket and embrace 'serious journalism'.

The distinction between politically and commercially motivated decisions is often blurred and difficult to maintain in practice. According to his former *Sunday Times* editor, Andrew Neil, Murdoch may put his business interests before his political beliefs if the two conflict (Neil, 1997: 208), but he also tries to ensure that commercial pragmatism and political leanings are in harmony. Thus, the praise heaped on Thatcher's neo-liberal crusade by the Murdoch newspapers in the 1980s reflected his belief that her government's policies did not just promote his company's interests, which they clearly did, but were also introducing much needed change in the country's economic attitudes and behaviour. Similarly, the support of the traditionally pro-Conservative *Daily Express* for New Labour in the late 1990s may have been part of a commercial strategy to try to win new readers in a market segment dominated by the *Daily Mail*, but it was also the case that the paper's owner, Lord Hollick, was a well-known supporter of New Labour.

Proprietorial intervention can be spectacularly direct; more usually the owner relies on the loyalty (or subservience) of the editorial staff who are well aware of their proprietor's views on major issues. Editors may be content to follow the proprietorial line and may even feel that ownership confers on proprietors the right to interfere. For example, when in 1989 Max Hastings, editor of *The Daily Telegraph*, was asked about his reaction to proprietorial interference, he retorted:

> I've never really believed in the notion of editorial independence as such. I would never imagine saying to Conrad [Black], 'You have no right to ask me to do this, I must observe my independence', because Conrad is, it seems to me, richly entitled to take a view when he owns the newspaper. (Bevins, 1990: 13–14)

Andrew Neil, appointed to the editorship of *The Sunday Times* in 1983, echoed these sentiments in his evaluation of the proprietorial style of Rupert Murdoch: 'why should the owner not be the ultimate arbiter of what was in his paper?' (Neil, 1997: 47). However, it was not so much a case of Murdoch laying down the law as of the proprietor appointing an editor who shared 'a set of common assumptions about politics and society' (Neil, 1997: 202) and then usually allowing Neil to get on with the job.

If an editor fails to conform, then their services can be dispensed with, as in the case of the conflict that pitted Murdoch against Harold

Evans, editor of *The Sunday Times* and then of *The Times* in the early 1980s (Evans, 1983). According to Neil's account his own relationship with Murdoch eventually broke down when news coverage by *The Sunday Times* in February 1994 of the Pergau dam affair in Malaysia threatened to interfere with the South East Asian interests and global media expansion plans of the parent company, News Corporation. Neil left his editor's post shortly afterwards (Neil, 1997: 509–45).

Proprietorial intervention may be particularly important with reference to the partisanship of a newspaper. In 1995 Murdoch asserted that in the following general election campaign both *The Times* and *Sunday Times* would back whomever the editors wished to support. Peter Stothard, appointed editor of *The Times* in 1992, contends that he was given no advice on the line to take with the Conservative government of John Major and that Murdoch subsequently did not try to interfere with his editorial decisions (Seldon, 1997: 710). However, with regard to *The Sun*, Murdoch quipped that 'I'm sure the editor will consult with me and I will have some input' (*The Guardian*, 22 May 1995). Neil argues that the two Murdoch tabloids – *The Sun* and the *News of the World* – were 'the two papers whose editorial lines are directly under his [Murdoch's] control' (Neil, 1997: xxii) and that their editors played almost no part in the decision that these two papers would back New Labour in the 1997 general election campaign. In a clear example of proprietorial intervention, the decision to switch sides was imposed on reluctant senior journalists at *The Sun* at the very start of the 1997 campaign (McKie, 1998: 119; Scammell and Harrop, 1997: 160). In 2002 Murdoch announced that all his titles (*The Sun*, *The Times*, *News of the World* and *The Sunday Times*) would support a 'No' vote in any forthcoming referendum on the issue of British membership of the single European currency.

At the other end of the spectrum is the situation at *The Guardian*, which is owned by the non-interventionist Scott Trust. While the trust was originally established as a means of avoiding death duties for the Scott family, the impact of which might have financially destabilized the newspaper (Scott, 1998), its chief purpose has been to ensure that *The Guardian* cannot fall into unacceptable predatory hands. A former editor of the paper commented:

> The only instruction given to the editor of *The Guardian* on appointment is to 'carry on the paper in the same spirit as before'. Editorial policy is discussed by the trustees only infrequently, and then generally on the initiative of the editor . . . [This] has in practice secured . . . the independence of [the paper's] editor. (Hetherington, 1985: 26)

The nature of the relationship between proprietors and editors varies from paper to paper and over time, making generalizations difficult (Negrine, 1998: 163–73; Tunstall, 1996: 77–135). As Tunstall points out, even a domineering proprietor like Maxwell did not always get his own way at the *Daily Mirror* and could be persuaded to give the editor a large measure of management control of the paper (Tunstall, 1996: 129). In similar fashion, in the 1997 general election campaign the *Daily Mail* supported the Conservatives, despite the fact that the paper's proprietor, Lord Rothermere, was personally supportive of Blair (Scammell and Harrop, 1997: 168; Seldon, 1997: 711–12). Nonetheless, in terms of the general strategic direction of a newspaper, there is considerable validity in the view that 'owners dominate their newspapers from the top down' (Franklin, 1994: 38).

Advertiser influence

Newspapers depend on advertising revenue for market survival. Advertising is, of course, enormously beneficial to national newspapers, keeping down the cost to the consumer by providing newspapers with an additional source of revenue to the cover price. Without advertising, newspapers would be significantly more expensive to purchase. Indeed, one of the success stories of the twenty-first century has been the *Metro* morning papers distributed freely in London and other cities, the total circulation of which topped one million in 2005 and whose revenue is derived entirely from advertising (Berry, 2005).

However, advertising may also distort the economics of newspaper publishing. Because of the different socio-economic composition of their readerships, advertisers in the tabloid sector need quantity, while advertisers in the broadsheet/compact sector are more interested in quality. As a result, popular and middle market newspapers may cease to be profitable even with what at first sight appear to be reasonably high circulations, as was the case with the *Daily Herald* in the 1960s. In contrast, 'quality' newspapers do not need huge circulations to survive, as the example of the *Financial Times* makes clear. In fact, paradoxically more readers may actually be detrimental to the commercial success of an upmarket newspaper. If the new readers are not of the socio-economic status sought by advertisers, the increase in circulation may be more than offset by a loss in advertising revenue.

Advertisers may also seek directly to influence media content. The case in 1978 of the Cunard shipping company, which withdrew advertising from *The Times* and *Sunday Times* in response to articles in the two newspapers critical of the company, can be viewed as an example of the attempted exercise of financial power by advertisers. However, since the articles were in fact published, the case can also be seen as an illustration of the inability of advertisers to influence content when faced by media resistance (Hollingsworth, 1986: 15). Indeed, rather than search for spectacular individual examples of advertiser interference, it is more useful to concentrate on the structural and agenda-setting influence of advertising for the news media. Curran and Seaton make a strong case for the impact of advertising both in limiting the range of newspapers operating in the market to the detriment of radical and left-wing titles and in influencing the content of newspapers generally (Curran and Seaton, 1997: 71–108). Moreover, broadening the analysis to embrace other news media, Street is probably correct in arguing that 'the political influence of advertisers may be identified, not in the specific content of any given magazine or paper or programme, but rather in the *kinds* of stories that appear' (Street, 2001: 141, emphasis in original). Thus, the huge growth in features and lifestyle journalism has been largely driven by the need to attract advertisers. Much of the media's reliance on advertising may also contribute to a tendency on the part of some outlets 'to marginalize politics, and to adopt a populist approach to scheduling and news coverage, in which "hard news" makes way for "human interest" stories' (ibid.: 143).

The market, the state and press freedom

Along with concentration of newspaper ownership (which we shall examine in Chapter 4), proprietorial power and the important role of advertising revenue in national newspaper funding are important characteristics of the market functioning of the press in contemporary Britain. None of these features may negate the claims of the press to be free in terms of its relationship with the state. However, by distorting the relationship between consumer and producer, they raise questions about the efficacy of the largely unrestricted market in delivering the levels of choice and diversity which proponents of the free press principle have traditionally claimed as one of its main strengths:

[H]istorically, the proponents of 'liberty of the press' directed their criti-cisms mainly against the *state* regulation of market-based communica-tions media. Today, by contrast, friends of the 'liberty of the press' must recognize that *communications markets restrict freedom of communica-tion* by generating barriers to entry, monopoly and restrictions upon choice, and by shifting the prevailing definition of information from that of a public good to that of a privately appropriable commodity. (Keane, 1991: 89, emphasis in original)

Yet whatever its limitations in practice, the principle of a free press seems well-entrenched as a reference point for policy-making in this sector of the media. For example, regulations on levels of newspaper ownership are either non-existent or, where they do exist, have been liberally interpreted (see Chapter 4). In addition, despite public concerns about aspects of press behaviour, the operations of the news-paper industry are subject to a system of self-regulation rather than monitoring by a statutory body (see Chapter 5).

The comparative lack of regulation has been accompanied by a refusal on the part of successive governments to provide any state financial assistance to newspapers to help promote diversity and pluralism, even though similar schemes exist in several, though not all, continental European countries. Such proposals have included the redistribution of advertising revenue to newspapers requiring finan-cial support and the establishment of a media enterprise board to assist the launch of new ventures. In this respect the principle of non-inter-vention stated by the Royal Commission on the Press in 1977 remains apposite:

We are strongly against any scheme which would make the press, or any section of it, dependent on government through reliance on continuing subsidies from public funds. (Royal Commission on the Press, 1977: 112)

One argument against state subsidy – that financial aid from the state might lead to governmental interference in editorial content – is not borne out by the experience of other European countries. A second argument – that state aid does not necessarily achieve the desired goal of increasing pluralism and diversity across the newspaper sector – may carry more weight (Murschetz, 1998: 303–4). So too may the argument that in an age of converging media technologies it is diffi-cult to defend technology-dependent subsidies, whereby financial aid is given to one type of medium that is published on one specific type of technology – print – while support to other types of media such as digitised services is rejected (Skogerbø, 1997: 115). In any case, the question of state assistance to the press is a purely academic one in contemporary Britain. Among political elites there appears to be a consensual view that the concept of a free press is incompatible with any notion of positive state assistance over and above the non-imposition of VAT on the sale of newspapers.

Public service broadcasting

The establishment of the BBC

In the broadcasting sector a set of values based on the concept of public service dominated the framing of policy for most of the twentieth century. The public service approach to broadcasting dates from the foundation of the BBC as a public corporation in the 1920s. Though the BBC was initially established as a private company by wireless manufacturers who needed a reliable source of programming to promote the sale of their radio sets to the public, the state soon became involved in the organization and regulation of the new medium. In 1926 the Crawford Committee recommended the transformation of the company into a public corporation, which in return for benefiting from a monopoly in programming would be regulated as a public service (Briggs, 1961: 327–48).

Various factors contributed to the application of the public service principle to government policy in these formative years of British broadcasting. First, there was the technical argument that the restricted nature of the frequency spectrum meant there could be no free market in sound broadcasting. Second, the US model of organization, in which radio was run by many competing commercial companies, was not considered suitable for Britain (Hearst, 1992: 62). Third, a government-controlled system was unacceptable for political reasons (Tivey, 1973: 30). Fourth, there was a belief among policy elites that 'the new medium was so powerful a means of disseminating knowledge and opinion that it should not be left to the market for its development' (Gibbons, 1998a: 56). Fifth, a commitment to ideas of the public corporation and 'public good' was prevalent among policy-makers (Curran and Seaton, 1997: 113–18). Finally, the views of the BBC's first managing director, John Reith, had an influential impact (Gaber, 2002: 32–5). Reith was an unashamed elitist who had a strong sense of the cultural and educative mission of the new medium. He believed that radio should be used to raise audience tastes and not just cater for what listeners wanted. Under Reith's stewardship the Corporation was to use 'the brute force of monopoly' to expand its reach and impose on its audience the sort of programming that Reith considered to be in their best interests (Reith, 1949: 99).

This Reithian interpretation of public service was highly moralistic, paternalist and even condescending. The output of BBC radio in the 1920s and 1930s scarcely catered for the range of audience tastes. Yet though in its original form such an elitist vision of broadcasting would be wholly unacceptable nowadays, it did allow the early BBC to foster a culture of broadcasting that was devoid of commercialism. For Reith the maintenance of the monopoly was crucial to the achievement of his mission and so state support for this principle was vital. While the relationship between the state and Reith's BBC was sometimes stormy, both parties recognised a shared interest in reaching a mutually acceptable *modus vivendi*. For the government, the monopoly simplified the organization of the medium and made it administratively easier to manage. Reith recognized that as a monopoly radio service the BBC could not be wholly independent of the state, while the monopoly allowed him to use radio for his social and cultural crusade. Yet at the same time he was keen to ensure that the government would not establish close editorial control of broadcast content on a day-to-day basis for fear that this would weaken the legitimacy of the Corporation.

Coverage of the 1926 General Strike by the nascent BBC was an early indication of both the scope of and limitations on the Corporation's independence from the state. Reith persuaded the government not to take over the airwaves of the BBC, while in return the BBC adopted a stance that was unashamedly pro-government and anti-strike. 'Reith felt that it was his duty as the managing director of a national company to act in the national interest, which he interpreted along the lines of not broadcasting anything which might help to spread the strike and thus damage the nation' (Sales, 1986: 49). From the very beginning of its corporate existence, therefore, the BBC sought to resolve the tension between its public face as a non-partisan broadcaster and its need to cultivate a working relationship with the state by operating as an institution within the Constitution. The effect on the BBC's coverage of politics was that up until the loss of its broadcasting monopoly in the mid-1950s the Corporation tended to eschew political controversy, avoid the discussion of anything too radical and treat establishment politicians with deference.

The regulated duopoly

After the Second World War the public service approach was carried over from radio and applied to the organization of television during the few years of BBC monopoly. Moreover, even when the monopoly was abolished with the introduction of ITV, competition between the two services was still highly regulated. Though ITV's programme output was clearly aimed at a more downmarket audience than the BBC's, the operations of the ITV companies were made subject to public service provisions (Curran and Seaton, 1997: 161–72). In a 'historical bargain' between the state and the new broadcaster, the ITV companies 'were granted sole access to public spectrum for the licence period and therefore a monopoly on television advertising revenue in the region. In return for the licence the ITV companies agreed to public service obligations including an independent news provider ITN' (Cowling, 2004: 63). ITV was obliged to show educational and information programmes in addition to its entertainment output; due impartiality in news programming was required; a ban on editorializing was enforced; programmes deemed unsuitable for children were to be excluded from early evening schedules; a requirement that proper proportions of programmes be of British origin and British performance was imposed; and the type and quantity of advertising were strictly controlled.

A new regulatory body, the Independent Television Authority (ITA), renamed the Independent Broadcasting Authority (IBA) after the establishment of Independent Local Radio in the 1970s, was created as a public corporation to ensure the compliance of the ITV companies with these and other public service regulations. As a result, though in many respects it appeared to operate like a commercial broadcaster, ITV was not free to programme what it liked to maximize its audience ratings and advertising revenue. While Reith may have viewed the establishment of ITV as comparable to an invasion of bubonic plague (McIntyre, 1993: 310), the new broadcaster came to be regarded by many as 'an extension of public service broadcasting, not an alternative' (Scannell, 1990: 18).

In the eyes of its defenders the regulated British public service broadcasting system had many successes. It proved itself to be adaptable, evolving in response to changing social climates and audience tastes. Its programme output was popular with British viewers and its programmes enjoyed wide international admiration, frequently carrying off the honours at international television festivals. It maintained programme range and quality by introducing a measure of competition among channels for viewers, while at the same time avoiding certain undesirable consequences of untrammelled competition – such as an all out ratings war – by ensuring the separate components different sources of funding.

Up until the 1980s the conventional view among policy-makers and broadcasting professionals was that the regulated public service approach was a successful compromise between a state-controlled and market-oriented system:

> Separate funding and an overall public service framework had secured diversity of programming, rather than the 'lowest common denominator' of commercially driven audience maximisation. Competition for audiences and one-remove control of public service had contributed to a more popular and less deferential approach to television. Secure funding and public service obligations had produced a professional culture of, and an audience taste for, high-budget, sometimes controversial, domestically produced programming. (Goodwin, 1998: 16)

Garnham also puts forward the conventional defence of the public servce duopoly (but only before going on to attack it for its complacency):

> By vesting the power to broadcast in two independent public service corporations run by bodies appointed to represent the public interest, we have successfully freed broadcasting from state control; by the device of the licence fee we have freed the BBC from crude commercial control and the chase for ratings thus allowing minority interests to be catered for as well as mass pleasures; by the device of competition and advertising revenue under firm public service control we have avoided the dangers of irresponsibility and elitism inherent in monopoly and enabled the public to control the broadcasters not only via parliament and the corporations but also via the exercise of choice. (Garnham, 1980: 15)

One should certainly be very wary of looking back to a supposed golden age of public service broadcasting in Britain. The system always provided limited choice to listeners and viewers; some programming was mediocre, even if some was very good; and the broadcasters were largely unaccountable to the public. Moreover, if direct governmental interference in political content was exceptional and not always successful – as was demonstrated in the 1956 Suez crisis – indirect pressures were certainly present and broadcasters were always open to the criticism, especially from the Left, of operating within the parameters of the prevalent elite middle-of-the-road consensus.

Definitional dilemmas

For all the tenacity of the public service principle in policy-making, the essentials of the public service approach have always been difficult to pin down with any precision (Scannell, 1990; Peacock Report, 1986: 130–3). The practical application of the principle not only evolved in response to social changes, growing broadcasting provision and new methods of funding, but was also adapted to cover a variety of different institutional arrangements and styles of programming. It embraced the BBC radio monopoly of the 1920s and the range of radio and television output of the early 1980s. The deferential BBC of the 1950s was a public service broadcaster of its time as much as the iconoclastic Corporation of the 1960s.

However, while the flexibility of the principle of public service may have allowed the British broadcasting system to grow organically, this was at the cost of a lack of definitional clarity with regard to the principle's core values. At one end of the ideological spectrum, Rupert Murdoch affirmed in 1989 that 'anybody who . . . provides a service which the public wants at a price it can afford is providing a public service' (Gaber, 2002: 60), thus placing the consumer's willingness and ability to pay at the heart of his interpretation of the concept. Fourteen years later, in its review of public service television broadcasting, Ofcom argued that the problem with the term 'public service broadcasting' is that it has at least four different meanings: good television; worthy television; television that would not exist without some form of public intervention; and the institutions that broadcast this type of television (http://www.ofcom.org.uk/consultations/current/psb/meaning/).

As the ideological dominance of the principle came under challenge in the 1980s, its defenders drew up a list of its defining features (Broadcasting Research Unit, 1985). These were:

- Universality: geographic – broadcast programmes should be available to the whole population
- Universality: of appeal – broadcast programmes should cater for all interests and tastes
- Minorities, especially disadvantaged minorities, should receive particular provision
- Broadcasters should recognize their special relationship to the sense of national identity and community
- Broadcasting should be distanced from all vested interests, and in particular from those of the government of the day

- Universality of payment – one main instrument of broadcasting should be directly funded by the corpus of users
- Broadcasting should be structured so as to encourage competition in good programming rather than competition for numbers
- The public guidelines for broadcasting should be designed to liberate rather than restrict the programme makers.

Critics argued that these elements were vague and that the list invited 'the suspicion that it offers ex-post justification for whatever broadcasters provide us with' (Peacock, 1989: 53). In any event, confronted by a pincer movement of new broadcasting technology and New Right ideology, the organization of broadcasting based on a controlled and limited supply subject to public service regulation began to break down in the late 1980s. As a result, an expanded, more competitive and less highly regulated broadcasting system became evident in the years that followed. By the second half of the Thatcher premiership the largely unchallenged dominance of public service values in influencing British broadcasting policy had come to an end.

Consumer sovereignty versus public service?

From the foundation of the BBC up until the broadcasting reforms instituted by the Conservative government in the second half of the 1980s, policy-makers in Britain generally accepted the desirability of broadcasting being organized and regulated as a public rather than a private good. Though other views were not absent from policy debates, they were either assimilated into the dominant public service principle or had little impact on decision-making. During the Thatcher premiership, however, the continued relevance of public service values in broadcasting was challenged by a new approach based on the principle of consumer sovereignty.

The Peacock Report and consumer sovereignty

The Thatcher premiership thus witnessed the emergence of a norma-tive conflict between those defending an established notion of public service and those advocating a more commercially-oriented, deregu-latory approach. The principle of consumer sovereignty was most explicitly outlined in the 1986 Peacock Report on financing the BBC and underpinned recommendations in the government's 1988 White

Paper *Broadcasting in the '90s: Competition, Choice and Quality* (Home Office, 1988). It also influenced the content of the 1990 Broadcasting Act, one of the main objectives of which was to create a 'light touch' regulator to supervise the ITV network.

Two main factors help explain the emergence of the principle of consumer sovereignty in policy debates at this time. First, new means of delivering television to households were beginning to make their presence felt in the broadcasting market (McQuail, 1995). The new technologies of cable and satellite changed the ground rules in television transmission. By expanding the potential range of programming available to households through multi-channel television, these 'new media' appeared to open up the possibility of a broadcasting system that would be more responsive to audiences and less dependent on public service type regulation. This allowed proponents of change to argue that consumers rather than regulators could now be the arbiters of public taste. It is true that in practice the provision and audience take-up of these new services, especially cable, were considerably slower than forecast. However, the anticipated arrival of multi-channel television featured strongly in the analysis of the Peacock Committee.

Second, an intellectual shift had taken place in British governing circles during the Thatcher premiership. The rise of New Right ideas among intellectual opinion formers facilitated the emergence of an alternative normative conceptualization of the relationship between the state, broadcasting and the audience. Public broadcasters were accused of being inefficient and ridden with restrictive practices, while their approach to their audiences was deemed paternalistic and condescending. Regulators were now presented as having been 'captured' by the broadcasters rather than serving the interests of the public. The Reithian legacy was challenged across a wide front, as a market liberal discourse sought to claim the intellectual high ground. Such a discourse was not in itself new. Previous examples of its use could be found in the publications of right-wing 'think tanks' such as the Institute of Economic Affairs (Altman, Thomas and Sawers, 1962). However, for the first time a new principle began to have a major influence in the framing of the broadcasting policy debate.

The advocacy of a market liberal approach to the organization of broadcasting was part of a broader shift in elite thinking on the role of the state in the economy and society. The policy impact could be seen in the assault on public sector institutions by a radical right-wing administration which was prepared to use the language of economic efficiency and 'value for money' to attack the public sector. The Conservative government's belief in the primacy of market mechanisms, its sweeping privatization programme (which embraced the telecommunications, gas, electricity and water industries among others) and its rejection of core elements of the bipartisan elite consensus which had governed Britain between 1945 and 1979 (Kavanagh and Morris, 1989) – all of these had important implications for the application of public service values to broadcasting. In particular, the Thatcher premiership demonstrated an undisguised hostility towards the main public service broadcasting organization, the BBC, not just attacking aspects of its political coverage on issues such as the Falklands war and the conflict in Northern Ireland (Seaton, 1994), but also calling into question its source of funding, the effectiveness of its management and its allegedly over-protected status (Barnett and Curry, 1994).

In recommending a sweeping reform of broadcast regulation, the Peacock Report put forward the most convincing intellectual case for the application of the principle of consumer sovereignty to broadcasting policy (Peacock Report, 1986; Goodwin, 1998: 69–92). Though the committee had been established with the limited brief of assessing the effects of the introduction of advertising or sponsorship on the BBC, its report went much further than this by setting out the intellectual case for a deregulated broadcasting system. While previous committees of inquiry 'had considered broadcasting in social, cultural, and political terms . . . Peacock . . . applied a stringent economic approach and in so doing completely shifted the grounds of discussion' (Scannell, 1990: 21). As a result, the report's significance lay 'as much in the manner in which it shifted the intellectual paradigm' of broadcasting policy as in any of its specific recommendations (Negrine, 1990: 154).

The report attacked what it termed the 'comfortable duopoly' of BBC and ITV which appeared to serve the interests of the broadcasters more than those of the viewer. The existing broadcasting set-up artificially restricted market entry and failed to maximize the welfare of consumers. Instead Peacock argued that 'the fundamental aim of broadcasting policy should . . . be to enlarge both the freedom of choice of the consumer and the opportunities available to programme makers to offer alternative wares to the public' (Peacock Report, 1986: 125). Peacock recommended the removal of entry barriers to producers and the use of subscription as a means of payment in an attempt to create conditions as analogous as possible to those of a perfect broadcasting market, in which pay-tv services would provide opportunities additional to advertising and tax-financed channels (Brittan, 1989: 33).

In the multi-channel television system of the future, content regulation – equated by some of the committee's members with censorship (ibid.: 27) – would be neither necessary nor practical. Instead Peacock envisaged a scenario in which there would be a television market similar to that which already existed for the press. In this new era of electronic publishing, viewers should be allowed to choose their own programme menu and not be compelled to swallow a balanced diet, however healthy such a regime were deemed to be. While the general laws applicable to press output and certain technical regulations might need to be enforced, there would be little or no necessity to uphold traditional public service regulations in a genuine consumer-oriented market (Wheeler, 1997: 118–26). Peacock thus advocated what one of the committee's leading members described as a 'phased programme of deregulation' (Brittan, 1987: 12).

While the radical scenario outlined by Peacock did not go unchallenged, the report's consumerist market-oriented principle was to have a significant impact in setting the agenda for the subsequent policy debate (Franklin, 2001a; Goodwin, 1998: 93–108). The 1988 White Paper argued that the avowed aim of television policy should be 'to open the doors so that individuals can choose for themselves from a much wider range of programmes and types of broadcasting' (Home Office, 1988: 1). The expansion in the number of television channels should be accompanied by a light regulatory commitment by the government. 'As new services emerge and subscription develops, viewer choice, rather than regulatory imposition, can and should increasingly be relied upon to secure the programmes which viewers want' (ibid.: 5):

> Wherever possible the Government's approach to broadcasting should be consistent with its overall deregulation policy. This is that the Government should help enterprises to set up, develop and meet the needs of consumers by removing unnecessary regulatory barriers. This implies both less regulation (removing restrictions which are outmoded or unnecessary) and better regulations (lighter, more flexible, more efficiently administered). (ibid.: 6)

Various policy initiatives in the 1990s pushed British broadcasting towards a more consumer-oriented approach. The 1990 Broadcasting Act sought to lighten the regulatory regime for ITV and create a 'light touch' regulator to supervise the commercial television sector. The system of allocating the ITV company licences was altered from a discretionary approach based on the reputation of the applicants to a process of competitive tendering whereby in principle franchises would be awarded to the highest bidder (Goodwin, 1998: 109–22). Before the 1990 Act 'public interest considerations were given a priority that allowed the market only a limited role in determining the framework of the service' (Gibbons, 1998a: 151). The 1990 Act changed this approach. Furthermore, independent producers were given a guaranteed quota of BBC and ITV output in a bid to reduce costs and open up the programme production side of the duopoly. In general, during the 1990s the ITV companies placed greater emphasis on company profitability and were more commercial in their programming policies as they sought to maximize advertising revenue (Wheeler, 1997: 149–55). In addition, the creation of an additional advertising-funded terrestrial channel, Channel 5, the gradual expansion of cable services and, most notably, the arrival of BSkyB as the unchallenged dominant player in satellite television (King, 1998) introduced a greater degree of competition into British television during these final years of the pre-digital era.

A revised concept of public service for the digital age

The conflict, which pitted the proponents of the consumer sovereignty principle against advocates of public service values in broadcasting policy, did not result in the total victory of the former or the unconditional surrender of the latter. As Britain began to embrace multi-channel television, defenders of public service values were partially successful in mitigating the full force of the neo-liberal onslaught, arguing that greater competition might lead to lower programme standards, greater reliance on American products, a reduction in diversity of opinions, a loss of cultural identity, the unacceptable commercialization of programming aimed at children and the possible loss of an educative and informative public sphere in mass communications (Blumler, 1992). The success of their damage limitation exercise was in part due to divisions within governing circles (see Chapter 3), in part because the sheer length of the policy-making process allowed them time to conduct their campaign and in part because of the strength, adaptability and interdependence of the established broadcasting institutions.

Despite the commercialization of the structures and functioning of a significant part of British radio and television in the 1990s, therefore, the deregulatory push was by no means all embracing. Broadcasters such as the BBC and Channel 4 continued to be given a public service purpose by government, while ITV retained some public service obligations; the ITV franchise auction included an important emphasis on programme range and quality as opposed to the purely financial aspect of the bids; and in its early years the new regulator for the commercial side of broadcasting, the Independent Television Commission, took its task of monitoring the programme output of the ITV franchise holders as seriously as its predecessor. It is probably fair to say, therefore, that while during the 1990s 'the broadcasting system became more market-oriented . . . it did not become, like the press, subordinated to the market' (Curran and Seaton, 1997: 330). Other commentators, however, have taken a more pessimistic line (Tracey, 1998), arguing that the regulatory minimalist approach undertaken by Conservative and Labour governments since the early 1980s effectively resulted in 'the game [being] up for public service broadcasting by the end of the twentieth century' (O'Malley, 2001: 28).

Whatever the assessment of developments in broadcasting policy in the final years of the analogue age, it is pertinent to ask whether public service values retain any relevance in the digital era. Clearly the technological rationale of spectrum scarcity no longer applies, while a Reithian vision of the civilizing mission of broadcasting appears wholly out of touch with audiences socialized in a leisure culture that emphasizes consumerism, choice and instant gratification:

> The ability to sell broadcasting, apparently like many other goods, has also made many question the need for public service broadcasting. This is now often seen as either unnecessary (spectrum scarcity has gone so there is no longer any case for public control), or as undesirable (because public service broadcasting is paternalistic), or as an anachronism (in the new world of competition and convergence, broadcasting policy should reflect the needs of industrial policy not the desires of a cultural elite), or as unsustainable (as other broadcasters expand people's willingness to pay the licence fee will disappear). (Graham and Davies, 1997: 8)

Yet an intellectual case for the continued relevance of public service values continues to inform media policy debates. Its supporters are not attempting to turn the clock back to an age of a restricted, integrated, public service broadcasting system. The argument is not that all broadcasting services in Britain should be managed with reference to public service values, as was effectively the situation up until the early 1980s. Rather, the objective is the more limited one of arguing the case for the retention of an important public service component in a mixed-media broadcasting and communications economy (Steemers, 1998). There are both economic and cultural/political parts to this case. Here we shall concentrate on the cultural/political arguments; we shall examine the economic ones in Chapter 4. From a broad cultural perspective one of the key mobilizing concepts employed by the supporters of public service values is the promotion of citizenship. It is argued, for example, that there are parts of our lives to which the market is simply not relevant, because we inhabit a public as well as a private realm (Lipsey, 2002: 21) and therefore watch television and listen to the radio not just as consumers, but also as citizens (Collins and Murroni, 1996: 13–14; Graham and Davies, 1997: 27). For Feintuck, addressing inequalities of citizenship is a central and legitimate aim for media regulation (Feintuck, 1999: 79), since 'citizenship, or full and effective participation in society, is dependent upon universal access to adequate sources of information' (Feintuck, 1999: 67). Within this citizenship framework Congdon stresses the role of a public service broadcaster like the BBC 'with a specific responsibility for providing high-quality news, offering a forum for debates about key issues of public policy and protecting certain conventions about the right conduct of such debates' (Congdon, 1995: 23).

Defenders of public service values also argue that the fragmentation of audiences that purely commercial broadcasting may produce could undermine both communities and cultures by limiting our shared experiences. Graham and Davies emphasize the importance of a common national culture (not synonymous with a single dominant culture), which equates to a set of shared values that are accommodating enough to accept on equal terms as many as possible of the minority group cultures that go to make up such a pluralist society, and thereby minimize its tendency towards fragmentation (Graham and Davies, 1997: 29; Lipsey, 2002: 22). Le Grand and New also contend that broadcasting provides a means of promoting a more integrated national community, through unifying activities, 'landmark' events and education in the widest sense (Le Grand and New, 1999: 115–16). One area under the heading of citizenship and community where a public service broadcaster might be expected to play a special role is in the broadcasting of national events (Graham and Davies, 1997: 29).

Within this overall approach that broadcasting has a public rationale which can be defined not just in terms of audience wants, but
with reference to a social purpose, Le Grand and New argue that
broadcasting should seek to support certain societal values such as
community, opportunity, responsibility and accountability.
Broadcasting can achieve this by facilitating the acquisition of essential skills, increasing awareness of health issues and holding government, institutions and individuals to account (Le Grand and New,
1999). While commercial broadcasting has much to offer in these
regards, they argue that public service broadcasters are best suited to
pursue these goals. In her role as Secretary of State for Culture, Media
and Sport, Tessa Jowell implicitly agreed with this analysis: 'I would
say that those episodes of *EastEnders* that tackle difficult issues of
child abuse, drug taking, teenage pregnancy, and so forth, are actually – when they do it responsibly – providing an important public
service' (Burrell, 2004: 8).

The capacity of broadcasting to protect against social exclusion is
also emphasized by defenders of public service values. For example,
Corfield argues that broadcasting has a particular responsibility to
serve the needs of the socially excluded, such as poor pensioners,
single parents, the unemployed and ethnic minorities, principally
through the provision of free-to-air services. Public service broadcasters in particular, as well as providing such a service, have a brand
that many people value and trust, offer value for money and run effective educational campaigns (Corfield, 1999).

In addition, public service broadcasting continues to occupy 'an
institutional space that has some independence from both the economy and the state' and 'potentially provides a national arena for a
diversity of social groups to communicate with one another'
(Stevenson, 1995: 63). Finally, it is claimed that public service broadcasters can act as instruments of positive regulation. In particular,
where a pubic service broadcaster enjoys a significant position in the
broadcasting system, it can exert 'a positive influence on the quality
and behaviour of the whole system', acting as a reference point for
standards and good practice (Graham, 1999: 44; see also Collins and
Murroni, 1996: 144).

In short, the positive cultural/political case for the retention of a
public service component in broadcasting in the digital era has been
largely underpinned by an emphasis on its contribution to citizenship,
its capacity for social and cultural inclusion, and the provision of high
quality political information and public education. Critics, however,

have asked whether broadcasting is necessarily an appropriate means for seeking to achieve some of these objectives, which may be more 'the function of the educational system in the widest sense' (Peacock, 1997: 312). In Chapter 5 we shall see how these arguments regarding the relevance of public service values in the digital era have influenced the New Labour government's policy on broadcasting and communications as enshrined in the 2003 Communications Act.

Conclusion

Three principal conclusions can be drawn from this overview of the main values that have influenced debates on media policy. First, for most of the twentieth century there was an apparently clear distinction between the press and broadcasting sectors. The dominant value in the press emphasized the importance of a largely self-regulating competitive market. As a result, attempts at intervention by the state had to overcome the strong ideological hold of the principle of a free press. In contrast, for a long time the market was not regarded as a suitable mechanism for the organization of radio and television. Instead a system based on public service values developed in the broadcasting sector. The dominance of different sets of policy values in these two media sectors can be explained with reference to various factors. These include contrasting elite evaluations of the social and political power of the press and broadcasting, the different technological conditions pertaining to their operations, the impact of historical events (such as the nineteenth-century campaign for a free press) and the influence of key actors (such as Reith at the BBC).

Second, whatever the differences between market-based and public service approaches to media organization and regulation, both have been defended by their supporters with reference to the pursuit of similar democratic ideals. Proponents of the market approach emphasize that through its focus on competition the market is best suited to achieving desired goals of pluralism and diversity. Meanwhile, advocates of public service stress not only the inadequacies and imperfections of the market, but also the superiority of the public service approach in ensuring that some types of media content are made available to all audiences and that the needs and interests of certain sections of society are adequately catered for.

Third, the two sets of values are not simply mutually antagonistic. Rather, in their application to the policy-making process, each has to some extent been influenced by the other. The influence of market values on recent interpretations of the public service principle in broadcasting has been particularly marked. The establishment of ITV in the 1950s ensured that public service broadcasting would be more responsive to audience tastes in its programming. This trend continued as more radio stations and television channels were created. Audience survey evidence and market research have been increasingly used for scheduling purposes by public service broadcasting organizations. In the 1990s ITV became a more overtly commercial broadcaster, while the operations of the BBC became more attuned to the needs of the marketplace.

Conversely the neo-liberal Peacock Report recognized the importance of protecting and promoting certain types of public service programming (such as high quality or minority programmes in the arts, current affairs, science and other specialist areas) which might be lost in the transition to a market system. The Peacock Report recommended the establishment of a Public Service Broadcasting Council along the lines of the Arts Council to fund such programming, an idea that was to re-emerge on the policy agenda over fifteen years later (see Chapter 5). Moreover, even the deregulatory 1988 White Paper on broadcasting recognized that rules would be needed to safeguard programme standards on such matters as good taste and decency and to ensure that the unique power of the broadcast media was not abused (Home Office, 1988: 5).

The influence of public service values in policy debates on the press is perhaps less immediately evident. However, the tightening up of the system of self-regulation in the 1990s (see Chapter 5) can be seen as an attempt by the newspaper industry to operate on the basis of a stronger concept of public interest than was previously the case. In short, while the extent of the mutual influence between the two sets of values should not be overstated, the fact that in the 1990s the BBC saw an integral part of its mission as 'extending choice' while the press accepted the need for greater social responsibility in newspaper coverage points to some cross-fertilization between the two approaches.

This chapter has argued that values make an important contribution to the process of media policy-making. They help to influence the conceptualization of policy debates, provide an ideological coherence to policy proposals and furnish a normative reference point for policy actors. However, it is also important to recognize their limitations as an explanatory tool in helping to make sense of the policy process.

First, they are general abstract concepts, open to differing definitions and interpretations by policy actors. In the real world of media policy-making it may be difficult, for example, for policy actors to operationalize the concept of public service in a way that maximizes the compatibility between general values and specific policy decisions.

Second, values have no mobilizing power on their own. They need to be taken up by influential political and media actors if they are to have an impact on the substance of policy-making. For example, whatever the power of the intellectual case for the application of the principle of consumer sovereignty to broadcasting policy, the arguments needed to be articulated in the policy debate by an actor with status and resources if they were to have any influence on policy formulation.

Third, this raises the point that a value-based discourse can be used by policy actors to give a principled respectability to the pursuit of their self-interest. For example, the support given to the neo-liberal cause by the Murdoch stable of newspapers may well have been driven by intellectual conviction. However, it is impossible to separate the force of the argument based on principle from the knowledge of the economic gains that his broadcasting interests stood to make if public policy reflected a Murdoch-inspired interpretation of market values.

3

Policy-making

Because they are vitally important information providers, cultural industries and economic entities, the media are the object of various specific public policy provisions. Conditions of market entry, patterns of ownership and aspects of content have all been considered legitimate areas for policy intervention in the past. More recently, the objectives, scope and efficacy of media regulation were matters of political debate in the run-up to the introduction of the 2003 Communications Act. Before we look at this debate in more detail (see Chapters 4 and 5), it is important to bear in mind the changed context of media policy-making in the digital era.

In the policy-making environment of the pre-digital age clear distinctions could generally be made between media, based on their use of different technologies, their operation in discrete markets and the relative lack of substitutability in their social modes of consumption. At the same time national actors overwhelmingly dominated the policy-making process, while the policy agenda concentrated mainly on issues of purely domestic concern, largely unaffected by wider international developments. Finally, policy outputs tended to be sector-specific, with different media and communication sectors subject to separate regulatory regimes.

In the digital era Britain's media and communication industries are more technologically and economically integrated than in the past. Technological convergence has undermined the integrity of sectoral boundaries, while several communication companies have sought to diversify their corporate holdings across a range of media markets. In addition, major media companies increasingly operate on a transnational basis (or at least have aspirations so to do), media content flows pay less respect to national territorial borders, and the European Union has acquired regulatory functions within the context of the single European market. These changes have called into question the maintenance of distinct regulatory regimes for different media sectors in Britain, while also introducing a supranational element into the regulatory sphere.

The objective of this chapter is to examine selected key features of the media policy-making process in the digital era. The chapter is divided into three sections. The first examines two developments which have been particularly influential in shaping the terms of the policy debate in recent years: technological convergence and transnationalization. Part two focuses on key actors in the policy community. The final section provides an evaluation of the media policy-making process in Britain.

Policy variables

In the digital era two developments in particular have altered the context of media policy-making in Britain. The first is technological convergence, which is linked to the transition from analogue to digital in the production and distribution of media content. The second is transnationalization, which refers to the declining importance of national boundaries in the structures, functioning and regulation of the British media.

Technological convergence

Technological change in the media has always had important consequences for the organization of production, means of distribution and patterns of audience usage. In the second half of the nineteenth century, for example, advances in techniques of newspaper printing contributed to the industrialization of the press and the creation of a mass market for newspapers. Most spectacularly, technological progress has led to the introduction of wholly new media of communication, such as radio and television in the first half of the twentieth century.

The 'digital revolution'

The most recent leap forward in communications technology is digitization (Murdock, 2000). The impact of digital can be appreciated at a variety of levels. First, through its capacity for signal compression, digital technology allows for significantly more efficient use of terrestrial, cable and satellite transmission platforms than was previously the case. The arrival of digital networks makes it possible to

deliver far more content over the same spectrum, with digital television, for example, usually delivering up to six channels in the spectrum previously used for one analogue channel. Digitization therefore
has massively increased the potential number of radio stations and
television channels available to audiences, giving a new impetus to
the distribution of multi-channel television to British households
(Graham and Davies, 1997). As a result, for many media users digitization has come to be associated with greater choice of broadcast
media provision.

Second, in increasing the number of specialist stations and channels
aimed at particular niche markets, the spread of digital radio and television further segments broadcasting supply. For instance, traditional
broadcasting companies have launched their own digital stations and
niche channels to trade on their established brand image. By 2005 the
BBC's publicly funded digital television services included BBC3,
BBC4, Cbeebies, CBBC, BBC News 24 and BBC Parliament. The
Corporation was thus using digital to target different societal groups
and interests, with children's programming, news, youth content and
arts programming prominent in its digital offerings (Iosifidis,
Steemers and Wheeler, 2005: 13). ITV had also established new digital channels (ITV2, ITV3 and ITV4) as had Channel 4 (Film Four, E4
and More 4). Overall, the television sector in the digital era is characterized by strong competition for audiences, revenue, programme
rights and product both across distribution platforms and among
content providers, while the expansion of supply has inevitably led to
a reduction in the market share of any single channel. For audiences,
digital technology also facilitates the capacity of audiences to plan
their own listening and viewing schedules through technologies such
as podcasting and the Personal Video Recorder. It has been argued that
with the spread of digital the viewing experience is moving towards a
more fragmented, interactive and personalized model.

The impact of digitization on the traditional broadcasting sector is,
however, only a small part of a larger picture. Digital technology has
contributed to a huge increase in the transmission capability and efficiency of communications systems as a whole and thereby expanded
the total supply of information services. It has 'greatly augmented
communications capacity, that is, the possible number of television
and computer channels and the overall bandwith available through
telecommunications, computing and broadcasting networks for
voice, still image, moving image and data communication' (Boyd-
Barrett, 1999: 59). The possibilities for interactive media usage, for

instance, are greatly enhanced by the use of digital. The British government's 2000 White Paper on the future of communications described the impact on television of the changes introduced by digital in the following terms:

> Digital television transforms the family set . . . The potential of teletext is unleashed by use of graphics and high speed updates, turning it into a multimedia information system. The current generation of set-top boxes, often provided free by subscription broadcasters, brings email and interactive programmes into homes without expensive computers. Many of the next generation of set-top boxes will bring full Internet access and increased interactivity. Around one in five of those with access to digital TV use interactive television services. In this way the television can become the information and entertainment centre of the home with two-way communication – the days are numbered in which a television is the passively watched box in the corner of the living room. (DTI/DCMS, 2000: 26)

In this broader context the most significant consequence of the arrival of digital towards the end of the twentieth century was the growing technological convergence among communications media (Cuilenburg and Slaa, 1993). By radically altering the ways in which information is reproduced, stored and transmitted, digital technology removes the barriers between the previously discrete communication sectors of broadcasting, telecommunications and information technology. Technological convergence means that the same media product can now be delivered through a range of different conduits, since digitization 'allows any content to be freely transmitted in any electronic transport mode' (Østergaard, 1998: 95). Online newspapers, electronic publishing, radio and television broadcasts on the internet, video images via the telephone and e-mail accounts via television sets are just a few examples of the cross-over of traditional sectoral boundaries in the contemporary communications media. In short, the growing convergence embracing telephony, television and broadband has meant that consumers may now access media content via an array of household and portable devices. In the light of its convergence capabilities, digital technology has been widely presented as the essential infrastructure of the knowledge-based economy, enabling the much-heralded shift from the industrial to the information society.

Technological convergence has consequences for economic markets and regulatory policies. In facilitating the movement of economic actors across previously distinct sectors, it has encouraged corporate mergers and new strategic alliances in the media and communications industries (see Chapter 4). 'The boundaries of industries are blurring: telecommunication companies want to become broadcasters, while broadcasters increasingly are moving into e-commerce, and Internet Service Providers are offering television channels' (DTI/DCMS, 2000: 9). In short, technological convergence has given rise to a significant degree of economic convergence.

Technological convergence has also helped change the regulatory landscape by undermining sector-specific regulations. It has become more difficult than before to differentiate between broadcasting and telecommunications, since the former might have an interactive component, while the latter might have a broadcast or video component. This change brought on to the policy agenda the possibility of regulatory convergence, whereby a more integrated regulatory framework would be established to cover all broadcasting and communications media (see Chapter 5).

The end of broadcasting?

Because of its impact on audience usage, technological convergence has also opened up the possibility of the end of broadcasting as previously understood:

> The communications revolution means that hundreds of *narrow*cast channels, specializing in particular programme types, such as news or sport, will constitute a plethora of niche markets. The viewers of the future will be charged only for the programmes they watch. They could even order and be sent programmes on demand . . . Given the ability to select and pay for individual programmes, why would anyone continue to use generalist broadcast channels, paying for a minority of unwatched, unchosen programmes? (Collins and Murroni, 1996: 140)

If such a change were to take place in consumption patterns, this would affect all broadcasting companies and would have a particular impact on the role and legitimacy of those broadcasting institutions with a specific public service mission.

Is technological convergence having such a revolutionary impact? The answer is 'no', or at least, 'not as yet'. Historically, established media sectors are not simply supplanted by the emergence of new media. Instead, they have frequently adapted to new market conditions, even if success cannot be guaranteed for every specific outlet. Newspapers and radio, for example, accommodated themselves to the sweeping advance of television in the second half of the twentieth century. Radio had considerable success in this regard, aided by its portability, widespread use in cars, popularity with the young and niche programming, while newspapers appeared to be engaged in a prolonged rearguard battle to retain traditional readers and attract new ones.

Moreover, even in an age of technological convergence media content from different outlets are not regarded as simply interchangeable by audiences. Collins and Murroni argue that established patterns of television programming and of viewer expectations will not change radically over a short period of time and, despite technological change, there will still be a consumer demand for broadcasting (as opposed to narrowcasting) even in a market of increased choice. In particular, there is a strong chance that consumers will continue to value 'broadcasting's *flow model* of distribution', whereby programmes are selected and packaged for audiences within the context of a constructed schedule (Collins and Murroni, 1996: 142). Allen also subscribes to the view that broadcasting will survive digitization. Indeed, he regards digital television as an extension of analogue television, arguing that consumers will continue to use screen-based media primarily for narrative material, that the most prevalent mode of consumer use will be passive and that such usage is largely satisfied by traditional media forms, including broadcast television (Allen, 1998: 61–4).

The British government initially adopted a cautious approach to the impact of digital technology on revolutionizing consumer usage of communications media. In its 1998 Green Paper on *Regulating Communications: Approaching Convergence in the Information Age*, the government argued that in the late 1990s convergence was more apparent from the perspective of the providers (the supply side) than of the consumers (the demand side):

> It seems likely that, while the converging market becomes more homogeneous in terms of providers, a spectrum of distinct segments of consumer demand, reflecting established patterns of consumption, will persist for some considerable time to come. At one end of this spectrum there is likely to be a segment which looks much like the universal broadcast television as consumers know it today. At the other, there is likely to be a segment with many of the characteristics of the Internet as we know it today. (DTI/DCMS, 1998: 11)

As a result, the government considered that broadcasting, including the packaging of programming in generalist channels, was not set to disappear under a tide of niche-oriented channels or particularistic, video-on-demand type services.

By the start of the twenty-first century, therefore, technological covergence had altered important aspects of the structures and functioning of the communications media in Britain as the impact of digitization began to make itself felt. Understandably policy-makers had to assess the consequences of technological convergence for economic and content regulation. At the same time, talk of a 'digital revolution' exaggerated the pace of change, especially on the consumption side. Policy-makers, therefore, were involved in a balancing act: trying to factor convergence into their policy proposals so that regulation would not be left behind by technological change, while simultaneously seeking to anticipate the more gradual impact of such convergence on current and future audience usage.

Transnationalization

In the digital era it is increasingly evident that media developments in Britain cannot be isolated from wider European and global trends. Transnationalization includes international, supranational and global developments, embracing such diverse phenomena as trade in programmes between countries, regulatory intervention by the European Union and the expanding commercial role of global multimedia companies. The term 'transnationalization' rather than the more frequently used 'globalization' is preferred in this section, in part because transnationalization embraces initiatives, for example at the EU level, which are more a supranational response to – rather than an integral part of – globalization, and in part because the term 'globalization' has become weighed down with positive and negative connotations. In this section three facets of the phenomenon of media transnationalization are analyzed: technology, content and ownership. A fourth aspect'– regulation – will be considered later in this chapter when we examine the policy-making input of the European Union.

Transnational technology

The first feature of transnationalization is linked to changes in media and communications technology. In the latter part of the twentieth century the proliferation of communication satellites orbiting the earth radically transformed the scope and speed of media content distribution. No area of the planet was now out of the reach of communications technology, with British audiences becoming accustomed to seeing images from the other side of the world transmitted instantaneously via satellite. In television news, for example, satellite communication allows established broadcasters, such as the BBC, to take live feeds from correspondents around the world and to cover breaking stories in different parts of the globe.

The more radical impact of satellite communication, however, has been to open up previously well protected national broadcasting systems to external newcomers. In their role as transmission platforms, satellites can revolutionize television distribution because their signals overspill national frontiers. This allows the possibility for audiences to access content from non-domestic service providers. Television channels such as CNN International have emerged to take advantage of this technological shift by targeting global (or global-regional) rather than purely national audiences. Branded channels, such as MTV, can be found on cable and satellite systems in different countries. The implication of this phenomenon is that it is 'now impossible to maintain national sovereignty in mass communications so long as the members of a society have access to satellite dishes' (Waters, 1995: 148).

The quintessential transnational communications infrastructure is the internet (Truetzschler, 1998). Though it originated in the United States, this network of computer networks has been transformed into a truly global medium of communication and information. In enabling the interaction of virtual communities in cyberspace, the internet is both a striking symbol and a powerful means of time-space compression. Its operations are not nationally bounded and regulation of content by any single national democratic government is impossible.

Transnational content and formats

A second aspect of transnationalization can be found in the field of media content and formats. The huge worldwide growth in media outlets has created a demand for a large amount of product. In television, for example, there is a global market in programming whereby series of programmes are traded between broadcasters in different countries (Steemers, 2004). In addition, programme formats cross national frontiers, accompanied by some fine-tuning to suit the tastes of local audiences. Ricky Gervais' BBC comedy hit, *The Office*, is a good example of both trends. By 2006 the original version of the programme had been sold to 33 national broadcasters and shown in more than 80 countries. A local variant was also distributed to the US market by NBC (*The Office: An American Workplace*) and to French audiences by Canal + (*Le Bureau*).

The British media are both significant importers and exporters of broadcast and audio-visual content, particularly to and from the United States. However, while 'the US has shown an interest in British ideas . . . they are unwilling to import the actual programmes as they are. The sale of formats, however, is of growing importance, particularly with recent developments in which British companies have been commissioned to produce American versions of British entertainment shows' (Tongue, 1999: 114). In recent years the formats of British quiz programmes such as *Who Wants to be a Millionaire?* and the *Weakest Link* have been successfully exported to the USA. British television companies are also involved in co-productions with US counterparts, notably in expensive programming genres such as drama and natural history programmes. Despite this export success, however, British television has a substantial trade deficit with the United States. This is due in part to a failure to market exports effectively and in part to the success of US imports. Whether the lack of success of British television to make significant inroads into the North American market is due to the nature of the content (too parochial and idiosyncratic for American audiences), production failures (the production runs of popular series are too short) or marketing problems, the balance of payments gap in UK–US programme trade is huge.

In terms of programme imports, during the 1990s the programme output of BSkyB and later Channel 5 relied heavily on American products, while on a much smaller scale Channel 4 has served as the British outlet for several US comedies and drama shows, such as *Friends*, *Frasier* and *ER*. Various thematic channels, such as children's channels and pop music video, also originate from the USA. Meanwhile, Australian programming has in recent years made some inroads into British television, notably the soap opera *Neighbours*.

Programme formats are also imported into Britain and adapted for domestic consumption. One of the best known examples of this was the hugely popular *Big Brother* programme, first screened on Channel 4 in 2000 and supplemented with internet coverage on a dedicated website. The format of this reality show originated in the Netherlands and versions adapted for local consumption were later shown in other European countries. Finally, the growing importance of the European dimension for the British media can be gauged by the increase in trade between Britain and the rest of the European Union in television programmes, whereby the EU has become the biggest market for UK exports (ibid.: 111–16). Within Europe, London is a prime location for media production and distribution.

Transnational ownership

Companies that operate transnationally have become major players in the production, packaging and distribution of media content, making a significant contribution to the status of the media as one of the fastest-growing industrial sectors around the world. The most powerful transnational media companies operate as vertically integrated conglomerates, using their domestic market as a core sector from which to expand into other markets or simply operating across different national markets without any dominant base in any specific one.

Most of the major transnational companies are either American-owned or have a significant presence in the United States (Herman and McChesney, 1997: 70–105). For example, it is American companies that are the main players in the global markets for computer operator systems, computer chips and gateway access to the internet (Boyd-Barrett, 1999: 60). In addition, global film and television markets are in general dominated by Hollywood productions (Tunstall and Machin, 1999: 127–85), the costs of which can be amortized in the large, affluent home market. Consequently, the major firms in the global entertainment media are also mainly American, notably Time-Warner, Disney and Viacom.

Nonetheless, some British media companies aspire to be global players, including most notably the BBC. Indeed, one of the strategic dilemmas for the BBC in the digital era is the reconciliation of its role as a national public service broadcaster with its ambitions to be a commercial media player in the global marketplace (Currie and Siner, 1999). The Conservative government's 1994 White Paper on the future of the Corporation approved its transition into an international multi-media enterprise and supported moves to develop its commercial services, especially in international markets (Department of National Heritage, 1994). BBC Worldwide was formed in the same year to manage the Corporation's international operations, including cable and satellite channels and programme distribution. In 1997 BBC Worldwide concluded agreements with the US cable company Telecommunication Inc (TCI), which included in particular a joint venture with Flextech (Steemers, 1998: 114). This resulted in the launch of several channels under the banner of UKTV. In 1998 the Corporation entered into a further partnership agreement with the US-based Discovery channel, which led to the launch of BBC America, available in 45 million cable homes in the US in 2005. These agreements 'represented a recognition by the BBC that its most significant potential market was the USA and that the BBC could only be a significant world player in the digital era if it was allied with at least one big American company' (Tunstall and Machin, 1999: 183). During the 1990s the Corporation also launched its 24-hour international news service, BBC World.

As well as British media companies seeking a stake in overseas markets, companies with their headquarters outside Britain, especially those used to operating in Anglophone global regions, have acquired major ownership stakes in the UK media. The most significant example in this regard is undoubtedly Rupert Murdoch's News Corporation, whose holdings in Britain are only part of a broad international portfolio of media interests. News Corporation has newspaper and television holdings in Australia, where the Murdoch empire has its roots, and has also expanded into the USA, Latin America, continental Europe and Asia. The company's media interests include the Twentieth Century Fox film studio, the Fox broadcasting network, HarperCollins publishers, Star TV and Sky Italia (Shah, 2004). By any criteria News Corporation is a truly global media company.

On a much lesser scale, a huge slice of the British cable market (television and telecommunications) is in the hands of companies whose main business is in the United States. During the 1990s American companies such as NTL and Telewest took a significant ownership holding in the running of British cable systems as network operators. In addition, while News International (a subsidiary of News Corporation) may be the best known press group in Britain not owned by a UK citizen, the *Telegraph* titles were until recently also in the foreign hands of its Canadian owner Conrad Black, while the Irishman Tony O'Reilly is the main owner of *The Independent*.

There is also evidence of closer ownership linkages involving the British media and continental Europe. Pearson, for example, the owners of the *Financial Times*, has had holdings in France and Spain as part of its commercial strategy to control the financial newspaper market across Europe (De Bens and Østbye, 1998: 12). In 2000 the company announced a merger with the Luxembourg-based CLT–UFA group, creating Europe's biggest broadcasting business (Street, 2001: 168). In 2005 RTL, dominated by the German Bertelsmann media group, increased its ownership stake in the British terrestrial television network Five (previously Channel 5) from 65 to 100 per cent.

The continuing importance of the national dimension

Transnationalization of technology, content and ownership are clearly important features of the British media in the digital era. The structures and operations of the media in Britain can no longer be satisfactorily explained with reference to purely national considerations. Yet it is also important to place the phenomenon of transnationalization in perspective. Two caveats in particular are in order: transnationalization is not wholly new and its contemporary impact should not be overstated.

First, in certain respects the media in Britain have been exposed to transnational developments for many years. Consider the following examples. First, in running the World Service the BBC has long operated a radio network with a global reach. Second, British audiences in the inter-war years regularly listened to radio programming from continental European stations such as Radio Luxembourg in preference to the more staid output of Reith's BBC. Third, well before they became part of the Murdoch empire in 1981, *The Times* and *The Sunday Times* had been in the hands of the Canadian media mogul Roy Thomson, who had purchased them in 1966 and 1959 respectively. In the 1950s the Thomson group also owned the ITV company Scottish Television and *The Scotsman* newspaper. Finally, Britain has for many years been a major importer/exporter of programmes from/to foreign television systems, especially the United States. ITV prime-time in the 1950s, for instance, was heavily dependent on American products. 'By 1956 the bulk of programming on ITV was either an imported American cowboy, crime, or comedy show or an American quiz-game or other format hurriedly recast with British faces and voices . . . And then there was the television advertising, which, also, was heavily influenced by American models and American-owned advertising agencies' (Tunstall and Machin, 1999: 154). In short, transnationalization is not new.

Second, it would be profoundly misleading to present a picture of the British media implicated in transnational developments to such an extent that the national (and sub-national) features of their structures and operations have somehow become submerged. Instead, the ramifications of transnationalization need to be offset against the continued strength of national and sub-national specificities across the British media. Britain is a sufficiently well populated and economically developed country with its own national language to support a highly sophisticated indigenous media system. Several media companies are wholly or predominantly British owned. In addition, in some media sectors ownership regulations have been enforced to counter aspects of transnationalization; for instance, non-EU companies were for a long time banned from owning more than a 20 per cent share in a UK terrestrial broadcaster.

Moreover, a significant amount of media content is not just produced in Britain but caters for the tastes and interests of the domestic audience. Market pressures ensure that much newspaper content covers British events and issues (crime, sport, politics and showbusiness), while regulation and convention have ensured that British broadcasting has catered for its national audiences with predominantly domestically produced output. Finally, in general British audiences show a distinct preference for media content with a British flavour (Goodwin, 1998: 5). The most popular programmes on British television, for instance, are the nationally produced 'soaps' such as *Coronation Street* and *EastEnders*. In short, in several key respects Britain still retains what Steemers calls a 'national television culture', albeit one influenced by wider global trends (Steemers, 2004: 1–19).

The central role of politics in policy-making

Media policy is shaped by a combination of technological, economic and socio-cultural factors. These interact to open up and close down policy options, pushing and pulling policy-makers in one direction or another. While frequently it is difficult to disentangle the relative contribution of each of these variables, at other times one of them tends to dominate the policy process. For example, economic and industrial considerations rather than social or cultural factors underpinned the Conservative government's enthusiasm for cable in the early 1980s (Hollins, 1984). Conversely, the changing nature of British society, notably its growing cultural differentiation, was a major factor in the policy proposals that reached fruition in the launch of Channel 4 in 1982. As an analogue terrestrial service, Channel 4 broke no new technological ground. In contrast, during the 1990s the new technology of satellite broadcasting changed the ground rules for television transmission, allowed a major new supplier of programming into British television and brought new regulatory issues on to the UK media policy agenda.

Yet while technological, economic and socio-cultural factors undoubtedly influence the agenda and issue framing of media policy, they do not determine policy outcomes. It is important, therefore, to emphasize the political dimension in policy-making. For example, the Thatcher government's refusal to put any public money into cable during the 1980s was a political decision, inspired by the ideological leanings of the government towards a market-led solution. A government of another political persuasion might well have acted differently by committing public resources to the project of cabling the nation. Similarly, the special regulatory remit given to the new Channel 4 was the product of a political choice. The government could easily have decided to create another channel catering for mass tastes by accepting the arguments put forward by those lobbying for the establishment of a second ITV network. Finally, the government could have been much less accommodating to the satellite broadcast service provided by BSkyB. Another government might have provided more support for the British direct-to-home satellite in its competition with Sky or imposed tougher regulations on BSkyB once it had gained dominance in the British market.

Two points need to be stressed here. First, technological, economic or socio-cultural variables do not impose their own irrefutable logic on the policy process in some independent fashion. Instead, policy outcomes need to be seen as the product of a process of conflict, cooperation, lobbying and negotiation by different actors in the policy arena. These actors pursue their own particular interests and/or claim to speak on behalf of the public interest, mobilizing arguments to support their case. Policy outcomes, therefore, are not inevitably determined in advance by impersonal forces; rather they are shaped by different actors who engage in bargaining to pursue their policy objectives. In short, the input of economic and political actors makes a difference (Winseck, 1998: 364). For instance, in his study of broadcasting policy during the Thatcher and Major premierships, Goodwin argues that decisions taken by the government made a significant contribution to shaping the structures and functioning of Britain's television system between 1979 and 1997:

> *Government policy counted.* Different policies would have produced substantially different outcomes. UK television in 1997 was by no means a simple result of technological or economic inevitability. For good or ill, its actual shape in that year was to a very large extent the result of the vagaries of Tory policy over the previous eighteen years. (Goodwin, 1998: 173, emphasis in original)

Second, it is also true that policy makers cannot just ignore changes in the technological, economic and socio-cultural contexts. Nor can they control them. Policy options may be influenced, therefore, by developments that have not been anticipated by policy-makers. Both the direction and pace of change may leave policy-makers trying to catch up, as existing policies are seen to be no longer appropriate to new conditions. This is particularly true in the case of media technology which often necessitates a re-evaluation of policy as previous responses are superseded by technological advances.

The New Labour government has had to formulate its policy on the media with reference to a more complex technological and economic environment than that faced by any of its predecessors. Indeed the title of the 2003 legislation as a *Communications* Act – in contrast to the 1990 and 1996 *Broadcasting* Acts – is itself testimony to the impact of change. Moreover, technological convergence and transnationalization are not simply 'objective realities' which both exert an influence on and are influenced by the decisions of policy-makers. They are also an integral part of the policy discourse of various actors who seek to play up (or down) the impact of convergence and transnationalization to further their own particular interests. To some extent, therefore, they are self-fulfilling concepts. If, irrespective of any objective indicators, a significant proportion of key policy actors believe that convergence and transnationalization are taking place, then this is enough for these factors to exert an influence on policy. Perception and 'spin' thus become an integral part of the policy-making process, as the rhetoric of 'convergence' and 'globalization' inform corporate strategy proposals and governmental policy statements alike (Held and McGrew, 2000: 5).

Policy actors

Media policies are the product of a process of interaction among different actors. A checklist of the main policy actors includes the following:

- Central government (ministers, top civil servants and special advisers), including the Department of Culture, Media and Sport; the Department of Trade and Industry; the Prime Minister and Number 10 advisers; and the Treasury
- Media organizations including press groups, public service broadcasters, commercial broadcasting companies, pay-tv companies, independent production companies and cable network operators

- Institutions of the European Union, particularly the Commission and the European Parliament
- National regulatory authorities
- The UK Parliament, notably the relevant House of Commons Select Committees
- Major political parties
- Special interest lobby groups, including professional bodies, employers' organizations, media trade unions and consumer associations
- Think tanks, official committees and assorted experts

Three points are worth noting about this list. First, it has expanded over time as a result of political changes (for example, growing intervention from the European Union), institutional developments (such as the establishment of parliamentary select committees and the emergence of think tanks) and changes in the media (including new outlets and content providers). Second, it excludes judicial institutions which have traditionally played little role in media policy-making in Britain. This stands in contrast to the policy process in certain continental European countries, such as France, Italy and Germany, where the supreme judicial authority has been an important media policy actor. Third, since media policy-making is overwhelmingly an elite process, the list omits any reference to public opinion. The public's participation in media policy-making is at best indirect and of marginal influence (Hutchison, 1999: 137–9). Moreover, media policy rarely features as an issue during general election campaigns. The most important policy actors in terms of powers, resources and organization are the UK government, the major media companies and in recent years the European Union. National regulatory authorities have also at times played an influential insider lobbying role. This section focuses on these four sets of actors.

The government

In formal terms at least central government plays the leading role in the process of media policy-making. Not only has it benefited from specific powers such as control of the level of the BBC licence fee and of key appointments to regulatory authorities, but it also enjoys a pivotal policy position through its dominance of the legislative process. Historically, legislation promoted by government has been particularly important with reference to the broadcasting sector, evidenced by the introduction of two major pieces of legislation on broadcasting in the 1990s. The 1990 Broadcasting Act imposed lighter touch regulation in the commercial terrestrial television sector and established new regulatory authorities for radio and television, while the 1996 Broadcasting Act introduced among other things a liberalization of cross-media ownership regulations. Regulation of media ownership and content regulation in broadcasting have been two key areas of governmental activity over the years.

Traditionally one of the most important policy functions performed by the executive has been overall control of market entry into broadcasting. Frequency scarcity meant that the allocation of spectrum to broadcasters had to be managed and in practice strategic policy decisions were made by the government. As a result, for most of the twentieth century the government effectively determined who was (and who was not) allowed to broadcast radio and television programmes originating from within the state's territorial jurisdiction. It was the government that granted the BBC its status as a monopoly broadcaster in the 1920s, approved the establishment of ITV in the 1950s, granted the BBC a second channel in the 1960s, gave the go-ahead for the creation of Independent Local Radio in the 1970s, authorized the launch of Channel 4 in the 1980s and allowed Channel 5 and three new national radio networks to come on air in the 1990s.

Yet, although clearly a central actor in the policy-making process, the government suffers from certain constraints in its attempts to command the field. First, the executive is not a monolithic entity and joined-up government in the media policy field may be particularly difficult to achieve. Apart from the normal in-fighting between ministerial departments intent on protecting and promoting their own fiefdoms, the media pose a particular problem to government because they are simultaneously information providers, sources of cultural output, leisure industries, means of educational dissemination and communication conduits. In particular, the cultural/industrial dichotomy, whereby the media are regarded predominantly in terms of either their content or their technological capacities, has often resulted in a tension at the heart of government policy.

Recent policy documents have attempted to address this turf-war issue. For example, the New Labour government's 1998 Green Paper and 2000 White Paper on communications policy in the age of convergence were both the product of a joint effort by the Department of Trade and Industry (DTI) and the Department of Culture, Media and Sport (DCMS). However, this evidence of departmental cooperation could not mask the differences in emphasis between the concerns of the two departments. In the case of the 2000 White Paper, for instance, the DTI was 'primarily concerned with promoting competition, creating a dynamic market (the title of chapter one of the White Paper) and encouraging the export potential of British businesses' (Barnett, 2001: 64), while the DCMS was left to redress the balance with its focus on issues to do with quality, the maintenance of public service broadcasting, and media plurality and diversity.

Second, the policy process may go off in a direction not intended by government. When it set up the Peacock Committee in 1985, for example, the Conservative government appointed neo-liberal economists Alan Peacock and Samuel Brittan (the brother of the Conservative Cabinet minister Leon Brittan) to help steer the committee to come up with the recommendation the government wanted. The Prime Minister was keen to see the BBC take advertising (Thatcher, 1993: 636), a policy goal which one of her ministers, Ian Gilmour, described as a 'Thatcherite article of faith' (Gilmour, 1992: 206). The Peacock Report, however, went off in a different free market direction and rejected this option. As a result, the findings of the report 'threw Tory televison policy into disarray' (Goodwin, 1998: 85).

This is only one example of the inability of the government to get its way. Goodwin, for example, points to the various failures of Conservative governments between 1979 and 1997 in achieving their policy goals in the cable, satellite and terrestrial television fields. For instance, the 'direct-to-home satellite industry that established itself in the early 1990s was a very different one to that envisaged by government satellite policy of the early 1980s. It did not use UK technology . . . it was dominated by a non-UK controlled concern; and it broadcast heavily non-UK programming' (ibid.: 53).

Even on an issue where the government appears to be in control – such as the date of the switchover of all broadcasting signals from analogue to digital – the outcome is not as straightforward as it might seem at first sight. At the start of the digital era the New Labour government clearly wanted to encourage the rapid take-up of digital technology by consumers, hence the decision not to introduce a higher BBC licence fee for digital television. The government's objective was quickly to free up the analogue frequencies used by terrestrial broadcasters and make them available at a price for other communication services, such as mobile telephony. However, forcing consumers to purchase new television sets to receive digital signals risked alienating those voters who remained sceptical of the benefits of digital. Consequently, the government was reluctant to announce a date for the switchover far in advance. The policy goal of a rapid, voluntary take-up of the new technology by consumers was clear enough, but the means to achieve it did not lie solely or even mainly with government.

Media companies

Media companies are important policy actors, lobbying decision-makers at national and supranational levels to promote their corporate interests. Their media outlets may act as public commentators on the policy process and can be used by owners and management to campaign for or against a particular policy option. On the issue of press intrusion into privacy, for example, newspapers have not just lobbied government as insiders in the policy process, they have also covered the issue publicly in their columns. O'Malley and Soley argue that on the issue of press regulation newspaper proprietors have been able to influence the outcome of media policy in line with their own interests, despite criticism of the system of self-regulation from various quarters over the years (O'Malley and Soley, 2000: 95).

Tunstall goes further, contending that national newspapers have had a major say in the formulation of media policy, not only for the press but also for the broadcasting sector (Tunstall, 1996: 375–417). In part this has been achieved through the privileged access owners and editors have enjoyed in the upper echelons of government (ibid.: 409). In addition, newspaper columns have been used to discuss policy options and provide advice to policy-makers. Sometimes newspapers have mobilized behind a policy initiative to whip up a sense of crisis in broadcasting. During the 1980s, for instance, certain sections of the British press pitched in to help in the destabilization of public service broadcasting in general and the BBC in particular. The Murdoch newspapers, especially the quality broadsheets *The Times* and *The Sunday Times*, ran numerous stories critical of the Corporation at a time when Murdoch was just beginning to build up his own satellite television interests. For example, *The Times* mounted a sustained attack on the BBC, typified by the publication of three critical consecutive leader articles in January 1985, only a few weeks before the establishment of the Peacock Committee (Franklin, 2001a: 23–5). While it is impossible to measure the influence of newspaper coverage on policy outputs, the negative copy certainly had an undermining impact on the management of the Corporation and helped to structure a press agenda which was largely hostile to public service broadcasting values and the institutions that embodied them (O'Malley, 1994: 31–46).

Large transnational companies with interests across different market sectors are the most powerful media actors in the policy process. Rupert Murdoch's News Corporation is the obvious example in this context. During the Thatcher premiership, for example, the Murdoch group benefited from sympathetic treatment in its takeover of the two *Times* titles, while its satellite television programming was able to bypass government regulations. Less economically powerful media companies, especially those with interests predominantly in only one market sector, may need to join forces to play an effective lobbying role in policy-making. For example, by working together the ITV companies Granada and Carlton were able to exert significant leverage on government policy during the 1990s over the issue of ownership consolidation in the ITV network, despite opposition from the very small franchise holders (see Chapter 4). Similarly, the British Media Industry Group, a lobby organized by several national newspaper groups excluding the Murdoch titles, was particularly influential on government policy on cross-media ownership rules in the run-up to the 1996 Broadcasting Act (Doyle, 2002: 95). 'This was achieved through discreet lobbying, high-profile conferences aimed at opinion formers, and a stream of articles and reports promoting the case for abandoning media ownership restrictions.' (Williams, 2001: 197–8).

The BBC is a prime example of a media company that seeks to influence media policy in line with its own interests. During the Thatcher premiership it was a beleaguered institution, held in great suspicion by government. For much of the 1980s, therefore, the Corporation was on the defensive in policy circles, reacting to an agenda largely set by others, as in the government's proposal to introduce advertising on its domestic services. In contrast, during the Major and Blair premierships the dialogue between government and BBC was more productive. The licence fee was preserved in the short term, the Major government's recommendation that the Corporation adopt a global perspective in its operations went with, rather than against, the grain of BBC management thinking and the New Labour government's recognition of the importance of public service values in the digital era bolstered the BBC's legitimacy.

Overseeing the BBC's pursuit of its domestic and global objectives in recent years were two figures with solid New Labour credentials.

Greg Dyke, Director General of the BBC until his resignation in 2004, had previously given the Labour party a £50,000 personal contribution when employed in the commercial television sector. The revelation of the donation by *The Times* in 1999 initiated a fierce but unsuccesful campaign, pursued by the Conservative party, to oppose his appointment to the top managerial post at the Corporation. The Chairman of the BBC Board of Governors, Gavyn Davies, was also known to have close links with leading Labour politicians, notably Gordon Brown. The interests of the Corporation in the media policy process for much of the first two New Labour administrations were thus promoted by figures with an insider track to government.

The example of the battered BBC during the 1980s shows that media companies may lack influence in the policy process because they are out of favour with government. Conversely, a company's commercial power may give it a privileged status in policy-making. For instance, under Blair's leadership the New Labour party and government have been accused of cosying up to Murdoch so as to secure the support of his company's newspapers. Though initially the New Labour government were prepared to enforce rules that prevented Murdoch from being allowed to take a controlling stake in British commercial terrestrial television, the 2003 Communications Act removed regulatory barriers to a News Corporation takeover of Five. Commercial power, however, does not always lead to policy clout. For example, the view held by Major's Conservative government that News Corporation was acquiring too dominant a position in the British media resulted in the introduction of ownership legislation in 1996 which sought to impede the Murdoch group's future expansion (see Chapter 4). These measures were introduced at a time when the Murdoch newspapers were pursuing a highly critical campaign against Major's leadership. In the short term the Major government clipped Murdoch's wings, but there was a price to pay in terms of continued critical coverage of the Major premiership by the Murdoch stable of newspapers.

The European Union

The European Union is a relative newcomer as a media policy actor. The origins of EU involvement in media policy can be traced back to the early 1980s, but it was the creation of the single market later that decade that really brought the media firmly on to the EU's policy agenda. This concern was intensified in the 1990s when the convergence potential of digital technology was perceived by EU policy-makers as having a key role to play in the creation of the information society in Europe.

Of the various areas of EU intervention in media and communications policy, three are particularly noteworthy. The first is the emphasis on ensuring the free flow of programmes within the EU through the mutual recognition of national licensing regimes. The 1989 Television Without Frontiers (TVWF) Directive, revised in 1997, is the major policy statement in this respect (Goldberg, Prosser and Verhulst, 1998: 56–75). This recognized that transfrontier television on satellite systems broke the hold of nationally based terrestrial broadcasters and overspilled the jurisdiction of national regulatory bodies (Negrine, 1988). Supporters of the initiative had two goals: 'to ensure that the circulation of broadcast signals and services emanating from member states was not impeded in other member states; and to harmonize Community broadcast regulation so that competition between signals and services took place on a fair and equal basis' (Collins, 1994: 58). The directive thus inhibited member states from restricting retransmission on their territory of television broadcasts from other member states (Collins, 1993: 13). As a result, although the directive contained some interventionist provisions such as European content quotas, its thrust was essentially liberal and anti-protectionist: the creation of a single broadcasting market (Negrine and Papathanassopoulos, 1990).

The second area of EU intervention lies in the operation of competition law, which is having an increasing impact on the structure and shape of Europe's media industries. Indeed Levy argues that it has been through competition policy rather than specific interventionist measures that the European Union has exercised greatest impact on Europe's broadcasting industry (Levy, 1999: 80). In the digital era competition policy has been particularly influential in its application to prospective mergers between leading European media companies in their attempts to control markets through the formation of strategic alliances (Michalis, 1999). For example, in 1997 the Commission played a role in having BSkyB removed from the consortium that made the successful bid for the digital terrestrial television multiplex, British Digital Broadcasting (first renamed ONdigital and later ITV Digital). The Commission's view (shared by the British telecommunications regulator, Oftel) was that BSkyB's involvement in the consortium might entrench its dominant position in pay-tv. In contrast, in 1998 the Commission approved subject to certain conditions the joint venture British Interactive Broadcasting (BIB) for the launch of digital satellite television and interactive services. Embracing BSkyB, British Telecom and the consumer electronics company Matsushita, the BIB venture brought together the UK's leading telecommunications giant and its most important pay-tv company (Levy, 1999: 91). Finally, in 2003 the Commission intervened to ensure that the bidding process for rights to screen 'live' coverage of Premier League football for the period 2004–07 complied with competition regulations. Since the Commission had objected to the way in which the rights had previously been consolidated in a single package, in 2003 these were unbundled to be sold in four separate packages (games on Saturday early afternoon, Saturday late afternoon, Sunday and Monday respectively). However, while the Commission's underlying objective was for more than one broadcaster to win the screening of 'live' games, BSkyB won all four bids. On this occasion making the process more competitive did not affect the outcome.

Finally, the European Union has played an important role in promoting discussion and shaping the terms of the debate on the impact of convergence for the construction of the Information Society. In particular, its 1997 Green Paper put forward a series of options with regard to the regulatory implications of technological convergence and it was within the context of the consultation process that the UK government published its own Green Paper on the subject in 1998. Liberal and deregulatory in its approach, the EU Green Paper adopted a telecommunications rather than broadcasting perspective in its emphasis on infrastructure rather than content. The main concern for the European Commission at the end of the twentieth century was to introduce consistency in the regulation of broadcasting and telecommunications infrastructure in the light of converging technology and increased competition. The Commission proposed new legislation for the converging electronic communications sector that would remove existing barriers to the single market. As a result, the same regulatory framework will apply to all electronic communications networks and services across member states (DTI/DCMS, 2000: 18–19). In the run-up to the passing of the 2003 Communications Act, the 'British legislative initiative for communications ran parallel to the EC's convergence initiative' (Harcourt, 2005: 172), with the UK being the first member state of the European Union to implement the new EC regulatory framework for communications following close collaboration between the relevant British and EU authorities.

In short, it is undeniable that there has been a growing European dimension to British policy debates on the media in recent years. The EU has acted as a forum for interest group lobbying (for instance, by public service and commercial broadcasters) and a site for national governments to promote their own domestic concerns at the supranational level. The operation of the single market has had consequences for UK media policy, especially in the application of competition provisions. However, the impact of the European dimension on media policy in Britain should not be overstated. Several EU initiatives have been a failure, such as the attempt to draft a coherent overarching European policy on media ownership across sectors and national boundaries (Commission of the European Communities, 1992, 1994; Doyle, 2002: 154–70; Levy, 1999: 50–8), while others, such as the support programmes for audiovisual production, have had limited impact. Most crucially, most aspects of media content regulation continue to reflect national priorities and standards.

National regulatory authorities

Participation in the policy-making process cannot be regarded as the main function of national regulatory authorities. However, nor should their role be interpreted as simply one of implementing decisions emanating from a political process from which they are excluded. The ITC, for example, had a significant influence on many features of the 1990 Broadcasting Act (Gibbons, 1998a: 251). The regulator effectively was involved in an insider political lobbying exercise, which also included among others the *ad hoc* pressure group Campaign for Quality Television, to try to mitigate some of the more financially driven aspects of the Conservative government's proposed legislation. For example, the regulator played a part in persuading government to give more weight to programme quality in that part of the legislation dealing with the competitive tendering process, rather than just focus on the size of the financial bid. Also in the early 1990s the Press Complaints Commission played a key role in lobbying the government to maintain self-regulation of the press, arguing that a beefed-up code of practice rather than statutory regulation was the best way forward.

Moreover, in the subsequent exercise of their discretionary power within the rules imposed by legislation, regulatory authorities may make decisions which themselves have important consequences for media structures and functioning. For example, in the ITV franchise auction in 1991 the ITC judged that no fewer than 13 of the 27 applicants had failed the quality threshold test, while in the case of the Channel 5 franchise allocation in 1995, the regulator awarded the franchise to the Channel 5 Broadcasting consortium, rejecting an equally high financial bid from Virgin TV and an even higher one from UKTV on grounds of lack of quality and diversity in their programme proposals. The new regulatory authority Ofcom has already established itself as an important actor in the policy-making process, not least because of its expertise and research-driven data resources.

Policy process

Policy cycle

A conventional way of analyzing media policy-making in Britain uses the concept of the policy cycle. This divides the process into three chronological stages (Tunstall, 1984). First there is the inquiry phase during which policy is formulated. This phase would frequently centre on an inquiry by a Royal Commission or other government-appointed committee which would work to a specified frame of reference, gather evidence from interested parties and publish a report containing a list of recommendations. Then would come the political phase. This would centre on the legislative process including the framing of legislation, relevant parliamentary debates and committee work, culminating in the enactment of legislation. Finally, there would be the operational phase in which decisions were implemented.

The concept of the policy cycle seemed reasonably appropriate as an explanatory framework when the deliberations and recommendations of a full-scale Royal Commission were influential in government policy initiatives. This was especially the case with regard to broadcasting policy up until 1979. For example, between the end of the Second World War and the start of the Thatcher premiership three Royal Commissions reported on broadcasting in Britain. The first postwar cycle began with the report of the Beveridge Committee in 1951 and its major legislative output, recommended by a minority of the committee, led to the introduction of ITV in 1955 (Beveridge Report, 1951). The second cycle started with the work of the Pilkington Committee, whose report bolstered the position of the BBC and successfully recommended that the Corporation should be allocated a second television channel to help it compete with ITV (Pilkington Report, 1962). The third cycle centred on the Annan

Report of 1977, which among other things supported the establishment of a new television channel with a special programme remit to cater for minorities (Annan Report, 1977). The subsequent 1981 Broadcasting Act authorized the creation of Channel 4 which began transmissions the following year.

The concept of a policy cycle has also been applied to the policy process on broadcasting during the Thatcher premiership, beginning with the establishment of the Peacock Committee in 1985. Wheeler, for example, explicitly uses the concept to frame a stage-by-stage analysis of the policy process through an examination of the 1986 Peacock Report, the 1988 White Paper, the 1990 Broadcasting Act, the 1991 ITV franchise auction and the subsequent process of consolidation within the ITV network (Wheeler, 1997: 118–56). The most recent policy cycle began with the publication of a Green Paper on communications convergence in 1998 (DTI/DCMS, 1998), continued with a White Paper in December 2000 (DTI/DCMS, 2000) and a draft Communications Bill in May 2002 (DTI/DCMS, 2002), and concluded with the introduction of the 2003 Communications Act.

However, while the concept of a policy cycle imposes a neat analytic framework on the policy process, it is scarcely a satisfactory explanatory model. The analytically separate phases of the cycle never did reflect the messy reality of policy-making in which the formulation and implementation of policy overlapped and 'much of the process was organic and evolutionary' (Seymour-Ure, 1996: 235). In any case, the policy cycle approach now seems much less relevant in an age where all-encompassing Royal Commissions on the media have fallen out of fashion (the last one on broadcasting was the 1977 Annan Report and the most recent on the press was the McGregor Report of the same year) and consequently the inquiry phase has become more diffuse.

Increasingly the government prefers committees to investigate specific aspects of media structures and operations (for example, the 1999 Davies Committee on the Future Funding of the BBC) or it publishes a Green Paper as a discussion document to trigger debate, which is then followed up by a White Paper (such as the 1998 Green Paper followed by the 2000 White Paper on communications regulation). In the 1990s, for instance, several official reports were published on specific aspects of media structures and functioning. Issues covered included the press and privacy, the future of the BBC, media ownership, digital television, the possible introduction of a top-up digital licence fee and communications convergence. It could be argued, therefore, that there has been a shift in the approach to policy-making away from a wide-ranging sectoral framework as adopted by the Royal Commissions to a more issue-based agenda. This reflects a more complex policy-making environment: convergence has helped to break down traditional sectoral boundaries, more actors now have a stake in the process of policy-making and the pace of technological change makes large-scale inquiries liable to be out of date before their reports are published.

Joined-up policy-making?

Yet these developments should not be taken to mean that in the digital era the process of media policy-making has somehow become less holistic or coherent than in the past. This is because there never was a golden age of coordinated, joined-up policy-making. Instead, the traditional sector-based approach produced many inconsistencies and unintended consequences in media policy across and even within different sectors (Curran and Seaton, 1997: 321; Seymour-Ure, 1996: 237). In part, the lack of an integrated policy approach reflected the importance of different underlying sets of values in the press and broadcasting sectors, which in turn led to contrasting appreciations of the appropriate role for the state and the market in their organization and functioning. In part, it also stemmed from the different histories of the two sectors, with the press being regarded as primarily a medium of information while broadcasting was viewed as a source of culture and entertainment (Curran and Seaton, 1997: 327–8). These sectoral differences were amplified by the institutionalized separation of the relevant public inquiries into the press and broadcasting. As a result, it has been argued that throughout the second half of the twentieth century the British government did not have a single coherent media policy, more a set of separate policy initiatives (Seymour-Ure, 1996: 240).

Even within one sector, a lack of coherence has frequently been evident. For instance, Goodwin argues that with regard to television policy between 1979 and 1997:

> there was quite simply no over-arching 'Thatcherite project' for institutional reform. There was no single, even remotely coherent plan of action which guided Tory policy from the beginning of Margaret Thatcher's administration to the end of John Major's. Quite the opposite. Over these eighteen years Tory television policy lurched from one 'project' of reform to another. (Goodwin, 1998: 163)

Why was this the case? 'First, a number of developments in the politics of the industry prompted opportunistic reactions by the government . . . Second, several major developments occurred in the television industry which, at the very least, were not the original intentions or expectations of previous government policy' (ibid.: 165).

Interestingly, Goodwin contends that a consistent thrust to Conservative policy during these years did exist: 'to make television more a matter of the marketplace, and less a matter of public service' (ibid.: 166). However, this drive towards 'marketization' was accompanied by zigzags and opportunism in specifics. Some commentators have emphasized the importance of inter-departmental conflict during the Thatcher premiership as evidence of a failure by government to reconcile different values. With its mixture of deregulation on the one hand and political and moral censorship on the other, the broadcasting initiatives of the Thatcher premiership appeared to betray an essential contradiction at the heart of the Thatcherite reform agenda between libertarian and authoritarian values (Gamble, 1988; Keane, 1991: 112). Translated into departmental terms, the inconsistencies in broadcasting and communications policy may have reflected 'a tension between the thinking of the more traditional, and perhaps, more culturally conservative, Home Office, and the more radical, deregulatory and free market-oriented philosophy of the Department of Trade and Industry' (Corner, Harvey and Lury, 1994: 5–6). Thus, in the eyes of some commentators Thatcher's Conservative government was unwilling to accept one of the logical consequences of deregulation – the end of government control over broadcast content, failing to square the circle of supporting a market approach to television on the one hand and wishing to retain a hold over an important medium of public information and social control on the other. As one of the leading members of the Peacock Committee attested:

> in putting forward the idea of a free broadcasting market without censorship, Peacock exposed many of the contradictions in the Thatcherite espousal of market forces . . . They espouse the market system but dislike the libertarian value judgments involved in its operation. (Brittan, 1987: 4)

In contrast, though Goodwin accepts that the conflict between market liberalism and moral paternalism within the Thatcherite value system did exist, he does not regard this as the main cause of the failure to pursue the market model of broadcasting. Rather, he emphasizes that the lurches in Tory television policy resulted 'from problems inherent in the one goal of reviving market liberalism' (Goodwin, 1998: 167). In particular, he points to three basic problems. First, there was the strength, adaptability and interdependence of the institutions of the UK television duopoly which the Tories inherited (ibid.: 167–9). Second, the general goal of reviving market liberalism concealed within it several different and often conflicting policy goals, such as whether market values should be used to make public service institutions more efficient or to replace public service goals entirely (ibid.: 169–70). Finally, there was no agreement among market liberals over the means to achieve the 'marketization' of British broadcasting.

A single ministry of the media

Would organizational change at government level make a difference to policy coherence? Curran and Seaton argue that public policy in the media remains beset by a series of contradictions which are the product of a lack of an integrated framework of communications policy (Curran and Seaton, 1997: 319–30). In a previous edition of their text, they called for the creation of a single ministry of Arts, Communications and Entertainments to overcome this fragmented approach (Curran and Seaton, 1991: 333). They argued that the rationalization of responsible government ministries would 'facilitate the development of an integrated policy, committed to more clearly defined goals, that could properly consider the political and economic implications of developments . . . in the information industries' (ibid.: 334). In 1992 they seemed to get their wish when the Department of National Heritage, the forerunner of the current Department of Culture, Media and Sport, was created. However, not only did this ministry still have to consult and negotiate with other government ministries and a motley collection of regulatory agencies, but also there was no coherence imposed by 'the external political environment' (Curran and Seaton, 1997: 329). Continuing divisions both within government and between government and other policy actors effectively scuppered the attainment of an integrated and coordinated approach to media policy-making.

The belief shown by Curran and Seaton that the creation of a single ministry would be a major step towards such an approach shows an optimism in institutional reform which has scarcely been justified by subsequent events. Conflicts do not disappear because of the creation of a unitary institutional structure; they are just played out within a different organizational setting and one step removed from the public gaze. In any case, since the media fulfil different purposes (such as news, entertainment, education and information), inconsistencies in media policy are to be expected (Seymour-Ure, 1996: 239).

Is this changing in the digital era? Technological and economic convergence may act as 'push' factors for greater rationalization and coherence. For example, the creation of a single regulatory authority for the media and communications industries, Ofcom, is symptomatic of a desire on the part of government to impose a more unified approach to economic and content regulation (see Chapter 5). However, a variety of factors will still contrive to make a coherent media policy difficult to attain: the number of actors and range of interests involved in media policy-making; the balance to be struck between national, supranational and global concerns; the pace of technological and economic developments; and changing social attitudes on issues such as censorship and public service values.

Conclusion

Media policy-making is characterized above all by complexity. First, a wide range of variables (economic, socio-cultural, technological and political) feed into the policy-making process, frequently driving policy in mutually incompatible directions. Technological convergence and transnationalization have exacerbated the situation in the digital era. Convergence has undermined the boundaries between media sectors, while transnationalization has introduced a supranational and global dimension to policy debates.

Second, a variety of actors have a stake in the policy-making process, each defending its interests and promoting its values. Tension and conflict are a feature of the inter-relationship between different actors. In addition, the actors are often internally divided on objectives, strategy and tactics. Division may be compensated by alliances between groups of actors in pursuit of a common goal, but such examples of cooperation are often tenuous and short-lived.

Finally, and understandably in the light of the above, media policy often has a fragmented and inconsistent feel to it. This is not just the result of a lack of institutional coordination, although this has frequently been present. It is also the consequence of the diverse nature of the media, which fulfil a range of different functions for their various audiences.

4

Ownership

Competition in the newspaper industry, growth in the broadcasting sector and the transition to digital technology have all contributed to important changes in the configuration of media ownership in Britain in recent years. Significant levels of ownership concentration – defined as 'an increase in the presence of one (monopoly) or a few media companies (oligopoly) in any market as a result of acquisitions and mergers or the disappearance of competitors' (Meier and Trappel, 1998: 41) – are evident. Some groups have expanded their share within a specific market sector (sectoral concentration) and/or acquired an ownership stake across different media sectors (cross-media diversification). In addition, leading companies have acquired an interest in the various stages along the value chain of production, programming, distribution and promotion of media content and related spin-off activities (vertical integration). Joint ventures and alliances between media and internet companies also appeared on the corporate agenda at the start of the twenty-first century, as the former with their stocks of content and the latter with a new means of distribution sought to exploit the apparent complementarity of their interests. Finally, as we have seen in Chapter 3, ownership of the media has been influenced by the phenomenon of transnationalization, with major companies now seeking to have media interests across national boundaries.

In the inter-relationship between economic markets and regulatory policy, changing patterns of media ownership have both helped to shape policy outputs and been constrained by them (International Institute of Communications, 1996). For instance, in framing their regulatory initiatives policy-makers have had to take account of corporate developments in media markets at national and transnational levels. Yet at the same time, the capacity of media companies to engage in new ownership initiatives has been restricted by the prevailing regulatory provisions. Thus, while commercial considerations may push media companies towards expanding their interests in one or more market sectors, public policy may either facilitate or impede the implementation of their corporate strategies.

Regulation to prevent unacceptable levels of ownership concentration and the abuse of dominant market positions has long been accepted as a legitimate component of government media policy. Key questions for policy-makers to address have included how to define relevant markets, whether there is a need for sector specific limits on media ownership in addition to general competition rules and what are the optimal means to measure market dominance within and across different media sectors. A more fundamental concern is how to balance economic/industrial considerations, which may favour concentration, with the democratic goals of pluralism and diversity, which may be promoted by anti-concentration measures.

This chapter is divided into two sections. The first describes and analyzes some of the main developments in media ownership and regulatory provision in Britain in recent years. The objective of this section is to provide an overview of the inter-relationship beween ownership patterns and relevant public policy. The second section examines some of the central issues informing the regulatory debate on media ownership. The objective here is to highlight some of the complexities of this debate, ranging from broad issues of principle to more detailed questions of formulation and implementation.

Concentration of ownership and regulatory provisions

Sectoral concentration

There is still considerable merit in looking at patterns of media ownership within specific market sectors. When combined with a historical framework, for example, such an approach can show important elements of continuity and change in ownership over time (Seymour-Ure, 1996: 16–117). Moreover, even in an age of convergence, it remains the case that some leading companies are best known for their presence in a single market sector. A sector-specific approach is also a recognition that traditional sectoral boundaries retain their importance for audiences and that ownership regulations continue to be applied within sectors as well as across them. Two examples are used here to illustrate the phenomenon of sectoral concentration in the British media: the national newspaper industry and commercial terrestrial television.

National newspapers

National newspapers in Britain are owned by a small number of press groups with five companies – News International (*The Sun, The Times, News of the World* and *The Sunday Times*), the Daily Mail and General Trust (*Daily Mail* and *The Mail on Sunday*), Trinity Mirror (*Daily Mirror, Daily Record, Sunday Mirror* and *Sunday People*), the Telegraph group (*The Daily Telegraph* and *The Sunday Telegraph*) and Richard Desmond's Northern and Shell group (*Daily Express, Daily Star, Sunday Express* and *The Star on Sunday*) – controlling well over 90 per cent of daily and Sunday sales. The most important group, News International, alone controls around one third of national newspaper circulation, with its unique position of owning a quality title and popular tabloid in both the daily and Sunday markets.

Applying commonly used instruments of monopoly analysis drawn from economic theory, Sparks has argued that there is a significant degree of market dominance by a small number of firms in the UK national daily press (Sparks, 1995). As a result, he contends that the national daily newspaper market 'is not an open but a more or less closed market. It is virtually impossible to make a successful new entry without very substantial resources and prior experience of the industry' (ibid.: 192). This is particularly the case in the popular and middle market segments, in both of which only three firms were present in the mid-1990s (a total that has been reduced to two in the middle market segment since the closure of *Today* in 1995). Sparks argues that 'changes in the production and distribution process for national newspapers have . . . tended to reinforce the power of the larger corporations' (ibid.: 198) which have organized themselves into 'vertical chains', consisting of newspapers published at the same time daily in the same location and differentiated primarily by their direction to different segments of the market:

> The expansion of companies across each of these markets and the formation of 'vertical chains' further reinforces the domination of the large companies and may be creating the conditions under which a further reduction in titles and further concentration of market share can take place. (Ibid.: 200)

In short, the national newspaper industry is dominated by a few press groups and in practice, because of the very high start-up costs, it is extremely difficult for a newcomer to enter the market, attract advertising and build up a viable circulation.

Regulations regarding ownership in the newspaper industry are not particularly stringent in either their substance or application. For example, there is no maximum statutory ceiling on newspaper ownership in Britain, in contrast to the position in some other member states of the European Union such as France and Italy. In 1995 as part of a raft of possible reform measures on media ownership, the Conservative government tentatively proposed the introduction of a threshold of 20 per cent of the total newspaper market (local, regional and national newspapers) for ownership by any single press group (Department of National Heritage, 1995a). While levels of concentration above this threshold would not automatically have been regarded as illegal, they would have triggered an investigation by an independent regulator to ascertain whether the resultant concentration of ownership operated against the public interest (ibid.: 24). In the end, however, these proposals were not enacted.

In fact, few statutory controls exist in this sector at all. Under the terms of the 1973 Fair Trading Act (FTA), takeovers and mergers in the newspaper industry for any acquisition that would result in ownership of newspapers with a cumulative circulation of over 500,000 were, in principle, subject to the prior consent of the Secretary of State for Trade and Industry, who could not give that consent without referral to the relevant competition authorities. However, there were a number of exceptions to the application of this procedure, notably where the newspaper was not considered economic as a going concern and as a separate newspaper (Ainsworth and Weston, 1995).

As a result, several changes in national newspaper ownership escaped investigation from the competition authorities. For example, when both *The Times* and *The Sunday Times* were sold to News International in 1981, no reference was made to the Monopolies and Mergers Commission (MMC) on the grounds that the papers were not economic as a going concern and the case was one of urgency. This reasoning has been hotly disputed, particularly in the case of *The Sunday Times*. Indeed, Tunstall argues that 'this 1981 use of the get-out clause to deny a reference to the Monopolies Commission is the most remarkable single example of how the government of the day was able to use the vague wording of the monopoly law for its own political purposes' (Tunstall, 1996: 386). In contrast it has been argued that 'the only bidder willing to keep both titles going was Murdoch and there was a genuine fear that referral would lead to closure of the *Times*' (Greenslade, 2004: 378).

News International's acquisition of *Today* in 1987 was also approved by the Secretary of State without a merger investigation, again on the grounds that the newspaper was not economic as a going concern. Neither the acquisition of *The Observer* by the Guardian Media Group in 1993, nor that of *The Independent* by a consortium led by Mirror Group Newspapers in 1994 was referred to the MMC because of the financial weakness of the newspapers concerned. In the latter case the Secretary for Trade and Industry, Michael Heseltine, also refused to make the takeover conditional on the protection of editorial independence, even though the original management of *The Independent* had stressed this as a key feature of the newspaper. In practice, therefore, 'the majority of important newspaper acquisitions have escaped MMC scrutiny, leading to the criticism that the principle of strict supervision of newspaper mergers has not been reflected in the application of the legislation to the most important sector of the market' (Ainsworth and Weston, 1995: 3).

Government ministers, therefore, have played an important interventionist role in the process of newspaper takeovers and mergers, effectively short-circuiting the referral process to the relevant competition authorities. The exercise of this power means that the government has had an important input in the economic structuring of the newspaper industry (Tunstall, 1996: 378). Agreeing with the view that the high degree of concentration of ownership and lack of pluralism in the British press has not been unduly restricted by the press-specific FTA provisions, Feintuck is particularly critical of the discretionary power assumed by the government in this regard:

> At present . . . within the permissive, discretionary structure of the FTA provisions and the nebulous construct of the public interest applied, the statutory measures on newspaper acquisitions, in so far as they have any effect, operate simply to leave the power of determination essentially within the hands of the government of the day; a prime example of ritualistic regulation masking raw political power. (Feintuck, 1999: 98)

Under the provisions of the 2003 Communications Act, the system of mergers and transfers in the newspaper sector was streamlined; the new regime would focus regulatory action on those newspaper transfers that appeared to raise competition or plurality concerns. Procedural responsibility was moved from ministerial authority towards the relevant regulatory bodies.

Commercial television

In our second example – commercial terrestrial television – significant market consolidation was actively facilitated by changes in regulatory provisions during the 1990s. The 1990 Broadcasting Act had protected ITV's regional structure with provisions that prevented a handful of companies from dominating network ownership, though a small number of big companies had always controlled programme production. Several of the ITV companies that emerged successful from the 1991 franchise auction (Davidson, 1992) soon lobbied for a change in the ownership rules, arguing that these were too inflexible and restrictive. In particular, the provisions came in for strong criticism from the four largest franchise holders (Carlton, Central, Granada and LWT) who argued that the limits were holding back desirable and necessary consolidation in the industry.

These four companies contended that mergers between the large franchise holders would create organizations of critical mass size, which in turn would encourage economies of scale in programming, make for more efficient management of resources and protect the network from predatory forays by continental European media groups. The objections of the smaller companies that consolidation of ownership would have deleterious consequences for programme range and quality, and that the local and regional dimension of some types of programming (notably news and magazine programmes) would be harmed by any move towards bigger franchise holdings, lost out in the political lobbying, with the government arguing that local and regional programming could be preserved through regulation on production source and programme output, rather than via provisions on company ownership. Whether large or small, all the franchise holders were motivated primarily by self-interest, as each sought to maximize its commercial viability in what was clearly becoming a less stable and more competitive television market than before.

In 1993 the government gave in to the four giants and announced a relaxation in the merger rules, whereby two large licences could be owned simultaneously, excluding the weekday and weekend London licences. The results of this liberalization of the ITV franchise ownership rules were soon in evidence. Three separate mergers (or takeovers) took place involving the two largest licencees (Carlton and Central), the third and fourth largest (Granada and LWT) and the fifth and sixth largest (MAI, which owned a controlling stake in Meridian, and Anglia) (Collins and Murroni, 1996: 69). This step-by-step consolidation continued throughout the late 1990s as Carlton took over Westcountry Television, Granada took over Yorkshire/Tyne Tees, and United News and Media, the new owners of Meridian and Anglia, took over HTV.

By the end of the 1990s Granada, Carlton, and United News and Media had emerged as the three dominant players in ITV. The next stage in the process of ITV consolidation came in 2000 after a proposed merger between Carlton Communications and United News and Media was blocked by the government. This left the way open for a deal to be struck between Carlton and Granada. United News and Media then sold off their three ITV franchises (Anglia, HTV and Meridian) to Granada Media, leaving Carlton and Granada as the two remaining dominant players.

In the light of these company manoeuvrings, the consolidation of ITV into a single company looked ever more likely. The government's 2000 White Paper *A New Future for Communications* proposed revoking the rule that prohibited single ownership of the two London ITV licences, a recommendation confirmed in its 2001 consultation paper on media ownership. It also foresaw greater consolidation of the ITV network, which would have the benefit of 'streamlining the strategic decision making process within ITV, and promoting the international standing of ITV companies' (DTI/DCMS, 2000: 41). In 2001 the government confirmed that it would scrap the rules blocking the merger of Granada and Carlton. At the same time as permitting consolidation in ITV, the government also stated that it wanted to ensure a plurality of at least four separately controlled free-to-air terrestrial broadcasters and so announced that it would block any proposed merger between ITV and Channel 5. The 2002 Communications Bill confirmed the government's willingness to allow ITV to become a single company, dominated by Carlton and Granada, and the two companies announced their merger in 2002, with a new logo (ITV1) marking the rebranding of their principal channel across England and Wales. The merger was given regulatory approval in the autumn of 2003.

Cross-media diversification

A second feature of media ownership in contemporary Britain embraces companies with interests across different market sectors. For example, facing the long-term decline of their core newspaper market, several major national press groups looked to diversify into broadcasting in the run-up to the digital era. In this context the first press group to build up significant cross-media interests in Britain was Rupert Murdoch's News Corporation, which began to diversify in the 1980s with the launch of its Sky satellite television service. During the 1990s the supply of direct-to-home satellite television to the British market was dominated by BSkyB, in which Britain's most powerful newspaper group was clearly the controlling force.

The interest of press groups in having a presence in the broadcasting sector is not new. When ITV was established in the 1950s, various newspaper groups took important financial holdings in the regional franchises across the country. After 1963 restrictions were imposed in successive pieces of broadcasting legislation on newspaper proprietors holding an interest in commercial television stations. The 1977 Royal Commission on the Press argued that 'it is right to maintain policies to ensure that newspaper companies do not control broadcasting companies' (Royal Commission on the Press, 1977: 146). The 1990 Broadcasting Act reaffirmed this general principle and set down the permissible degree of cross-media ownership. In particular, the Act specified that national newspapers were allowed to hold up to a maximum of 20 per cent of one licence within each category of national radio, terrestrial television and domestic satellite broadcasting and up to a maximum of 5 per cent in any further such licences (Ainsworth and Weston, 1995: 6).

However, since these thresholds did not apply to press groups acquiring a share in companies delivering cable or non-domestic satellite services, these provisions did nothing to hamper the Murdoch group's cross-media expansion. Though its programme output was aimed primarily at the British market, BSkyB was officially regarded as a non-domestic broadcaster and so News Corporation was not affected by the relevant cross-media ownership legislation. Profits from the Murdoch stable of national newspapers could be used to subsidize losses in satellite television in the early 1990s, while his papers plugged BSkyB's programming to their readers in a sustained cross-media promotion. Murdoch thereby stole a march on competing newspaper groups who had to wait for legislative changes later in the decade before being given the opportunity to build up a significant stake in British television.

As BSkyB's audience reach increased during the first half of the 1990s, other national newspaper groups vigorously protested that the existing ownership rules effectively prevented their own cross-media diversification, while doing nothing to limit the growth of Murdoch's media empire. Between 1990 and 1995 most of the major non-Murdoch press groups worked to build up their cross-media interests, but only within the constraints of the prevailing legislation. More importantly, in 1993 four press groups (Associated Newspapers, the Guardian Media Group, Pearson and the Telegraph) established the British Media Industry Group (BMIG) to lobby for a relaxation of the rules restricting newspaper holdings in television. The force of the arguments of the BMIG informed the government's 1995 White Paper on *Media Ownership* and the subsequent legislation:

> The Government believes that it is essential that the media ownership regime should allow the media sector to develop. The similarity of the functions which newspapers and broadcasters undertake in terms of collecting, editing and disseminating information, news and entertainment, means that there are obvious and natural synergies between companies within each sector, and that it is in the interests of both the industry and the consumer to allow larger media companies to develop. (Department of National Heritage, 1995a: 20)

Consequently, the 1996 Broadcasting Act set out new provisions for cross-media ownership (Gibbons, 1998a: 222). While in the 1996 Broadcasting Act the government recognized that there was still a case for specific regulations governing media ownership beyond those that were applied under general competition law, it liberalized existing ownership regulations both within and across different media sectors. In particular, it removed many of the former upper limits on cross-ownership and allowed for the possibility of takeovers and mergers between newspaper groups, radio stations, commercial television companies and new media. The objective of the legislation in this respect was to pave the way for more broadly-based competitive UK media groups.

In particular, numerical limits on the holding of television licences were abolished. Holdings would now be restricted to 15 per cent of the total television audience. The rules limiting ownership between terrestrial television, satellite and cable broadcasters were also swept away. The rules whereby some players were restricted to a maximum 20 per cent shareholding in certain licences were mostly abolished. Only newspaper groups with a market share of 20 per cent or more were not permitted to hold a licence for a regional or national ITV service, Channel 5 or a radio licence. In addition, discretionary power was granted to the relevant regulatory authority to prevent the granting of a licence for a broadcast service to a body corporate that is (or is connected with) the proprietor of a newspaper 'if the relevant authority determine that in all the circumstances the holding of the licence by that body corporate could be expected to operate against the public interest' (Feintuck, 1999: 105–6).

These liberalizing provisions represented a victory for the lobbying activities of the BMIG and the big ITV companies. At the same time, they ruled out News Corporation and Mirror Group from significant expansion into commercial terrestrial television, though these two companies were not prevented from expanding their cable and satellite interests and they would be permitted to apply to run digital television services. The restrictions did not require the break-up of any pre-existing cross-media groups, such as News Corporation's newspaper and satellite television interests, and referred only to future acquisitions (ibid.: 105).

Yet despite the lobbying success of the BMIG in the 1990s in bringing about regulatory change, press groups in general did not find it easy to make significant inroads into the broadcasting sector. At the start of 2000 only two groups with a national newspaper presence, Pearson and United News and Media, had taken a significant stake in broadcasting. Later that year, however, United News and Media withdrew from ITV and then sold off their newspaper holdings in the two *Express* titles and the *Daily Star*. The new owner of these titles, Richard Desmond's Northern and Shell group, does not have any interests in the broadcasting sector. Consequently, by the start of the twenty-first century the extent of the cross-over by newspaper groups into television was much less than might have been anticipated a few years earlier. The notable exception was, of course, News Corporation, which had entered the television sector well in advance of the competition and which, despite regulation to limit its market power, had become a major player in the ownership of both national newspapers and pay-tv channels in the British market.

During the New Labour administration media ownership rules, both single sector and cross-media, have been liberalized in a continuation of the policy direction evident during the Major premiership (Doyle, 2002). The government has favoured competition as the best way to develop and sustain a dynamic market and has therefore placed considerable emphasis on the importance of general legislation such as the 1998 Competition Act. The 2003 Communications Act argued for significant deregulation and encouraged industry consolidation, with the retention of only a few basic structural limits on ownership.

On the thorny issue of cross-media ownership, the government relaxed regulatory constraints – in general, newspaper companies are no longer prohibited from owning broadcasting companies – while retaining some rules to prevent undue concentration of interests. In practice, this means that at the national level no company controlling more than 20 per cent of the newspaper market (for example, News International) may hold any licence for ITV or more than a 20 per cent stake in any ITV service. The new cross-media rules allowed Murdoch, for the first time, the possibility of owning Five, but kept ITV out of his reach. In addition, a 'public interest' clause would be evoked in any major cross-media merger or takeover that might result in an unacceptable concentration of media ownership, with the new media regulator, Ofcom, being given a key oversight role. The 2003 legislation also allowed the UK broadcasting market to be opened up to non-EU ownership, notably from US media conglomerates such as Disney and Viacom. This controversial initiative, defended by the government on the grounds that it was an essential component of its plan to attract new investment into the industry, made the British broadcasting system more open to non-EU interests than that of any other major Western European country.

Vertical integration and strategic alliances

Vertical integration and strategic alliances form the third component of media concentration, with the growth of digital broadcasting and the expansion in internet services underlining the apparent importance to media companies of combining ownership of content with control of the means of distribution to audiences. The US megamerger in 1999 between the media giant Time-Warner and the internet company America OnLine (AOL) seemed to demonstrate the mutual compatibility between traditional media organizations and new internet companies. This particular conjunction of interests may have failed to live up to stock market expectations following the end of the speculative dot.com boom only a few months after the merger. Nonetheless, in general terms there seem to be clear economic gains to be made in the digital era by companies with a controlling interest in the various stages of content production, programming and distribution (Murdock, 2000: 38).

As a vertically integrated player with significant cross-media interests in national newspapers and pay-tv, News Corporation is a hugely powerful player in British media markets. BSkyB's early dominance of the British pay-tv market placed it in an enviable position in the scramble for ascendancy in the new broadcasting markets of the digital era. The company runs several of its own television channels, including general entertainment channels, a rolling news network, and various sports and film channels. The company also has (or has had) an ownership interest in other channels such as Nickelodeon UK, the QVC shopping channel, the History channel and National Geographic. Its channels are also available on digital cable and terrestrial platforms.

Channel ownership is only one of the company's strengths. In the field of programme production, for example, BSkyB is able to benefit from News Corporation's control of the Twentieth Century Fox film business. It has also secured control of rights to the screening of major Hollywood blockbusters, regarded as key content in the battle to win viewers. It is a major player in the competitive bidding process for television sports rights, picking up first transmission rights for events such as the Ryder cup in golf and England's test cricket matches abroad. Its major sporting conquest, however, has been in domestic football. In 1992 the company first won the right to screen 'live' matches from the English Premier League and it has for the most part retained control of 'live' coverage of these games in subsequent biddings for the rights. In 2003, for example, BSkyB paid a total of just over one billion pounds to secure exclusive screening rights for 138 'live' Premier League games per season for a three year period from the start of the 2004–05 season. In 2006 BSkyB paid £1.3 billion for the rights to screen 92 matches a year and while another company, Setanta Sports, won the rights to screen another 46 matches, it agreed to pay Sky for the use of its broadcasting platform for distribution. Sky, therefore, still retains its dominance of 'live' Premier League football coverage on television.

BSkyB has also sought to influence the marketing of the product. In 2000 it even attempted to buy a controlling stake in England's most successful club in recent years, Manchester United. The club itself has promoted a phenomenally successful global brand image, which drives the marketing of various club-related merchandise. BSkyB's ownership of Manchester United would have allowed the media company effectively to control programming rights of the club's matches if these rights were ever to be negotiated at the level of individual clubs rather than collectively by the Premier League. Conversely, if the Premier League retained the negotiating rights, then through its ownership of the club BSkyB would have been ideally placed to exert leverage on any collective deal. Though opposed by many United supporters, the bid was approved by several of the club's major shareholders and initially looked as if it would be successful. In the end, however, on competition grounds the government refused to give approval to BSkyB's bid. Nonetheless, the episode illustrated the extent to which a financially powerful media company was prepared to go to control what it regarded as a key audience-winning and commercially lucrative sporting brand.

In addition, BSkyB has developed considerable expertise in content distribution. It controls the Sky digital satellite platform and has a stake in the Freeview terrestrial platform. It has also become involved in a series of joint ventures with internet companies, acquiring the broadband provider Easynet in 2005, while its parent company, News Corporation, owns the social networking site MySpace. Moreover, by virtue of entering the market early BSkyB secured a first mover advantage in the businesses of encryption technology and subscriber management systems, two key areas of activity in digital television.

BSkyB's strong position across the production/programming/ distribution chain has posed problems for competing companies in the digital pay-tv market. A graphic illustration of BSkyB's potential to abuse its market position was raised in the debate in the late 1990s regarding conditional access systems and electronic programme guides (EPGs). BSkyB's competitors in both distribution and programme provision feared that Murdoch would use his company's privileged position in both fields to discriminate against his competitors. The danger in their eyes was that BSkyB would be able to exploit its control of the key digital gateways (or bottlenecks) in the system for its own benefit:

> If control of distribution and access is combined with control of significant amounts of programming material (in particular sport and feature films), the emergence of alternative distribution systems can be restricted, as control of the distribution system underpins the ability to acquire premium programming in the first place and maintain a dominant position. (Steemers, 1998: 105)

Universal access to public service broadcasting services has been an important regulatory issue for the government. In 1995 the EU introduced the Advanced Television Standards Directive which 'requires Member States to take all necessary measures to ensure that operators of conditional access services offer services to all broadcasters on a

fair, reasonable and non-discriminatory basis and to comply with
Community competition law' (Goldberg, Prosser and Verhulst, 1998:
93; see also Levy, 1999: 63–79). This directive, to ensure that vertically integrated operators of conditional access systems did not
discriminate against competitors, has been left to Ofcom to implement in Britain. In its 2000 White Paper the government proposed that
the UK regulator should ensure that obligations to secure the carriage
of public service channels over cable and satellite would be maintained and extended, if necessary by the use of 'must carry' provisions. In addition, the government pledged to prevent control of
electronic programme guides being abused by the operator to privilege the content of some programme providers at others' expense
(DTI/DCMS, 2000: 19–20). The output of public service broadcasters
in particular would be guaranteed due prominence in EPGs so that
consumer access to public service channels would be facilitated. Yet
despite these good intentions, in 2005 broadcasters such as ITV were
still complaining to the regulator about the level of charges they had
to pay to BSkyB to have their services carried on its satellite platform.

Will the expansion of the internet have a radical impact on media
ownership configuration through its capacity to allow new smaller
sized companies to enter communications markets? Chadwick argues
that while there are very competitive subsectors, there are also 'pock-
ets of substantial market concentration in the Internet media sector'
(Chadwick, 2006: 299). Already powerful media conglomerates will
have a distinct advantage in establishing and maintaining a strong
presence in the sector because of their existing resources and expertise in production and distribution. Thus, far from encouraging the
entry of new market players, the internet may even accelerate both
horizontal and vertical integration (ibid.: 297). If correct, then
Chadwick's analysis applied to the British case is good news for both
News Corporation and the BBC.

The policy debate: issues and arguments

What is at stake in the policy debate on media ownership? The first
issue for polic-makers to address is whether there is any need for
sector specific regulation over and above the general competition
rules applied to all markets for goods and services. The case for such
minimal regulation is largely based on three arguments (Green, 1995).
First, additional regulation is unnecessary in an age where scarcity of

resource has been replaced by media plenty. From this perspective ownership provisions to ensure pluralism and diversity are out of date, since the attainment of these highly desirable goals is now sufficiently guaranteed by the proliferation of outlets in the marketplace. Second, regulation has become ineffective and unenforceable in an era of technological convergence and transnational communications. Put at its most simple, the age of the internet has rendered media ownership restrictions null and void. The third argument is founded on the view that national restrictions might disadvantage the emergence of large multimedia conglomerates capable of competing in an increasingly interdependent global media market (Humphreys and Lang, 1998). The opposing case argues that the age of media plenty has not yet arrived and in any case there is no simple correlation between the expansion of media supply on the one hand and greater pluralism in ownership and diversity of content on the other.

UK policy-makers have sought to address three objectives in the formulation and implementation of regulatory policy on media ownership for the digital era: first, to maintain and promote competition in national media markets; second, to provide conditions for the emergence and sustenance of companies capable of competing in international markets; and, third, to ensure adequate levels of pluralism of ownership and diversity of content. Since these objectives are frequently in conflict, there are inevitably cross-cutting tensions at the heart of policy-making in this field. For example, given the size of domestic media markets in Britain, it is not always easy to reconcile the first and second objectives outlined above. The formation of national champions to compete in global markets requires significant concentration of resources, while the maintenance of a competitive domestic market tends to support limits on such concentration. Ownership restrictions designed to ensure a highly competitive national market may hamper the capacity of British media companies to compete effectively at the European and global levels. Even the pursuit of the third objective is not without its difficulties, since there is no simple correlation between pluralism of ownership on the one hand and diversity of content on the other – a point to which we return later in this section.

The economic debate

The economic perspective regards the media as an industrial or commercial sector like any other. Concentration of ownership may be economically beneficial for the industry. For example, as in the case of any market, consolidation may result in efficiency gains from economies of scale and scope and as a result of new synergies. There are clear economies of scale (advantage of size) and scope (advantage of diversified supply) for companies that have a significant share of a specific media market (Doyle, 2002: 45–65). For instance, an assessment of the implications of more liberal ownership regulations in the commercial television sector in Britain in the late 1990s argued that opportunities for an improved use of resources had been created, enabling 'terrestrial commercial television companies to avail themselves, to a greater extent than before, of the economies of scale and scope which naturally arise in broadcasting' (Doyle, 1999: 149).

More generally, it has been argued that as far as ownership in a single media sector is concerned, there is a strong potential for additional economic efficiency gains through a relaxation or liberalization of regulations on concentration. From an economic perspective, therefore, in single media sectors big may well be beautiful, since consolidation gives rise to a more cost-effective use of resources. 'The higher ownership ceiling allows for a consolidation of administrative, managerial, technical and other support functions within the UK television sector, which, at least in theory, should not detrimentally affect any broadcasters' on-screen programme offerings' (ibid.: 150).

In addition, large media companies are better able to overcome high barriers to market entry and establish new media products and services. Ownership concentration may help a media sector secure new sources of investment to rise to the opportunities presented by technological and commercial developments. 'Risky new media markets require venture capital and market power in order to launch new products' (Collins and Murroni, 1996: 58). Finally, for national companies to compete effectively in European and global markets critical mass size may well be crucial. The 1995 White Paper on media ownership argued that if Britain were to develop major international media companies, both to achieve export success and to protect the home market from foreign domination, then these major UK international players would be created only by consolidation within the domestic industry (Department of National Heritage, 1995a).

Economic arguments can also be employed to support concentration of ownership *across* sectors. Essentially the case here is based on the view that the operations of different media industries such as the press and broadcasting involve the performance of similar or related functions, notably the collection, editing and dissemination of information, news and entertainment. Economic gains can be made from the transference of skills across sectors. Technological convergence further reinforces the case for allowing more liberal cross-media ownership patterns than in the past, since it can be argued that as the barriers between traditionally distinct media sectors are broken down, the synergies are likely to be even greater.

Critics have pointed out, however, that ownership concentration may not produce the economic benefits claimed by its supporters. For example, Doyle has emphasized an absence of operational synergies between television broadcasting and newspaper publishing, apart from the possible, but by no means certain, benefit from the opportunity to cross-promote products. As a result, her study concluded that no economic benefits could be expected to result from the deregulation of cross-media ownership restraints between television broadcasting and newspapers (Doyle, 1999: 153). In her view, the economic case just did not stand up. 'This finding is crucial since it flatly contradicts the main arguments in favour of liberalizing cross-media ownership restrictions' (Doyle, 2002: 78).

More important still are those economic arguments that emphasize the negative aspects of ownership concentration, whereby far from being beneficial or merely neutral, concentration may actually be economically harmful. These arguments stress the undesirable effects that arise from the establishment and abuse of monopoly or dominant market positions, as a result of which the market imperfectly reflects consumer preferences. Large media companies are capable of taking over or driving out smaller companies and may engage in uncompetitive practices, including predatory pricing and cross-subsidy of products, which make it difficult for competitors to enter or survive in the market (Meier and Trappel, 1998: 46).

For example, some critics have pointed to the way in which new communications technology creates strong pressures towards a broadcasting industry in which ownership is concentrated (Graham and Davies, 1997: 11–18). Concentration is the result of high fixed costs and low (or even zero) marginal costs, resulting in economies of scale for producers and barriers to new entrants into the market. Economies of scope (when activities in one area either decrease costs or increase revenues in a second area) also push towards ownership concentration. Yet while ownership may be more concentrated, audiences will fragment and, it is argued, this will have undesirable consequences for the system as a whole in terms of programme choice because minimum cost production in broadcasting is large. In short, one line of attack on the reliance on market provision to provide pluralism and diversity concentrates on the *imperfection* of the market. This approach accepts an economic paradigm for the framing of the regulatory debate, but argues that in practice the market mechanism is flawed. Imperfections in the market – market failures – prevent it from delivering the level of choice to consumers which is central to the neo-liberal case (Gibbons, 1998b: 74–6; Keane, 1991: 64–91).

The concept of market failure has also been used by some commentators to justify the retention of a public service component in British broadcasting (Fairbairn, 2004; Lipsey, 2002). Here the economic argument is that without pubic service broadcasters the television market in Britain would not necessarily supply particular types of programming or meet certain quality standards. Market failure has also been employed specifically in support of an economic case for the retention of the BBC as a provider of mass public service broadcasting in a market where the trend is towards 'fewer, bigger players, with Sky in particular being likely to exert increasing market power' (Davies, 2004: 25). In particular, Davies argues that broadcasting will remain a public good even in the digital world, that the most serious market failures are in the fields of news, information and education and that the BBC is one way – 'the way that Britain has chosen' (ibid.: 29) – of addressing market failure in broadcasting. In contrast, in its review of television in Britain in 2003, Ofcom argued that as digital take-up progressed, with multichannel provision, encryption systems and a wide variety of different models of consumption, the market failures associated with consumers not being able to watch the programmes they would willingly buy were diminishing fast.

Overall, the debate regarding market failure, whether in the media in general or broadcasting in particular, is highly economistic and technical, with great play made of ideas from welfare economics such as 'externalities' and 'merit goods'. Perhaps the important point to grasp for the non-specialist is that the initial expectation is one that favours the media being organized as a private market. It is then up to those who support ownership regulations or a continued role for public service broadcasting to respond with a counter-case couched in economic terms. This economistic framing of the debate on media regulation and broadcasting reform is linked to wider ideological changes which have given greater prominence to neo-liberal views in many areas of public policy in Britain.

The political debate

A second line of attack emphasizes the *inadequacy* of a market approach to the question of media ownership, arguing that an assessment of the economic costs and benefits of concentration in terms of consumer welfare is too narrow in scope. This approach seeks to widen the terms of the debate away from an emphasis on purely economic variables to include a social and political perspective, arguing that the media are qualitatively and even quintessentially different from other goods and services since they deal in the provision of information and cultural products. The media play an essential role in society in informing citizens, increasing democratic knowledge and promoting debate about values, policies, and the means and ends of politics. We have already seen in Chapter 2 how these types of arguments have been employed by supporters of public service values in the policy debate on broadcasting. They also have a wider application to media regulation, notably in the area of ownership rules:

> Media pluralism serves democracy by providing the citizens with a broad range of information and views needed for the effective exercise of citizenship; it gives minorities the opportunity to maintain their separate existences in a larger society; it limits social conflict by increasing the chances of understanding between potentially opposed groups or interests; it adds generally to the richness and variety of cultural and social life; it opens the way for social and cultural exchange, especially where it takes the form of giving access to new, powerless or marginal voices. (Meier and Trappel, 1998: 42)

Such a perspective informed the analysis of the 1995 White Paper on media ownership, which argued that:

> a free and diverse media are an indispensable part of the democratic process. They provide the multiplicity of voices and opinions that informs the public, influences opinion, and engenders political debate. They promote the culture of dissent which any healthy democracy must have. In so doing, they contribute to the cultural fabric of the nation and help define our sense of identity and purpose. If one voice becomes too powerful, this process is placed in jeopardy and democracy is damaged. Special media ownership rules, which exist in all major media markets, are needed therefore to provide the safeguards necessary to maintain diversity and plurality. (Department of National Heritage, 1995a: 3)

In the national newspaper industry, for example, concentration of ownership has a political dimension separate from its economic implications. This was recognized by the first postwar Royal Commission on the Press, which stated that:

> the dangers of too much concentration of ownership in the newspaper field are, first, that there may be insufficient channels for the expression of opinion and, second, that it may become possible for a very few men to influence the outlook and opinions of large numbers of people by selecting and presenting news in such a way as to project a particular view of the world or to support a particular policy. (Royal Commission on the Press, 1949: 55)

These dangers are as relevant today as they were in 1949. Newspapers are important sources of information, help to set the political agenda and act as agencies of opinion formation. They exert an influence on the political attitudes and behaviour of their readers, however difficult it may be to assess the precise impact. Concentration of ownership in the hands of a few large press groups may stifle diversity and restrict consumer choice.

This does not mean that media concentration is indefensible from a socio-political perspective. Indeed, some advantages may flow from a certain concentration of resources. Large media companies, for example, are more likely to have the personnel and financial backing to devote to extensive coverage of news and current affairs. In driving down costs, a market with a multiplicity of competing outlets may result in none of them having sufficient resources to devote to specific news beats (such as foreign correspondents) or to certain types of coverage (such as in-depth current affairs programming). Extensive coverage of a prolonged international event, such as the war in the Balkans or the conflicts in the Gulf, can stretch the resources of even a major news organization like the BBC. The New Labour government's 2001 consultation paper on media ownership also saw merits for content diversity in some consolidation, without which it argued there was a risk that a number of small companies would all tend to aim their content at the same middle ground, all seeking the largest possible share of the mass audience.

Nonetheless, from a political perspective concentration would be regarded as harmful if it had a deleterious impact on levels of pluralism and diversity (Feintuck, 1999: 76). It is important to disentangle the different dimensions involved in this equation. Pluralism and diversity can be analyzed as operating on three levels. The first is diversity of content, which is concerned with the substance of media material and in particular the range of different output available to audiences. Diversity in media content may be valued as a desirable goal in itself or 'as a mechanism for serving the needs of citizenship' (ibid.: 93). The second is plurality of source, which consists of different producers, editors and owners of information. The third is plurality of outlet which entails a variety of delivery services (or media outlets) that select and present material directly to the audience (Gibbons, 1999: 157). The relationship between these three dimensions is neither simple nor straightforward.

First, it is possible that a plurality of outlets and of sources will not necessarily result in diversity of content. Different owners and editors operating through a variety of media outlets may still produce and transmit to their audiences a rather uniform and one-dimensional view of the world. For example, during the 1980s there was a diversity of outlets in the national newspaper industry in Britain and, in terms of ownership, at least some diversity of source. However, in terms of newspaper attitudes towards the Thatcher premiership, there was considerably less diversity in content, since with only a few notable exceptions most national newspapers articulated strong support for Thatcherite values, reflecting the sympathy of their owners for such an ideological stance.

Conversely, it is possible to have a range of diverse content from a single media outlet and source. For example, a public service broadcaster such as the BBC is obliged to reflect in its coverage a spectrum of political and social viewpoints, albeit in practice within the general parameters of mainstream opinion. In this case, because of the application of content regulations, a single media organization through its different outlets may be considered as practising a form of what commentators call 'internal pluralism'. At a lower level of significance, some 'quality' newspapers allow a plurality of views to be expressed in their news and commentary columns.

A third possibility is a single media proprietor allowing different outlets owned by the company to adopt different and even contrasting political positions; for example, with regard to partisanship during a general election campaign. This was the case in the 1997 general election when the Murdoch papers disagreed in their voting recommendations to their readers: *The Sun* and *News of the World* supported Labour; *The Sunday Times* backed the Conservatives; and *The Times* urged its readers to vote for the most Eurosceptic candidate in their constituency. However, while this example might point to proprietorial tolerance of diversity in partisanship, it could also be pointed out that on the issue of Europe all the Murdoch papers have championed the Eurosceptic position. This might indicate that while on some issues different newspapers from the same ownership stable may articulate a diverse range of opinion, on other issues closer to the proprietor's commercial interests this possibility is denied them.

Finally, it should be noted that legislation to limit concentration of ownership does not necessarily lead to increased diversity in editorial opinion – it might just result in the closure of some outlets as owners divest themselves of some of their interests, as Murdoch did with the *Today* newspaper in 1995. While the decision to close *Today* was made predominantly on commercial grounds, it had implications for diversity of choice. A proprietor may prefer to see a newspaper being liquidated rather than sell it to another potential owner (it was revealed that the businessman Mohammed Al Fayed, chairman of Harrods, was interested in taking over *Today*). Such a decision may well be economically rational in that it allows a press group to concentrate its activities on its other media activities. In the short term the closure of *Today* reduced the circulation share of the Murdoch group among national newspapers, even if some of the paper's readers did switch to other Murdoch titles. But it did not increase overall consumer choice in the market – rather, the reverse.

In short, since there is no simple link between pluralism of source/outlet on the one hand and diversity of content on the other, ownership regulations designed to ensure the former cannot be guaranteed to secure the latter. Nonetheless, there must be a danger that the more ownership is concentrated in fewer privately owned companies, the less likely it is that a range of opinions will be given means of expression via the media. The potential for the abuse of ownership power increases in proportion to any growth in media concentration, as does the risk of a narrowing of views and arguments placed into the public sphere. Thus, despite the lack of a clear relationship between ownership and content, a case can still be made for the retention of regulations on ownership as part of a broader regulatory framework, including regulation of content and protection of editorial and journalistic independence, designed to promote diversity of opinions and the free exchange of ideas.

How to measure concentration?

This is the position adopted by Collins and Murroni who point to two chief potential harms which may result from concentrated ownership and control of the media. First, some important viewpoints may be unrepresented or under-represented (and others over-represented). Second, an interest group, whether political, commercial or otherwise, may use its media influence and power to exercise political influence and power. While they argue that effective, national competition regulation should be the primary plank of media policy, they also consider that competition policy of itself is not sufficient to deliver a democratic marketplace for ideas and to provide a comprehensive basis for the regulation of media markets (Collins and Murroni, 1996: 63). Essentially, this is because competition policy is concerned with economic competition rather than with pluralism or diversity (Michalis, 1999: 163). For example, competition policy lacks sensitivity to problems posed by media enterprises that compete in several markets but are dominant in none, while even competitive media markets, with more than one firm supplying relevant products and services, may not deliver diverse, quality media products (Collins and Murroni, 1996: 62). This is why according to Collins and Murroni specific ceilings on ownership concentration in the media are needed.

They propose to allow companies a 40 per cent ceiling in not more than one of several distinct markets, with the maximum share declining the more sectors a company has a stake in. They emphasize four media sectors on the grounds that these are the main sources of news and opinion for the public: national newspapers, regional newspapers, television and radio. The percentage shares are based on the judgement that no media company should have more than 15 per cent of the total media market (i.e. the four sectors combined). Thus, their proposed ceilings are:

- Maximum share in one of the four sectors: 40 per cent
- Maximum share in two of the sectors: 30 per cent
- Maximum share in three of the sectors: 20 per cent
- Maximum share in all of the sectors: 15 per cent.

What is the rationale for the 15 per cent total? The authors contend that a market of ten media owners does not threaten pluralism, but that a market of five would. How do Collins and Murroni intend to measure market shares? Circulation figures would be used in the case of newspapers, audience figues in the case of free-to-air radio and television, and subscription figures for pay-tv.

The use of traditional means of measuring market share certainly avoids the problem of trying to construct a complex system of cross-media comparison. Various such schemes to measure market share in and across designated media sectors were debated in the 1990s when the government was actively considering its cross-media ownership legislation. These included, for instance, measurement by the size of the audience, by the length of time spent in media usage and by the revenue media obtained from different sources. Within any one market sector, however, different means of measurement (audience, time or revenue) produce different results (Robinson, 1995). When one then tries to aggregate the media sectors to estimate the overall size of the media market and the shares of companies within that single market, then the methodological problems become truly daunting. As Robinson points out when trying to create a satisfactory approach in terms of audience-based measures, 'there is no obvious solution to the problem of creating an *overall* market share. If a particular company has 10 per cent of the television market and 20 per cent of the newspaper market and nothing in radio, what is its share of the total media market?' (Robinson, 1995: 59, emphasis in original).

The Collins and Murroni approach to market share has the merit of simplicity and clarity. However, Feintuck (1999: 104) has criticized their list of recommendations on the following grounds:

- It contains implicit assumptions regarding a 'media exchange rate'. In other words in failing to address the problem of comparison across media sectors, it ducks an important issue.
- It appears to understate the difficulty in establishing market share even within one sector.
- It remains questionable whether the minimum level of diversity secured across the media as a whole is adequate.
- In the modern context such a measure must be expanded to factor in control of key aspects of the technological infrastructure, which appears at least as significant as control of production companies.

This last criticism is particularly pertinent for Feintuck who regards the digital gateways as forming an important new media sector in their own right. In his eyes the failure of the 1996 legislation 'to integrate multiplexes for DTT [digital terrestrial television] into the calculation of cross-media holdings . . . may allow powerful groups or individuals to shape the new market' (ibid.: 107).

Gibbons (1999) is also concerned about the protection of media pluralism in an era of convergence. He accepts that competition law

does not recognise a firm's dominance, in itself, to be a problem, but
'only begins to take effect when dominance is abused or competition
is significantly impeded' (ibid.: 168). As a result, the application of
competition law is inadequate to protect media pluralism. However,
for Gibbons 'ownership regulation by industry structure will no
longer be appropriate as existing market sectors merge' (ibid.: 169).
Instead other means to regulate for pluralism are required. Gibbons
puts forward three approaches for consideration (ibid.: 171–3). The
first is to rely on public service broadcasting to ensure pluralism.
However, he recognizes that whatever the strengths of the public
service tradition in Britain, this will be only one source of content in
the converged media markets and 'the protection of pluralism cannot
depend on virtually fortuitous audience exposure to one, increasingly
smaller, kind of programming'. A second option is 'to target
programme production and supply in order to guarantee diversity of
output'. The aim in this context would be 'to ensure that the supply of
material – the crucial element of the value chain in a converged media
– does not fall into too few hands'. More specifically, Gibbons
proposes that a threshold of 10–15 per cent of audience share might be
established to prevent undertakings from achieving more than such a
share of editorial or scheduling control over content. A final approach,
'which could be used to supplement the second, would be to focus on
the delivery to the audience and ensure that a choice of material was
available'. This might include the possibility of imposing quotas on
the source of supply, although Gibbons recognises that this would be
cumbersome to implement across fluid, converged delivery platforms. In short, Gibbons wishes to ensure through regulation that
'major media players do not control more than a significant share of
the audiences' experience'. His solution is to adapt behaviour-based
competition regulation to impose a threshold for media domination
that differs from, but complements, notions of economic dominance
(ibid.: 173).

Conclusion

The policy debate on media ownership is concerned not with how
media proprietors run their organizations or even how they may use
media outlets for the transmission of their political views to the
public. Rather its focus is directed towards the broader issue of the
concentration of economic and political power in and across market

sectors. The expression of divergent views from policy stakeholders and commentators on how to proceed on the issue of media ownership policy is not surprising, since regulation raises a host of complex questions. Should the media be regarded primarily as economic concerns or as political communication actors? At what level does concentration of ownership become harmful to the realization of the goals of pluralism and diversity? How can ownership concentration across different media sectors be measured? It is easier to agree on the desirability of certain general principles than on how specific policies should be formulated and implemented.

Moreover, these are not simply managerial or technical questions; the issue of media ownership is fundamentally political. One of the problems any government faces in this context is how much criticism it is prepared to tolerate from media companies if its proposed owner-ship policies run counter to the promotion of their commercial inter-ests. To put it crudely: to what extent can a government risk alienating a powerful communications group which might then use its media outlets to launch a series of hostile political attacks? Recent British governments have tended to emphasize a regulatory approach to media ownership based primarily on grounds of competition and on economic and commercial considerations rather than the need to protect pluralism and diversity (Doyle, 2002: 137). Whether from a sense of conviction or fear, they have shown themselves unwilling to place strong limits on the ownership shares of the major media companies operating in the UK. Indeed, the latter have to a significant extent dominated the agenda construction and framing of this issue to their own commercial benefit.

5

Regulation

Rules on ownership form one part of the regulatory equation in public policy on the media. The other consists of rules on content. All media in Britain are subject to content regulation to some extent: no communications medium is totally free simply to produce or distribute material without any legal impediment. For example, on an issue such as incitement to racial hatred, the media are subject to the same general legislation which sets limits on the behaviour of all persons with regard to the exercise of their freedom of expression in the public domain.

The objective of this chapter is to examine selected key aspects of the political and policy debates on media content regulation in recent years. Such regulation has long been sector-specific, with the press and broadcasting subject to separate and distinct regulatory regimes. This difference reflected the respective dominance in each sector of a regulatory logic based on either the principle of market freedom or the values of public service (see Chapter 2). Some of this sector-specificity is breaking down as a result of digital convergence (see Chapter 3), especially in the area of broadcasting/communications. At the same time, different regulatory obligations and modes of regulation still persist across the media as a whole, especially between the press on the one hand and broadcasting on the other, while the internet is to a large extent a case apart.

The chapter is divided into three sections, which cover broadcasting, the press and the internet. This approach allows for the consideration of different levels and modes of content regulation in declining order of the extent of the exercise of formal authority. We begin with regulation by government and independent agencies in the case of broadcasting; then self-regulation by the industry in the case of the press; and, finally, a variant of co-regulation, predominantly by the user with some support from both service providers and public authorities in the case of the internet.

Broadcasting

A multi-level regulatory model

To ensure that broadcasters operate in the public interest the government has traditionally imposed specific content regulations in the form of both negative constraints and positive requirements, with compliance monitored via a system of state-appointed regulatory authorities. While public service values used to underpin the regulation of *all* broadcast outlets, differences in regulatory obligations began to appear in the 1980s encouraged by new systems of distribution such as cable and satellite and a different ideological approach on the part of policy-makers. A major challenge faced by the New Labour government in regulating for broadcasting in the digital era has been to establish a regulatory framework sufficiently flexible, transparent and coherent to cope with an ever growing number and range of content and service providers.

The expansion of broadcasting supply entrenched in the eyes of government the need for a multi-level approach to regulation. In its 2000 White Paper on *A New Future for Communications* it proposed to create a three-tier structure over and above the basic laws of the land. This, the government argued, 'would allow broadcasters to adapt quickly and effectively to change, and to reflect the specificity of each broadcaster, while creating more of a level playing field that is fair between different broadcasters, taking into account their differing missions and funding sources' (DTI/DCMS, 2000: 46). This approach was enshrined in the 2003 Communications Act.

The first tier sets minimum standards for all broadcasters. These include: negative minimum content provisions set by the regulator; rules on advertising and sponsorship; and the obligation to provide fair, impartial and accurate news. The two further tiers are applicable only to public service broadcasters (BBC, ITV1, Channel 4/S4C in Wales and Five), taking into account their particular remits. In the second tier, consisting of *quantitative* provisions, the regulator is responsible for ensuring the delivery of those public service obligations that are easily quantifiable and measurable, such as independent production quotas, targets for regional productions and regional programming and the fact of the availability of news and current affairs in peak time (ibid.: 55). The third tier covers the *qualitative* public service remit of these free-to-air public broadcasters. They are still required to produce a mixed and high quality range of programmes, variously including educational material, children's programmes, religious output and coverage of arts, science and international issues, with the BBC having the most onerous obligations and Five the least.

The key points of this regulatory model can be summarized as follows. First, the application of a specific tier of regulation to all broadcasters above the application of the general law of the land recognizes the continued special status of broadcasting even in an age of convergence. Moreover, broadcasting as a whole continues to be subject to more stringent regulation than the press. Second, there is an acceptance that much broadcast output should be subject to fairly minimal content regulation, especially in terms of positive programming requirements. In particular, those commercial broadcasters with no public service obligations are subject to 'light touch' regulation. Finally, while public service broadcasters are still expected to meet heavier programming obligations than other broadcast content providers, even here there is the expectation that in future such obligations may be delivered and monitored to a significant extent through self-regulation. Overall, therefore, the New Labour government's approach to content regulation in broadcasting is characterized by a significant degree of liberalization in terms of both specific provisions and underlying ethos.

New Labour's commitment to public service values

Notwithstanding this general commitment to liberalization, in various policy documents published since it came to power New Labour has accepted that public service broadcasting would retain an important role in the digital era. For example, the 2000 White Paper reaffirmed the government's commitment to public service broadcasting on three main grounds: economic, democratic and cultural. First, it accepted the argument regarding the imperfection of the market and the continued need for public service networks with mixed schedules, free at the point of use, funded through advertising or a licence fee as the best way of funding the production of mass audience, high quality, varied, UK-originated programmes (DTI/DCMS, 2000: 49). Second, public service broadcasting was held to have an important democratic role in terms of its educational and information functions. In particular, public service broadcasting was deemed to have an important role in the provision of news and current affairs as 'the key foundation of an open, balanced public debate' (ibid.: 49). Finally, the government argued that there are strong cultural justifications for the retention of public service broadcasting. Public service broadcasters have provided a guarantee and benchmark of quality for the rest of the market, halting any slide towards lowest common denominator content (ibid.: 51). More widely, public service broadcasters would be expected to continue to celebrate and reflect Britain's culturally diverse communities, and broadcast programmes that appeal to a wide range of tastes and interests (ibid.: 38).

The 2003 Communications Act offered support for the continued existence of public service broadcasting and attempted to define what sorts of programmes should be provided. On behalf of *consumers* the Act asks the designated public service broadcasters to offer a wide range of programmes, catering for a variety of tastes and interests and sustaining high quality, original and innovative programming. On behalf of *citizens*, the Act requires the terrestrial channels to provide a range of socially beneficial programming – education, news, information and content that reflects different UK communities and cultures.

According to Ofcom, the four basic objectives that the Act identifies for public service broadcasting can be summarized as:

- *Social values*: education, cultural identity, informing the democratic process, supporting a tolerant and inclusive society
- *Quality*: production values, standards, innovation
- *Range and balance*: treatment of a range of subject matters across different genres, sub-genres and formats at all times
- *Diversity*: catering for different/minority audiences and communities.

With many of the consumer market failures that justify intervention in the broadcasting market set to disappear in the digital world of multi-channel provision, Ofcom argued that there were enduring citizenship concerns which would continue to call for some public intervention in the television market.

The policy debate on public service broadcasting

The New Labour government's acceptance of a continued role for public service broadcasting in the digital era raises several policy questions. How can public service content be rigorously defined? How should such content be provided in future? How should its provision be funded? In practice, much of the political debate has tended to focus on the BBC as the principal established public service broadcaster. However, precisely because of the BBC's central position in the UK broadcasting ecology, the policy debate has ramifications for all other broadcasters.

This is particularly true of the current advertising-funded public service television channels – ITV1, Channel 4 and Five – which are seeking to square the circle of complying with public service programme requirements, maintaining audience share and retaining secure funding streams. The example of ITV1 is particularly illustrative of the difficulties these broadcasters face. When in the days of the regulated duopoly the ITV network had a monopoly on broadcast advertising revenue, one of its company chairmen argued that it provided 'a licence to print money'. This is far from true now. In the run-up to full digital switchover, the value to commercial public service broadcasters of their place on the terrestrial spectrum will decline to the point where 'the costs of the public service obligations . . . may one day outweigh the benefits of access to spectrum' (Cowling, 2004: 65). Meanwhile, the increase in advertising opportunities offered by other fully commercial broadcasters (i.e. those with no public service obligations) combined with the commercial public service broadcasters' falling audience share 'could undermine their revenue stream and ability to afford costly public service content' (ibid.). In short, producing and transmitting public service content in a digital world may lose commercial public service broadcasters both audiences and money. Even Channel 4's special status as a public corporation will not protect it from the impact of the economics of the digital marketplace (Rossiter, 2005: 6–7). As multi-channel television took hold in Britain, evidence showed that 'the more popular genres of programming – soaps, drama series, "lifestyle" programming and (to a certain extent) entertainment – have come to account for a larger share of terrestrial channels schedules, at the expense of the traditionalist public service broadcasting genres: arts, current affairs, classical music and religion' (Bergg, 2004: 12).

It is likely, therefore, that all the current advertising-funded public service broadcasters will be obliged to adopt increasingly commercial strategies to attract audiences and generate revenue. This does not necessarily mean that all public service content will be automatically jettisoned – for instance, *Channel 4 News* with its serious coverage of national and international events might still survive in a more commercial marketplace. However, some public service genres currently available on commercial public service channels will certainly come under threat and without public intervention will disappear. In 2005, faced with a sharp fall in audiences for its ITV1 service, ITV called for the lifting of its entire remaining public service broadcasting obligations, including regional news, in a bid to cut costs. A few years previously the company had tried to drop its flagship evening news progamme, *News at Ten*, from its regular viewing slot so as to make way for uninterrupted prime-time entertainment (Tumber, 2001) – an eloquent illustration of the tension between commercial push and regulatory pull in a more competitive market. With the decline in the force of regulatory levers, one possible policy response might be to allocate these broadcasters a tranche of public funding to support public service content (see below). An alternative would be to accept that public service content will in future be the prerogative of the BBC, supported by Channel 4.

Sport on the box

Sports coverage on television offers a broad illustration of the difficulties public service broadcasters face in a competitive market and the relative inability of regulation to act as a protective defence. In the days of the regulated duopoly the free-to-air terrestrial broadcasters faced no competition outside their own ranks in their attempts to secure the rights to cover major sporting events on television. Sports coverage was regarded as part of their balanced programme scheduling and the BBC in particular regarded coverage of major national sporting events as integral to its mission as the nation's broadcaster. The entry into the television market of BSkyB altered for ever the relationship between television and sport in Britain. Sport is one of the most competitive programme genres in the digital era, with coverage of premium sporting events regarded by broadcasters not just as attractive content for viewers, but also as a means of branding one's organization as a major broadcaster.

The government has taken steps through regulation to protect coverage of some sporting events for free-to-air terrestrial broadcasters. The 1996 Broadcasting Act protects coverage of certain listed sports events on free-to-air television. Broadcasters who broadcast to at least 95 per cent of UK viewers (i.e. the BBC, ITV network and Channel 4) and who offer reception at no additional cost, can acquire the rights to these events on fair and reasonable terms. In the case of Group A events such as the FA Cup Final and the Grand National horse race, full 'live' coverage is protected. In the case of Group B events such as the Ryder Cup and the Commonwealth Games, secondary coverage only is protected, reflecting the scheduling problems caused either by their duration or the number of games or matches involved. In its 2000 White Paper the government remained committed to protecting coverage of key sporting and other events on free-to-air television and pledged to review the list of events regularly.

The government's regulatory commitment in this regard is testimony to the lobbying power of free-to-air broadcasters in both national and supranational policy fora. Yet it would be naïve to expect that governmental intervention through regulation can turn the clock back. Certain sports are now linked in a symbiotic relationship with pay-tv, from which both stand to gain financially. Cash rich commercial broadcasters can afford to direct a significant proportion of their resources to sports coverage. This is a choice denied free-to-air broadcasters because of their more limited funds and their general regulatory remits. Regulation may be employed to protect for free-to-air broadcasters a few sporting events considered of importance to a wide national audience. However, even here the concessions have been described as 'largely token' (Goodwin, 1998: 153). More importantly, financial power now dictates which broadcaster picks up the spoils.

The future of the BBC

Contributing to the debate on the renewal of the BBC's Charter in 2006, the New Labour government's 2005 Green Paper proposed six public purposes for the Corporation (DCMS, 2005: 20–53). These were:

- *Sustaining citizenship and civil society*: informing ourselves and others and increasing our understanding of the world through news, information and analysis of current events and ideas
- *Promoting education and learning*: stimulating our interest in and knowledge of a full range of subjects and issues through content that is accessible and can encourage either formal or informal learning; providing specialist educational programmes and accompanying material to facilitate learning at all levels and for all ages
- *Stimulating creativity and cultural excellence*: enriching the cultural life of the UK through creative excellence in distinctive and original programming; fostering creativity and nurturing talent; promoting interest, engagement and participation in cultural activity among new audiences

- *Reflecting the UK, its nations, regions and communities*: reflecting and strengthening our cultural identity through original programming at local, regional and national level, on occasion bringing audiences together for shared experiences; making us aware of different cultures and alternative viewpoints, through content that reflects the lives of other people and other communities within the UK
- *Bringing the world to the UK and the UK to the world*: making UK audiences aware of international issues and of the different cultures and viewpoints of people living outside the UK; bringing high-quality international news coverage to a global audience through radio, television and new media.

These represented an attempt to update the traditional public service values of information, education and entertainment to make them appropriate for a multi-channel, global era. The last public purpose was:

- *Building digital Britain*: helping to bring the benefits of digital services to all households and providing hiqh quality content to drive take-up of those services; taking a leading role in the process of digital switchover in television.

The achievement of these purposes by the BBC depends to a significant extent on managerial, editorial and production decisions taken within the Corporation – a matter largely of internal strategy and organization. There remain, however, issues pertinent to public policy which continue to feature in the wider political debate about the future of the BBC. Three are highlighted here: the range of services to be provided by the Corporation, its means of funding and its structure of governance. The terms of this debate serve as a reminder that the acceptance of the principle of a continued role for public service broadcasting 'should not be confused with support for the BBC's current governance structure or existing financial and institutional arrangements' (Pratten and Deakin, 2004: 83).

The first issue concerns the range of services the BBC should provide in the digital era. To achieve its public service mission should the BBC seek to be present in all areas of broadcasting and new communications or should it restrict itself to certain specific types of programming and service provision? Critics of the BBC argue that the Corporation tends to define public service content as anything it chooses to be involved in. This allows BBC executives to defend as public service content what may in reality be an unwarranted incursion by the Corporation into areas of programming either already delivered perfectly well by private sector operators or that could be so delivered if the BBC did not distort market competition. This is a viewpoint that is frequently put forward by the Corporation's commercial rivals, who argue that they are being unfairly 'crowded out' of programming sectors by the BBC's abuse of its market power (Collins, 2004: 141–4).

Let us take an example to illustrate the argument. Can popular music on radio be subsumed within a definition of public service content? Or to put it another way, are Radios 1 and 2 an integral part of the BBC's public service mission? Critics argue that these radio services are unnecessary because they do not add to consumer choice ('there is enough pop music on radio from non-BBC providers') and that their 'protected' existence under the BBC aegis makes it more difficult for commercial competitors to prosper and for potential new suppliers of this type of programming to enter the market. In response, defenders of BBC Radio 1 point to its 'eclectic approach to music and its commitment to mixing speech programming with music output' – in short, that Radio 1 offers listeners a service that is different to that of commercial broadcasters and which is successful with its target audience, reaching 'half of the 15–24 year old age group each week' (Barnett, 2004: 42). Ofcom is now empowered to carry out a market impact assessment to evaluate the effect on the Corporation's commercial rivals of new BBC services and significant changes to existing services. This should address the competition concerns of possible BBC 'crowding out'. However, the question of whether the Corporation should be involved in some areas of broadcasting, such as Radios 1 and 2, is not just a competition issue. It returns us to the fundamental question of what activities are appropriate for public service broadcasters in the digital age.

If many types of programming are made available in the marketplace by commercial providers to the satisfaction of consumers, then some argue that the BBC should concentrate simply on addressing public needs in areas where market provision has demonstrably failed – a variant of the market failure argument we examined in Chapter 4, but this time used to support only a minor role for the BBC. This might result in a highly restricted public service provision – a quality service for the upmarket, educated elite, with the BBC shrinking in size to become a much smaller organization than it is currently.

Opponents of this 'ghettoization' of the BBC argue that such a role would so limit its contribution as a public service broadcaster that it would be unable to fulfil its mission of serving the public as a whole by offering 'free, high quality, universally available material with a decent element of innovation to everyone regardless of where they live, what they can afford or whether they are attractive to advertisers' (Barnett, 2004: 44). This latter position might be seen as a vigorous justification for a wide-ranging BBC within a mixed broadcasting economy. Critics would argue that it can also be interpreted as a self-serving defence of whatever the Corporation chooses to do.

For some commentators, the BBC's growing commercial interests pose a possible competition problem and also present the Corporation with the dilemma of how to avoid its public service commitment from being adversely influenced by its commercial activities. These are issues that have increased in significance since the development of the BBC's role in global media markets (see Chapter 4). Currie and Siner, for instance, argue that it makes good sense for the BBC to realize the value of its products in the broader commercial market, both at home and overseas, through sales, licensing and joint ventures, so as to increase the resources available to plough back into public service broadcasting (Currie and Siner, 1999: 74). The BBC argues that the flow of revenue does go in this direction: from its commercial to its public services. Certainly to ensure fair competition in the domestic broadcasting market it is important that the Corporation's commercial services should not be cross-subsidized by its publicly-funded activity.

A different concern is that the Corporation's focus on commercial activities may divert it from its public service mission. Steemers, for instance, argues that an emphasis on commercial activities 'could compromise the public service mission in the long term' (Steemers, 1998: 113). She argues that 'it may be too tempting in the end for commercial (and increasingly global) goals to take over from public (and domestic) goals, resulting in a narrower cultural diversity concentrated in the hands of one dominant public supplier' (ibid.: 116). Goodwin agrees, arguing that 'despite all the formal safeguards the government and the Corporation had introduced in the new charter and licence . . . there was the real prospect that the (mainly international) commercial tail of the BBC would soon start wagging the (primarily domestic) public service dog' (Goodwin, 1998: 138). Graham and Davies go further, stating that 'faced with a squeeze on its relative position the BBC should *not* seek to expand commercial income because the scope for doing so without prejudicing the public service role is extremely limited' (Graham and Davies, 1997: 64, emphasis in original).

The dilemma for the BBC as a public service broadcaster frequently seems stark. If public service broadcasting increasingly emulates the management practices and resembles the output of commercial rivals, then the defence of a specific public service component in broadcasting and communications on the grounds of its particular contribution to the achievement of socially desirable objectives is severely weakened, along with the claim to a secure source of public funding (Iosifidis, Steemers and Wheeler, 2005: 11). Conversely, if the BBC retires to a small public service ghetto of 'worthy' broadcast ouput, it runs the risk of losing many listeners and viewers and so the case for public funding via the licence-fee is again undermined. To put it bluntly, 'either the BBC services the masses, in which case it is no longer distinguishable from the commercial broadcasters, or it does not service the masses, in which case it cannot possibly deserve to be financed by an unjust tax on them' (Lipsey, 2002: 2). The squaring of the circle requires the BBC to distribute content across a range of stations, channels and online services which is both different from that of commercial rivals and yet is still attractive to an aggregate of varied audiences – to be popular without 'dumbing down', to be distinctive without being elitist.

This leads us on to the second issue in the public policy debate: the funding of the Corporation. The BBC overwhelmingly depends on licence fee revenue to finance its domestic services, with the level of the licence set by the government. The advantages of licence fee funding include providing the Corporation with 'a stable predictable income, independence of commercial pressures, programming uninterrupted by advertising and programmes free at the point of use to all who want to watch them' (ibid.: 7). The BBC continues to push the case that part of the broadcasting system should not be simply subject to commercial imperatives. It claims that its services represent a public space that acts as a forum for the interchange of differing views and opinions, and that the licence fee is a sound mechanism for ensuring that the Corporation is not tied to one segment of the audience, a particular social class or business group. The licence fee system, however, has also raised questions in the past about the Corporation's independence from government with regard to both political interference and financial control. Critics of the licence fee system have pointed to the possibility of a government using its hold over the purse strings to seek to influence the Corporation's output and/or to deprive the Corporation of much needed financial resources.

Notwithstanding these aspects of the licence fee method of funding, the most worrying problem for the BBC in the digital era is the continued legitimacy of this means of revenue raising. As the 2005 Green Paper on BBC Charter Review made clear, the licence is a regressive form of taxation – a poll tax in everything but name – where everyone pays the same flat charge regardless of their income and consumption. The Green Paper noted other drawbacks with the television licence fee: revenue from the licence is used by the BBC to pay for other services, including radio and new media; the costs of collection and evasion are high; subscription will become an even more common form of payment for television programming than currently, making the licence fee appear out of date; and, since television viewing may no longer be confined to traditional television sets, but could take place via computer terminals or mobile phones, a licence fee based on television ownership might become redundant (DCMS, 2005: 59).

The fear among BBC executives is that if the Corporation's share of the audience falls back significantly, then its claim to funding through the licence system may be severely undermined as public and political support for a universal charge ebbs away. There is an obvious issue of whether (and, if so, how much) consumers will continue to use public service stations and channels in an era of expanded choice. One way in which the Corporation has responded to this situation is by redefining its links with the public in terms of 'audience reach' rather than 'audience share'. This is the argument that whatever its overall share of the market, which is bound to decline, the BBC will continue to be used regularly by a high proportion of the audience for at least *some* services *some* of the time. There is, however, also the question of what types of content on public service outlets these audiences access. For instance, there is some evidence that in multi-channel households some public service television *genres* are not especially valued by audiences, even if the public service *channels* are still used by them. If so, 'audience reach' may indicate only that a particular public service outlet is being used, but not necessarily that public service content is being accessed (Tambini, 2004).

Some have argued that in these circumstances it might be preferable not to fund a specific public service broadcasting *organization* from the licence fee, but rather to finance public service *content* such as news and current affairs programming across a range of providers.

These might compete for revenue from a Public Service Broadcasting Fund (Peacock, 2004: 46) with the revenue allocated by an Arts Council of the Air (Lipsey, 2002: 8). Ofcom has also talked about the possible establishment of a new Public Service Publisher which might commission and distribute public service content using a variety of technologies. It would distribute licence fee revenue and other public funding beyond the BBC to sustain plurality and competition in public service broadcasting and might even take the form of a new, separate public service channel. Unsurprisingly, the BBC argues that it should retain the totality of licence fee funding (Rossiter, 2005: 20) and for now it seems to have won the political debate in this respect, not least because of the practical difficulties involved in introducing a system of contestable funding among different providers of public service broadcasting content.

Despite its disadvantages, the principle of the licence fee for BBC funding has been accepted by successive Conservative and Labour governments since the early 1990s. In part, this is because the options to the licence fee – such as direct funding from government, commercial income via advertising and sponsorship, or viewer subscription – also carry potentially significant drawbacks in terms of political intervention, economic uncertainty and the undermining of the principle of universal access (plus in radio no subscription facility exists or is likely to in the foreseeable future). It has also been argued that in any case most users benefit from a licence fee funding system, since they gain programming and services that they value and at less cost than they would through a system of voluntary subscription (Barwise, 2004: 31). It may be the case that some citizens – 'probably concentrated among the minority ethnic groups, the lower income groups, and those outside the south east of England' (Davies, 2004: 29) – lose out, compelled to pay the licence fee for services that they rarely use or do not value. However, for Davies this problem needs to be addressed by the BBC re-orienting some of its output to take account of their requirements, not through an abandonment of the licence fee system itself. The 1992 Green Paper on the BBC argued that while the licence fee was an oddity, with all television viewers being obliged to pay it irrespective of whether they watched or liked many BBC programmes, 'so far, no-one has devised an obviously better system' (Department of National Heritage, 1992: 31). This view was reiterated in the 2005–06 Charter review process which confirmed that the licence fee would remain for the following decade.

Finally, there is the issue of the BBC's governance. Until recently, the BBC Board of Governors was formally entrusted to represent the public interest. However, three main problems with this arrangement were frequently alluded to by critics. First, although in terms of the governance of public broadcasting the BBC has been regarded as an exemplar of the 'professional model', whereby broadcasting should be 'largely insulated from political control and run by broadcasting professionals' (Hallin and Mancini, 2004: 31), there remained the danger of politicization because the Governors were appointed by the government. During the Thatcher premiership, for example, the government nominated political sympathizers to the Board, including the Chairman, Marmaduke Hussey, to help restructure the management of the Corporation and stiffen its political backbone on issues such as BBC coverage of the conflict in Northern Ireland. Second, the Board of Governors was not representative of the diversity of British society. Entrenching the representation of particular socially relevant groups such as community organizations and ethnic associations was seen as a step towards a different, 'corporatist' model of governance and hence incompatible with the retention of the 'professional' model. The possibility, therefore, of electing the Governors by an electoral college to ensure their 'representativeness' and to make them more responsive to the public (Collins, 2004: 139–40) has never been a serious policy option. Finally, there may have been a tendency for the Governors to 'go native' and to see their role as defending the BBC rather than representing the public. This is what seems to have happened in the furore surrounding aspects of BBC coverage of the Iraq conflict in 2003. The Governors provided a stolid defence of BBC management in its response to the government on the subject of Andrew Gilligan's infamous broadcast on the Radio 4 *Today* programme when he accused the government of 'sexing up' the case for going to war (see Chapter 7). In so doing, the Governors laid themselves open to the charge of confusing the interests of the Corporation's management and staff with the wider public interest.

In the 2006 White Paper on the BBC's Charter review the government proposed that a new board, provisionally called the BBC Trust, should replace the Board of Governors. The Trust would not be involved in day to day management of the Corporation. Among its new functions, the Trust would have to take competition issues into account while ensuring that the BBC acted in the public interest. It would also be able to approve new services through a public value test, previously the responsibility of the appropriate government minister. The Corporation would be subject to the oversight of the

Trust in delivering obligations that are unique or central to its own remit and purposes. These include ensuring accuracy and impartiality in all BBC programmes and protecting the editorial independence of the Corporation. While the importance of the independence of Trust members was emphasized, the method of their appointment would be the same as that used in the case of the Governors. It remained to be seen whether the new body would be a marked improvement on its predecessor in representing the public interest within the Corporation and how the Trust would interface with Ofcom on those regulatory issues where the BBC is subject to Ofcom oversight.

A new regulatory authority for broadcasting and communications

At the end of the twentieth century the main regulatory bodies for the broadcasting and communications media included:

- The ITC, which licensed and regulated non-BBC television, including ITV, Channel 4, Channel 5, cable, satellite and digital terrestrial television
- The Radio Authority, which licensed commercial radio
- The Radio Communications Agency
- The Broadcasting Standards Commission, which adjudicated on matters of taste and decency in broadcasting, including the portrayal of sex and violence
- Oftel, which regulated the telecommunications sector
- The BBC Governors

Thus the overall picture was one of considerable fragmentation of regulatory agencies, with some dealing predominantly with issues of content and others with concerns about competition (Leam, 2002).

Some commentators had long thought that such regulatory fragmentation was not sustainable in the digital era. For example, writing in the early 1990s Cuilenberg and Slaa contended that government media policies could no longer be exclusively guided by cultural values, while telecommunications policy should also pursue objectives outside the technological and economic field (Cuilenberg and Slaa, 1993). They concluded that an integration of media and telecommunications policy was called for (policy convergence), leading to one national communications policy. If not, then what they termed 'boundary conflicts' between the telecommunications, broadcasting and cable sectors would spread, as 'the traditional provider of a specific service seeks to protect its original domain, while at the same time extending it into new forms of services' (ibid.: 165). In similar vein Collins and Murroni argued for the creation of a super-regulatory authority, responsible for the broadcasting and communications sectors (Collins and Murroni, 1996: 158–81).

In its 2000 White Paper and 2002 Communications Bill the government accepted the force of the regulatory convergence case, arguing that there was a need to make economic regulation of the market and regulation of content go hand in hand. This was an acceptance of the view that content and distribution networks were becoming more inseparable. 'Networks are often worthless without content, but, in the early stages of network development, a company can't sell content unless it can build out its own network or get access to someone else's' (DTI/DCMS, 2000: 77). In particular the goverment proposed the establishment of a new unified regulator for the communications sector, the Office of Communications (Ofcom), which would be responsible for economic regulation, content regulation and spectrum management.

Ofcom has replaced the previous regulatory bodies listed above, with the exception of the BBC Trust. Its central regulatory objectives are to protect the interests of consumers, in particular through promoting open and competitive markets; to maintain high quality of content, a wide range of programming and plurality of public expression; and to protect the interests of citizens, for example by ensuring appropriate protection of fairness and privacy (ibid.: 79). Its mission is to roll back regulation promptly where increasing competition renders it unnecessary, while it encourages co-regulation and self-regulation where these best achieve the regulatory objectives (ibid.: 82). In short, with a brief to minimize regulatory intervention where possible, Ofcom has responsibility for ensuring a competitive marketplace in communications media and also monitors the application of 'light touch' content regulation in the broadcasting sector.

The creation of a single regulatory authority represents the acceptance of a new integrated approach to broadcasting and communications regulation in Britain. Supporters of a single authority point to the advantages in achieving greater regulatory coherence and avoiding disputes between different regulatory authorities whose modes of operation had been left behind by the impact of technological convergence. Indeed for some the new integrated approach does not go far enough, since certain aspects of the governance of the BBC remain the prerogative of the new BBC Trust rather than of Ofcom. Opponents, however, contend that substantive conflicts do not disappear as a result of institutional change; rather, these may be conducted in private rather than in public. Moreover, for some critics there is also the fear that a single super-regulator might take too much of an economic rather than a content-based perspective on regulation, with the result that content regulation might be relaxed more quickly than they consider desirable in the light of the media's democratic responsibilities (Gibbons, 1998b: 93).

The press

From a long-term historical perspective the press in Britain 'has moved from being a highly regulated medium of communication to one that operates in a largely deregulated environment' (Meech, 1990: 232). As a result, the contemporary newspaper industry is principally responsible for regulating its own affairs. Although the capacity of the press to regulate itself satisfactorily has been the subject of critical scrutiny from assorted politicians and sections of the public over the years, its self-regulatory status has been fiercely and, to a large extent, successfully defended by newspaper owners and management (O'Malley and Soley, 2000).

The history of the postwar debate on press regulation can be characterized in terms of a spiral. Criticisms are made of the newspaper industry for its unacceptable standards in reporting; the industry reluctantly responds with self-regulatory measures and a promise that matters will improve; further offences continue; the system of self-regulation is beefed up slightly and the cycle recommences at a new level. Present-day concern with newspaper standards is therefore nothing new (see Table 5.1). Back in the late 1940s the first postwar Royal Commission on the Press commented unfavourably about sensationalist newspaper coverage, arguing that 'an aspect of this form of sensationalism which has attracted much attention is the intrusion on the privacy of individuals necessary to satisy the appetite for intimate personal detail about the lives and affairs of people who are, perhaps quite accidentally, in the news' (Royal Commission on the Press, 1949: 132).

The 1949 Royal Commission addressed this issue by recommending the establishment of a General Council of the Press, one objective

Table 5.1   Press, privacy and regulation 1945–2003

1949	First Royal Commission on the Press recommends the establishment of the General Council of the Press.
1953	Press industry belatedly agrees to establish a General Council of the Press on a voluntary basis.
1962	Second Royal Commission on the Press criticizes the General Council's failure to implement the recommendations of the first Royal Commission.
1972	Younger Committee on Privacy recommends changes in the composition of the Press Council.
1977	Third Royal Commission on the Press criticizes inadequate role of the Press Council in maintaining acceptable standards.
1989	The Home Secretary, Douglas Hurd, appoints David Calcutt to chair a review 'to consider what measures . . . are needed to give further protection to individual privacy from the activities of the press'.
1990	The *Sunday Sport* invades hospital room of the seriously injured *'Allo 'Allo* actor, Gordon Kaye. Efforts to prevent publication fail in the High Court.
	The first Calcutt Report on *Privacy and Related Matters* recommends that 'the press should be given one final chance to prove that voluntary self-regulation can be made to work.' The report makes thirteen recommendations concerning the proposed new Press Complaints Commission (PCC) to replace the discredited Press Council.
	David Mellor, Home Office minister with responsibility for press matters, states that the press is 'drinking in the last-chance saloon'.
1991	The PCC, chaired by Lord McGregor of Durris, replaces the Press Council.
1992	Liberal-Democrat leader, Paddy Ashdown, confesses to a previous affair with his secretary after the story is published in *The Scotsman*.
	Press coverage of the 'loveless' royal marriage between Prince Charles and Princess Diana follows publication of Andrew Morton's book *Diana: her true story*. *Sunday Times* serialization of Morton's book prompts Lord McGregor to condemn journalists for 'dabbling their fingers in the stuff of other people's souls'.
	Sir David Calcutt is asked to conduct a review of press self-regulation by the National Heritage Secretary, David Mellor.
	The Independent reveals that the Health Secretary, Virginia Bottomley, had been an 'unmarried teenage mum'. *The Sun* criticises *The Independent* for invasion of the minister's privacy.
	The People publishes details of an amorous liaison between actress Antonia de Sancha and David Mellor.
	The *Daily Mirror* and *The Sun* publish topless photos of the Duchess of York.

→

Table 5.1 continued

1993	The second Calcutt report, *Review of Press Self-Regulation*, is published. The report recommends the introduction of a statutory regulatory body for the press.
	The National Heritage Select Committee proposes a press privacy bill, a tougher self-regulatory body and a statutory Press Ombudsman.
	Weakness of PCC widely criticized. PCC beefs up its code of practice and opts for a majority of non-industry members on the commission.
	Details of Royal phone conversations published in press.
	Sunday Mirror and *Daily Mirror* publish 'peeping tom' photos of the Princess of Wales exercising in a health club. PCC comes close to collapse.
	Princess Diana announces her retirement from public life, blaming media intrusion for her decision.
	Government announces its intention to introduce new laws on privacy.
1994	PCC appoints Professor Robert Pinker as its 'privacy commissioner' with powers to discipline editors for breaches of its code.
	Lurid details concerning the death of Conservative MP, Stephen Milligan, from autoerotic asphyxiation are widely published in the press.
	The Guardian publishes details of a stay at the Ritz in Paris by government minister, Jonathan Aitken, which was paid for by Saudi businessmen and not declared by the minister.
	The newspaper industry publishes an alternative White Paper entitled *Media Freedom and Media Regulation*, which restates the case for continued voluntary self-regulation of the press.
	Former Conservative government minister, John Wakeham, is appointed new head of the PCC.
1995	Rupert Murdoch publicly rebukes Piers Morgan, editor of the *News of the World*, on the paper's reporting of the medical condition of the wife of Earl Spencer, brother of the Princess of Wales.
	Non-press industry majority membership of the PCC introduced.
	Government White Paper on *Privacy and Media Intrusion* published. Government rejects statutory regulation and supports tougher self-regulatory regime.
1997	Death of Princess Diana leads to newspaper re-evaluation of their role in covering the lives of celebrities. Intrusive media coverage of the life of the Princess is criticized by her brother, Earl Spencer, during his funeral oration.
1998	Labour Cabinet minister, Ron Davies, resigns from government and criticizes subsequent media coverage of the incident on Clapham Common which prompted his ministerial resignation.
2000	The PCC condemns the *Daily Sport* and *The Mail on Sunday* for separate intrusions into the privacy of the Blair family.
2003	Report of House of Commons Culture, Media and Sport Committee on *Privacy and Media Intrusion* calls for the introduction of a privacy law

of which would be to encourage the growth of a sense of public responsibility in newspapers. However, this body was not established until 1953 and 'was weaker and significantly less pro-active in intent than had been recommended by the Commission' (O'Malley and Soley, 2000: 59). In particular, it had limited powers of sanction and was generally unwilling to impose a code of journalistic practice on the industry. Its successor, the Press Council, created ten years later, not only had wider powers but was also composed in part of lay members. However, it too came in for criticism for its failure to curb the excesses of newspapers operating in a highly competitive market (Greenslade, 2004: 535–8). While the 1977 Royal Commission did not favour statutory regulation, it did recommend a stronger approach to self-regulation, including a recommendation that the Press Council should have an equal number of lay and press representatives.

Calcutt, privacy and press regulation

The continuation of the self-regulatory status of the press did not go unchallenged and a debate on press regulation featured prominently on political and media policy agendas during the 1990s, when it appeared that newspapers had finally exceeded the limits of public and governmental tolerance. Designed to boost newspaper sales in a flagging market, press intrusion into the lives of politicians, royalty and stars of the entertainment world led to renewed calls for tighter regulation of newspaper content (Snoddy, 1992). In 1991 the Press Council was replaced by the Press Complaints Commission (PCC), as the industry attempted yet again to respond to the climate of critical opinion. The abolition of the Press Council was one of the recommendations of a government-sponsored committee of inquiry under the chairmanship of David Calcutt. The *Report of the Committee on Privacy and Related Matters* recommended that the press should be given one final chance to prove that voluntary self-regulation could be made to work (Calcutt Report, 1990).

Nonetheless, the controversy over press regulation refused to go away. In 1992 the Secretary of State for National Heritage, David Mellor, asked Calcutt to conduct a second inquiry, the *Review of Press Self-Regulation*, specifically to assess the effectiveness of non-statutory self-regulation of the press and to make recommendations. Ironically, while Calcutt was deliberating, *The People* newspaper printed a salacious story alleging that Mellor had had an extra-marital affair with the actress, Antonia de Sancha – exactly the type of content that was fuelling some politicians' concern about unwarranted media intrusion into their private lives.

The second Calcutt Report, published in January 1993, concluded that the PCC had proved a failure. Calcutt argued that press coverage of Royalty, particularly the 'loveless marriage' of the Prince and Princess of Wales, and of the amorous adventures of certain leading politicians such as Paddy Ashdown and Mellor had shown the ineffectiveness of self-regulation. For Calcutt the PCC was not sufficiently independent of the industry it was supposed to be regulating to command public confidence:

> The Commission, as constituted, is, in essence, a body set up by the industry, financed by the industry, dominated by the industry, operating a code of practice devised by the industry and which is over-favourable to the industry. (Calcutt Report, 1993: 41)

The report recommended the establishment of a statutory regulatory authority for the press which would have the power to issue a press code of conduct, stop publication of offending material, receive complaints, require the printing of apologies, fine newspapers that broke the code of practice and award compensation to complainants. The proposed code of practice was also tougher than that used by the PCC, for example in its narrower interpretation of a public interest defence put forward by newspapers. Calcutt also wanted to see the enactment of three new criminal offences: entering or remaining on private property without consent; the use of surveillance devices on private property; and the taking photographs on private property without consent. The newspaper industry reacted with horror and in a display of unanimity rushed to condemn Calcutt.

In a separate report on *Privacy and Media Intrusion* published soon afterwards, the House of Commons National Heritage Select Committee also regarded the PCC as an inadequate regulator (National Heritage Select Committee, 1993). Though it was not in favour of a statutory press complaints tribunal, the Committee did support new controls. For example, it proposed abolishing the PCC and replacing it with a new Press Commission. This new body would be dominated by lay members and have the power to fine newspapers, order corrections and award compensation. In addition, the committee favoured the creation of a statutory Press Ombudsman, who would act as a final court of appeal and have the power to impose fines and order apologies. It also recommended a Protection of Privacy Bill, making it an offence to infringe individual privacy by outlawing practices such as taking photos on private property without consent, intercepting mobile phone calls and using surveillance devices on private property. It further argued that these constraints on press freedom should be balanced by greater public access to official information. Once again, the newspaper industry was indignant and attacked the Committee's report.

Conscious that the industry might be having its final drink in what Mellor had previously called 'the last chance saloon' of self-regulation, the PCC sought to reinforce its code of practice and ensure newspaper compliance. In 1993 it was announced that the PCC would be revamped to give its membership a lay majority and a telephone helpline was to be set up to receive public complaints. New rules were added to the code of practice, including outlawing snatch photos and limiting the use of long lenses on private property. Following the publication in two Mirror Group Newspapers of 'peeping tom' photos of Princess Diana exercising in a gym, the government gave a heavy signal to the PCC that it should create the position of press ombudsman to adjudicate on matters of privacy, with the power to recommend correction and compensation. Thrown on the defensive by the publication of the Princess Diana photos, the PCC had no alternative but to accept the government's proposal. In January 1994 Professor Robert Pinker, already a member of the Commission, was appointed by the PCC as the newspaper industry's first privacy ombudsman – the 'privacy commissioner'. He was given the power to initiate inquiries into extreme cases of breaching privacy rules, though he did not have the right to impose fines on errant newsapers.

Meanwhile in response to Calcutt the press industry launched its own alternative 'White Paper', *Media Freedom and Media Regulation*, which argued the case against both statutory regulation of newspapers and new privacy legislation. Much of the debate on the issue of press regulation and protection of privacy naturally reflected the self-interest of the participants. On the one hand, tabloid newspapers, caught up in a circulation war, were striving to sensationalize coverage and titillate their readers in pursuit of increased sales. It seemed to be a commercially successful approach. For example, in 1992 'the story that brought the biggest sales boost featured topless pictures of the Duchess of York, adding 583,000 sales to the *Mirror* on August 22' (Peak, 1993: 17).

On the other hand, politicians clearly wanted to protect certain aspects of their behaviour from press scrutiny because of the resultant damaging consequences for their careers. Newspaper coverage of their extra-marital 'sex romps' seemed to be an unwarranted intrusion into their private lives, attracting the interest of the public but not serving the public interest. Yet it could reasonably be argued that those politicians who championed 'family values' had placed their personal lives in the public realm. They had politicized the personal and could not reasonably complain if this rebounded to their disadvantage.

In the case of the Royal family the issue was particularly complicated. The monarchy had increasingly sought to use the media to enhance its legitimacy and public popularity. At the same time sections of the press were coopted by Prince Charles and Princess Diana during the final stages of the breakdown of their marriage, as both protagonists struggled to put their case across to win the battle for public opinion. This process culminated in two television programmes (the first an ITV documentary featuring Prince Charles screened in 1994 and the second an interview with Princess Diana on BBC *Panorama* in 1995), which were effectively public relations exercises in the marital conflict between the Prince and Princess of Wales. The latter's complaints about media intrusion were more than a little undermined by the way in which she blatantly used sections of the press (and then television) for her own image-making purposes.

The policy debate: issues and arguments

Yet while self-interest underpinned the positions of the main players, there were clear issues of principle at stake. At the heart of the debate was the need to reconcile two desirable but mutually incompatible objectives: the individual's right to privacy and the media's right to free expression (Cloonan, 1998). In a democracy the balance between the two will always be a question of judgement.

Subscribing to the Calcutt line, supporters of the case for statutory regulation argued that self-regulation had failed. They contended that for commercial reasons some newspapers would always seek to go beyond the limits of the self-regulatory regime, even if necessary cocking a snook at the regulators in the process. The PCC remained too tied to the newspaper industry to be an effective regulator and lacked the requisite authority and power to have its views enforced. Only statutory regulation could shield member of the public from the intrusive excesses of some newspapers. Moreover, those favouring legislation denied that statutory regulation was inimical to press freedom. Rather it was a justified curb on press licence which would raise press standards and make newspapers more socially responsible.

Opponents of statutory regulation tended to emphasize the following points (Franklin, 1995). First, statutory regulation was wrong in principle and constituted censorship. While Calcutt was dismissive of those who argued that a statutory press tribunal would lead to a loss of press freedom, his opponents in the newspaper industry argued precisely that. They pointed to the dangers inherent in a system of statutory regulation in inhibiting the ability of the press to investigate matters of legitimate public interest, such as corruption, malpractice and inefficiency.

Second, statutory controls would be impractical and unworkable in contrast to self-regulation which was more flexible and offered the most effective sanction against potential offenders. For example,

> a statutory tribunal, with powers to award damages and impose fines would immediately and inevitably become involved in more legalistic and formal proceedings. Newspapers exposed to such statutory proceedings would be bound to react in a more legalistic way. We do not believe that involving lawyers in more formal proceedings would be in the best interests of the kind of private individual who now complains successfully to the Press Complaints Commission. (Stephenson, 1994: 23)

Third, there were already too many statutory controls on press freedom. The newspaper industry's alternative 'White Paper' listed no fewer than forty-six separate pieces of legislation which it argued already constrained the media in Britain. These included the 1959 Obscene Publications Act, the 1976 Race Relations Act, the 1989 Official Secrets Act and the 1987 and 1988 Criminal Justice Acts (ibid.: 26).

Finally, there was no case that statutory regulation was necessary or warranted. In particular,

> there is no evidence of such widespread dissatisfaction with the present general balance in law between privacy and freedom of investigation over the whole spectrum of privacy as to warrant primary legislation to create an entirely new civil wrong of infringement of privacy. (Ibid.: 12)

Whatever the pros and cons of the debate in the abstract, in the real world of politics the Major government had to take account of the partisan leanings of the press in the run-up to the 1997 general election. The government had no great desire to enter into direct conflict with the newspaper industry. The certainty of the whole press, including traditional pro-Conservative newspapers, mobilizing against proposed legislation on statutory regulation can be reasonably expected to have weighed in the balance in ministerial calculations. An unpopular government with a slim parliamentary majority was understandably in no hurry to push ahead down the statutory route, even though many newspaper revelations about the sexual behaviour of Conservative politicians were scarcely designed to enhance the party's electoral fortunes or endear the newspapers responsible to the Conservative party.

The newspapers themselves were, of course, perfectly aware of this power relationship and several seemed prepared to exploit the situation to their advantage. Thus, while salacious stories about politicians were partly an ingredient in the circulation war, 'there was also a hint in several of them that any politicians trying to impose laws on the press might find themselves as the next exposed celebrity' (Peak, 1993: 13). In this particular battle between governmental authority and newspaper power, both sides knew not only their own strengths and weaknesses, but also those of their opponents.

Government proposals on the issues of press regulation and new privacy legislation were expected throughout 1994, but publication was delayed several times and the government's response finally appeared only in 1995 (Department of National Heritage, 1995b). In its White Paper the government welcomed the various self-regulatory changes which had been introduced by the industry with the backing of the PCC under its new chairman and former Conservative minister, John Wakeham. These included the lay majority on the Commission, the independent appointments body to the Commission and the PCC's revamped code of practice. The government rejected the option of a statutory complaints tribunal as recommended by Calcutt and of a statutory Press Ombudsman as proposed by the National Heritage Select Committee. Instead tougher self-regulation was advocated including a tightening up of the code of practice, tougher sanctions for breaches of the code, a compensation fund for those whose privacy had been unjustifiably infringed by the press, the exercise of preemptive pressure on newspapers to head off press abuses and greater publicity for the work of the PCC.

The government also rejected the option of new criminal offences to deal with invasion of privacy, on the grounds that it was impossible to draft legislation in a way that would satisfactorily balance the requirement to defend the practice of responsible investigative journalism and the right of the individual to personal privacy. Nor did the government intend to legislate a new civil remedy for infringements of privacy:

What has emerged . . . is a renewal of the commitment to voluntarism; a reiteration of the distaste of jurisprudence; and a restatement of the liberal belief that the considerable disadvantages do not outweigh the often hidden benefits of tolerating a largely unfettered press. (Stephenson and Bromley, 1998: 6)

Newspapers generally welcomed the government's proposals. In 1997, however, the editor of *The Guardian* wrote that he would be willing to accept the introduction of privacy legislation in return for positive safeguards concerning related aspects of newspaper coverage:

I would happily sacrifice the freedom to expose the love life of a BBC weather forecaster to 11 million prurient eyes if it meant that the courts would give greater protection to papers or broadcasters reporting corruption or dishonesty in public life. (Rusbridger, 1997: 22–3)

Politicians were much less happy. While the rejection of a statutory tribunal was welcomed by the Labour party, the lack of measures to protect privacy was widely condemned by representatives of all major forces. The shadow National Heritage Secretary, Chris Smith, summed up what appeared to be a widely held view among politicians: 'It does seem the Last Chance Saloon has had a substantial extension given to its drinking hours'.

From the mid-1990s onwards the issue of press regulation did not feature quite so prominently on the media policy agenda. In part this was because the PCC proved reasonably effective in defusing the issue by being (or appearing to be) more responsive to concerns than its regulatory predecessors; in part because newspapers had cleaned up their act, notably through a Code of Conduct which now covers issues such as 'privacy', 'harassment' and the use of long-lens photography in private places without the subject's consent; in part because governmental policy makers recognized the risks involved in taking on the entrenched power of the press; in part because the arguments for and against statutory regulation appeared to have been given such a thorough airing between 1989 and 1995; and, finally, in part because any imposition of statutory controls would go against the recent general trend in favour of 'self-regulation wherever possible and light-touch regulation wherever necessary' (Deacon, 2004: 19).

However, the alleged excesses of newspaper behaviour continued to form part of political and public debate. For example, the circumstances surrounding the death of Diana, Princess of Wales, in 1997 brought the role of the press back into question:

> When it emerged that prior to her car accident a number of photographers had been in pursuit of the car she was in, the whole issue of the responsibility of the press on questions of privacy came to the fore again. Her brother, the Earl Spencer, articulated this by accusing editors of having 'had blood on their hands'. (O'Malley and Soley, 2000: 169)

In the wake of Diana's death, the code was again tightened up. In the world post-Diana the issue of press intrusion may appear to have lost some of its salience. However, coverage of royal figures such as Prince William and of the children of Prime Minister Blair continued to give cause for concern. For example, sections of the media in 2001 argued that information about whether the Prime Minister's baby son, Leo, had been given the triple MMR vaccination was of public interest given the government's official support for this policy and the possible link between the vaccine and autism. Blair, however, refused to provide any information on what he argued was a personal family matter. The basic ingredients for the renewal of the policy debate over press regulation are still there: a competitive and shrinking newspaper market; journalists' fascination with human interest stories; and public obsession with the lives of celebrities and elite figures (Deacon, 2004).

In 2003, for instance, a House of Commons select committee again made the case for the introduction of a privacy law and a strengthened PCC with the right to impose fines and vet stories before publication (House of Commons Culture, Media and Sport Committee, 2003). This was in response to recent high profile cases involving celebrities such as the actors Michael Douglas and Catherine Zeta Jones, the supermodel Naomi Campbell and Radio 1 presenter Sara Cox. The government, however, insisted on its support for self-regulation, while the PCC promised to increase its independence, transparency, visibility and accountability to deliver what it called 'self-regulation plus'. Thus while in the early years of the twenty-first century the possibility of statutory intervention looked much less likely than a decade previously, reform of self-regulation continued to be an issue on the political agenda. At the same time any move in the direction of privacy legislation was more likely to be made through judicial interpretation based on Article 8 of the European Convention on Human Rights rather than by an Act of Parliament.

The internet

Both the press and broadcasting started out by being heavily regulated by national government before their regulatory regimes were subjected to a process of liberalization. This model of regulatory evolution is not applicable to the internet (Chadwick, 2006: 230–4). As a medium of communication the internet cannot be regulated by national government and some would argue cannot be effectively regulated at all. This is partly because of the transnational nature of the infrastructure and partly because of the sheer weight of material available on the worldwide web, which makes it impossible to monitor in any comprehensive fashion.

For policy-makers there are various issues connected with the growing spread of the internet. One of these most debated by the media and the public is the spread of offensive and obscene material, including most notoriously child pornography (ibid.: 272–4). Media stories of paedophiles using the net for their criminal activities have become commonplace, made more horrific by references to their use of internet chat rooms to groom unsuspecting children. More generally, many parents are worried about the possibility of their children accessing adult sexual material on the net. It is important not to confuse these two issues. Child pornography is illegal, whatever the medium of communication involved; the problem here is one of general law enforcement. Conversely, a lot of sexual material made available for the adult market on the internet is quite legal; the regulatory issue here is how to prevent it being accessed by minors.

The latter is not a new issue for policy-makers, regulators and media organizations. In the field of free-to-air terrestrial television, for example, the relevant authorities have long placed restrictions on the sort of material that can be shown at particular times, especially in the case of violent or sexually explicit content. Free-to-air television has traditionally separated material into pre- and post-watershed, with the post-watershed period running from 9 pm until 5.30 am the next day. The convention of the watershed signifies the point in the evening's television when programming shifts from being suitable for a general audience including children to being appropriate for an adult audience only. Similarly, film classification ratings by the British Board of Film Classification are used by pay-tv and pay-per-view channels to inform viewers of the sort of material a film contains. Some digital television providers have configured their equipment so that parents can control what their children are watching by using a password or PIN, thus allowing parents to block access to unsuitable material even when not present in person to supervise their children's viewing.

With regard to internet content, a number of proprietary rating and filtering systems exist to manage user access. Some bar access to certain sites, while other systems attempt to block material based on certain words or phrases (although since the system cannot allow for the context of the material, this may prevent access to innocuous content). Material can also be blocked that has been rated by the site itself. The government is keen to encourage rating and filtering systems on the internet to help users control the content they and their children use. This throws some of the regulatory burden on to the industry, notably internet service providers. At the same time the consumer is expected to assume some responsibility for regulating their own usage. Such an approach seems to be accepted by the public, who have become quite sophisticated in their expectations regarding media content on different distribution systems. Consumers have become accustomed to applying different standards according to the nature of the service (push/pull), the means of distribution (free-to-air or restricted access) and the financial contract involved (free or paid-for services). Consumers generally understand and accept that internet content cannot be regulated to the same extent as traditional broadcasting.

Conclusion

Media content has long been subject to different levels and modes of regulation, notably between the press and broadcasting sectors. Clear sector-specific regulatory distinctions between the press and broadcasting can still be drawn. First, the press is subject to a system of self-regulation by the industry, while broadcasting is the object of formal regulation by external regulatory authorities. Second, the press has been bound by fewer and generally less onerous regulations than broadcasters, particularly those with a public service remit. The spread of the internet further complicates the regulatory picture, with more responsibility being placed on consumers to regulate their own usage of a medium that is devoid of many of the regulatory constraints and content obligations traditionally imposed on other communications media.

In this context it may appear difficult to draw any general conclusions about future regulatory issues and trends. Nonetheless, three points are worth noting in this concluding section. First, because of the socio-political importance of the media, contrasting views on the need for content regulation will continue to inform public and political debate. From one perspective there is strong pressure on policy-makers to relax regulatory provisions on content. In an updated version of the 'consumer sovereignty' argument put forward by the Peacock Report, supporters of minimal content regulation argue that in an age of expanding media supply and changing social attitudes, the case for extensive regulation has been severely weakened. Only minimal regulation is now required in a market where producers supply a wide range of content and consumers can make their selection from the variety of information and entertainment made available. According to this view, not only does the huge choice provided by digital media make much content regulation unnecessary, but in an era of satellite and internet communication, national regulation is no longer a feasible proposition.

In contrast, defenders of content regulation argue that rules are still required: to prevent certain types of material from being distributed via the media; positively to promote the distribution of some content, for example in broadcasting, which a market-oriented system might omit or marginalize; and finally, to ensure balance and impartiality in broadcast news coverage. Moreover, with regard to some aspects of media behaviour, such as invasion of privacy and protection of confidentiality, strong demands have been made by sections of the public for tougher regulation to protect their rights from 'media intrusion'.

Second, it is likely that for the foreseeable future distinctions will continue to be made by policy-makers and public about the appropriate extent and level of regulatory intervention across and within different media sectors. Technological convergence has not swept away previous distinctions between media in terms, for example, of audience usage and expectations. Even within media sectors, audiences are capable of applying different standards with regard to the acceptability of material. Adult content that might not raise an eyebrow if screened on a pay-per-view channel late at night would not be considered acceptable on free-to-air television, especially if transmitted before the watershed. At the same time, audiences expect uniformity of standards from the same media organization, whatever means of distribution is being used. In the case of an organization like the BBC, for example, the same standards are expected of its online services as of its broadcast output. It is, of course, in the commercial and political interests of the Corporation to ensure that this remains the case.

Finally, where does this leave the argument that increased technological convergence would of necessity result in regulatory convergence? As the above analysis has demonstrated, in important respects sector-specific regulatory provisions are still relevant. Yet it is also the case that the creation of a single super-regulatory authority in Ofcom and the general emphasis on light touch regulation does provide evidence of some regulatory convergence, both in terms of institutional structures and normative provisions. In general, there is a 'growing trend towards relying more on competition law rather than sector-specific regulation to deliver economic and public policy objectives' (Iosifidis, Steemers and Wheeler, 2005: 78), combined with more emphasis on co-regulation and self-regulation by the industry and consumers.

6

News

The news media provide audiences with an enormous and varied amount of political information. The production of some of this material – such as a newspaper advert by a government department, a party election broadcast on television or a website run by a pressure group – is the responsibility of the relevant political actors, who have control of the key decisions regarding content and presentation. A great deal of political information, however, is processed and filtered by news media personnel, who act as intermediaries between political actors and the public. In the performance of the functions of news gathering and production, for example, journalists are intimately involved in the collection and selection of material, the formation of news agendas and the framing of issues.

The crucial importance of this mediating role raises questions about the economic, organizational and cultural contexts in which journalists function, the relationship between sources and the news media, the criteria of selection for news stories and the nature of the resulting output. The objective of this chapter is critically to analyze, explain and evaluate selected features of news production, content and reception. The chapter is divided into three sections: the first covers different variables that influence news production; the second deals with issues of bias and impartiality; and the final section examines key features of the news environment in the digital age.

News production

What is news? News is not a reflection of the world, with journalists simply holding a mirror to events and transmitting the resultant image to the audience (Gans, 1980). Nor is news a series of almost random reactions to unpredictable happenings (Hetherington, 1985: 21). Instead, news can be seen as the product of a definitional process by the media, which involves both selection and construction on the part of editors and journalists. As a result, if an event or issue is not covered by the media, then it is not news. Moreover, while some newsworthy events may be unpredictable, the production of news is centred on prediction and routines – what some commentators have called 'the routinization of the unexpected' (Fishman, 1980; Golding and Elliott, 1979). The processes of news gathering and production are influenced by the interaction of a variety of different factors. This section groups these under four analytic headings – economic, organizational, cultural and source-related – though in practice these variables are interdependent, with the result that in the case of any particular news story it is frequently difficult, if not impossible, to disaggregate their relative impact.

Economic variables

An analysis of news production that focuses on economic variables places particular emphasis on the importance of the means of ownership and control of news media organizations, the financial power of communications conglomerates and the commercial profit-motive of media companies operating in competitive markets (Herman and Chomsky, 1988). As the manager of a US television station owned by Rupert Murdoch asserted: 'We paid $3 billion for these television stations, . . . We'll decide what the news is. News is what we say it is' (Cohen, 2000: 139). From an economic perspective, therefore, news can be regarded as a commodity. The influence of interventionist proprietors on news content is relevant in this context (see Chapter 2). So too is that of advertisers. Campbell, for example, argues that advertising may affect the production of news in two distinct ways: first, at the systemic level it may reduce diversity by squeezing out some news outlets from the marketplace; second, there may be instances where advertisers attempt directly to influence editorial content (Campbell, 2004: 59–64).

There is no denying that news in contemporary Britain is produced in a media environment characterized by a high degree of competition for audiences and advertising/subscription revenue. Even the BBC, whose domestic services are not dependent on commercial income, is still obliged to compete in the market and secure audiences to justify its call on the licence fee. News may have a vital role to play in a media company's overall commercial strategy. This is particularly true in the case of the broadcasting media, whose primary function is to provide entertainment rather than information. Television news, for example, may be used by a media organization to furnish it with a particular brand image so that it stands out in the sea of competing channels and services. In similar fashion, dedicated news channels, such as Sky News, help give a media company the image of a serious broadcaster and so also contribute to the branding process.

News programmes on generalist television channels can be used to attract audiences by providing a product that the company hopes will act as a point of reference for the rest of the channel's output, especially important in an era of audience zapping. Television news programmes increasingly use anchor presenters to build up audience recognition and loyalty (Harrison, 2000: 88), while the need to attract and retain audiences puts pressure on news programmes to be entertaining. In 2004 the BBC political editor, Andrew Marr, commented that a television news bulletin 'is like a piece of music. It must have variety, pace and rhythm' (Marr, 2004: 295) to keep audiences watching. Changes in audience tastes and expectations can also influence news output. For instance, there is some evidence of less political content in television news as a proportion of total output than was the case thirty years ago, while there has been an increase in the reporting of crime, human interest stories, sport and entertainment. Political news has to compete for space in television's news agenda. This change reflects both a declining public engagement with political issues and an increased interest in lifestyle and consumer issues.

Yet notwithstanding the importance of economic variables in contributing to an analysis of news production, their explanatory force is also frequently limited. The most fundamental weakness is their high level of generality. Economic factors help in the construction of the 'big picture', focusing attention on the communications environment in which news media function and on the importance of the financial imperative. However, it is often difficult to establish the precise nature of the linkages between the economic context on the one hand and the day to day process of news production and specific aspects of news content on the other. As Schudson argues, 'it should be apparent . . . that private ownership, even coupled with a dominant profit orientation, is not a structural factor sufficient in itself to explain news production' (Schudson, 1991: 145). There is, therefore, a need to unpack the nature of the linkages between ownership and funding and news production to analyze 'the way that meaning is made and re-made through the concrete activities of producers and consumers' (Golding and Murdock, 1991: 19; see also Boyd-Barrett, 1995: 186–92).

Organizational variables

Since the news media are bureaucratic organizations with their own professional routines, institutional norms and socialization practices, news production is clearly influenced by a host of organizational variables. These include the size, complexity and decision-making structure of the news organization, the impact of technology, the pressures of deadlines and the limitations of the news format. From an organizational perspective news can be viewed as a socially manufactured product.

Early American studies of news production concentrated on the 'gatekeeping' function of key media personnel who decided which items were included or excluded from news coverage (White, 1950). The 'gatekeeping' metaphor is a useful one, since it emphasizes the importance of the filtering process in news production. It is, however, flawed in at least three key respects. First, early 'gatekeeping' studies tended to stress the personal, technical and professional aspects of the selection and rejection of potential news items, emphasizing the subjective nature of the process and marginalizing the organizational setting and wider political, economic and ideological contexts within which the gatekeepers operated (Boyd-Barrett, 1995: 271–2; Herman, 1986: 172–5). Second, the 'gatekeeping' analogy tends to focus attention on the *selection* of news, but ignores its *construction* by both sources and the news media. Finally, the 'gatekeeping' approach underestimates the capacity of sources to adapt their behaviour to try to ensure that their messages pass through the screening process of the 'gatekeeper' by anticipating the latter's response and adjusting their message accordingly.

News values are an important ingredient in many explanations of news production: journalists' decisions as to what makes a 'good story' – what is 'newsworthy' – are informed by their interpretation of a set of news values. Professional criteria of newsworthiness have been described as 'terse shorthand references to shared understandings about the nature and purpose of news' which influence both the selection and presentation of issues and events (Golding and Elliott, 1979). As a result, 'news is not simply that which happens, but that which can be regarded and presented as newsworthy.' (Fowler, 1991: 13). The classic study of news values is that of Galtung and Ruge (1965) who hypothesized with reference to coverage of foreign news that eight culture-free factors underpin the selection of news items: frequency, amplitude, clarity, meaningfulness, consonance, unexpectedness, continuity and composition. An obvious problem, however, in trying to apply this list to the news coverage of any particular media outlet in contemporary Britain is its high level of generality.

For Hetherington, seven factors influence the newsworthiness of an item (Hetherington, 1985: 8). These are:

- *Significance*: social, economic, political, human
- *Drama*: excitement, action, entertainment
- *Surprise*: freshness, newness, unpredictability
- *Personalities*: royal, political, showbusiness
- *Popular ingredients*: sex, scandal, crime
- *Numbers*: scale of the event, numbers of people affected
- *Proximity*: on our doorstep or 10,000 miles away

And in the case of television news:

- *Pictures* or visual attractiveness

This list is certainly more user-friendly than that of Galtung and Ruge. However, it too raises questions about the operationalization of news values in any specific context. For example, who decides what is socially significant and by what criteria? Are not freshness and unpredictability frequently offset in the news by coverage of routine events? How are trade-offs between the scale of an event on the one hand and its proximity on the other negotiated and resolved; for example, the newsworthiness of a large earthquake in Asia versus a small rail accident in Britain?

The explanatory utility of a general set of news values is, therefore, open to question. Certainly the operationalization of news values by journalists working for different media outlets does not lead to conformity in news agendas, the framing of issues or the style and tone of coverage. For instance, Harrison argues that despite the existence of a shared journalistic culture and a common adherence to the practical application of objectivity, a diversity of news values exists in British terrestrial television news (and by implication across the news media as a whole) (Harrison, 2000: 181). She contends that 'different conceptions of newsworthiness and what is in the public interest relate very strongly to different news programmes, different news organisations, and wider influences relating to the increasing commercialisation of broadcast television news' (ibid.: 161). These different conceptions have an impact on – among other things – the commitment to coverage of international stories, the length of news stories, their place in the running order and the emphasis on human interest elements within a story.

An explanation for the selection of certain news stories may also use the notion of an issue-attention cycle on the part of the media (Downs, 1972). Coverage of a particular type of story frequently spawns a run of similar stories for a few days as media interest is heightened, until news fatigue sets in, the issue drops out of the headlines and a fresh cycle on another topic may develop. 'The occurrence of a striking event will reinforce a stereotype, and reciprocally, the firmer the stereotype, the more likely are relevant events to become news' (Fowler, 1991: 17). Fowler gives the example of the major nuclear accident at Chernobyl in 1986 which he argues was not just newsworthy in itself, but also 'consolidated the stereotype "nuclear accident" in public consciousness, thus increasing the number of relevant events which were to figure in the news' (ibid.: 18).

Conventions and constraints emphasized from an organizational perspective include the news form, which covers the available space for an item, the layout of a newspaper and the running order of a broadcast news programme. Time is a crucial factor in this context, since as a product news has the transient and ephemeral quality of a perishable good. In his ethnographic study of BBC news production in the late 1970s, for example, Schlesinger emphasized the importance of what he termed the 'stop-watch culture' and the bias towards immediacy (Schlesinger, 1978: 83–105). In similar vein, Roschko talks of timeliness, whereby news is distinguished from other kinds of information by the intimation that it is shared as soon as possible after it is learned (Roschko, 1975).

The notion of time influences news production in different ways. First, deadlines tend to impose certain work practices on journalists, helping to foster a reliance on official, institutional sources which are particularly geared up to meet news production schedules. Second, traditionally in broadcast news the length of a news programme is fixed, only in exceptional circumstances extended and almost never shortened, except at weekends. As a result, news usually has to be compressed to fit the tight constraints of the broadcasting schedule. Conversely in the coverage of rolling news channels, the padding out of stories has become more noticeable as the media variant of Parkinson's law kicks in: news expands to fill the time available. Finally, the time frame of the twenty-four-hour news cycle means that the media tend to focus on events rather than more complex longer-term trends and processes. For example, in news coverage of the environment the media tend 'to be preoccupied with dramatic events such as oil spills', while environmental issues such as global warming normally involve 'slow, drawn-out processes' (Anderson, 1997: 123). Usually long-running events will need to reach some kind of dramatic climax if they are to be reported (Galtung and Ruge, 1965), while the event-driven nature of news often leaves little time or space for wider contextualization or explanation, especially in traditional broadcasting formats (Morrison, 1992: 68; Schlesinger, 1978: 105).

In the light of these time pressures, forward planning is important for news organizations. Much news is to some extent predictable in that it consists of pre-scheduled events such as official ceremonies, summit meetings and political speeches. These 'diary events' allow newsroom staff a certain level of foresight in the process of selection and construction. An early pioneering study of journalists in Britain (Tunstall, 1971) revealed 'the extent to which news was not an unpredictable and chaotic universe of events but was the steady and reliable prediction, preparation and routine management of "institutionalized" news' (Boyd-Barrett, 1995: 274). In addition, news stories sometimes explicitly include considerable speculation on the part of specialist correspondents and invited experts about what might happen – the anticipation of developments – rather than analysis of what has already occurred.

Technical factors also need to be borne in mind under this organizational heading. In the television sector, for instance, the introduction of new technology over the past couple of decades has had a significant impact on news gathering, editing and screening. Technological change has had an impact on the organizational make-up of the newsroom, for example on the balance between specialists and generalists among journalists. Negrine quotes a news executive with experience of several broadsheet dailies, who argued that 'newspapers are veering far more towards specialists and away from generalists partly because the wire services are so good and the technology allows us to get wire copy so quickly that we can get most of our general news stories that way' (Negrine, 1996: 80). News agencies such as Reuters with their authoritative reputations and global reach are particularly important for the supply of foreign news to financially constrained news operations (Boyd-Barrett, 1980) and much online news content is particularly dependent on news agency material (Chadwick, 2006: 301). In addition, each news media organization changes aspects of its newsgathering activites over time in response not just to technological developments but also to external changes in society, the economy and politics. Former journalist specialisms have declined (for instance, the industrial correspondent) while new ones have grown (business, media, legal affairs and the environment to name but a few) (Manning, 2001: 132–5; Negrine, 1996: 78–100).

Socialization processes within the newsroom, whereby journalists internalize the prevalent norms and values of the profession and organization, also feature strongly in the organizational approach. Here it is argued that the corporate culture of the news organization fashions journalistic behaviour, with most journalists conforming so as to be accepted by their peers and superiors. Schlesinger's study of decision-making at the BBC in the 1970s emphasized the importance of production routines and of the hierarchical editorial system as important organizational variables (Schlesinger, 1978). In addition, Tuchman has pointed out the way in which newsroom procedures are actually strategies through which journalists protect themselves from critics and lay professional claim to objectivity (Tuchman, 1972).

Socialization may also include the acceptance of the political partisanship of a newspaper as a key organizational value, while in the broadcasting sector norms of balance and impartiality formally underpin decision-making and validate the news production process (Schlesinger, 1978: 163–204). The different regulatory environments in which they operate and their positioning within their respective markets are only two of several factors that ensure the organizational culture and practices of BBC News are not the same as those of *The Sun* newspaper.

In general, organizational studies of news production have tended to play down the importance of the sociological composition of the newsroom. It is true that some authors have argued for a greater focus on the notion of the 'journalist as person' (Morrison and Tumber, 1988: p. x). In addition, institutional responses – such as the Cultural Diversity Network established by television broadcasters in 2000 – have been made to lobbying campaigns calling for fairer employment opportunities for disadvantaged social groups. However, organizational practices and constraints are generally deemed to be more significant in shaping news production than the personal views of individual journalists or the dominant sociological characteristics of the newsroom. If this view is valid, then concerns about the employment of women or members of ethnic minorities in the mainstream news media, especially in key positions, are wholly justifiable on grounds of equity, fairness and the provision of role models. However, there is less reason to believe that a shift away from white, male-dominated newsrooms would have a significant impact on the news agenda, although it might influence the framing of some issues.

Cultural variables

In the foreword to *Bad News* Hoggart writes that one of the filtering processes in news selection is 'the cultural air we breathe, the whole ideological atmosphere of our society, which tells us that some things can be said and others had best not be said' (Glasgow University Media Group, 1976: p. x). This comment alerts us to the importance for the process of news production of the wider societal culture (and subcultures) in which news organizations function. British society and its constituent communities have a variety of symbols and reference points which may frequently be taken for granted by media professionals and which may influence news production at both the conscious and subconscious levels, for example in the use of language or visual imagery. From this perspective news can be understood as a cultural narrative and there is a strong academic tradition of analyzing news as a cultural text.

In their study of news values, Galtung and Ruge (1965) argue that four culture-bound factors are deemed to be important in the 'north-western corner of the world'. An event is more likely to become a news item the more it concerns:

- Elite nations
- Elite people
- Individual persons (as opposed to impersonal social forces)
- Negative (rather than positive) stories

For example, Galtung and Ruge argue that news in societies such as Britain has a tendency to personify events rather than presenting them as the outcome of 'social forces' or the result of structural factors. They explain this personification partly in terms of cultural idealism, according to which man (sic) is the master of his own destiny and events can be seen as the outcome of an act of free will. Personification also facilitates empathy or antipathy on the part of the audience; it is easier for audiences to identify with persons than with impersonal structures or processes. In other cultures Galtung and Ruge contend that structural factors and social forces would be given greater emphasis. Similarly, while negative news focusing on conflict and crisis (Roschko, 1975) will be preferred to positive news in cultures such as Britain's, in other societies (for example, developing nations) more emphasis might be placed on positive 'feel-good' news stories.

According to Schudson, an approach to news production that highlights cultural variables also 'helps explain generalized images and stereotypes in the news media . . . that transcend structures of ownership or patterns of work relations' (Schudson, 2000: 189). These might include the prevalence of stereotypes based on gender, ethnicity and sexual orientation in some news stories. A cultural approach might also be usefully employed to ask which societal subcultures are reported and which ignored in the news (Gans, 1980). It has been argued that some environmental issues gain media coverage because 'they resonate with wider cultural values and fears of the unknown' (Anderson, 1997: 125) in a society increasingly concerned with risk in a variety of areas, from terrorism to food safety, from nuclear pollution to global warming.

Attention to the importance of a cultural approach might help explain certain ethnocentric aspects of news coverage, such as some British tabloid press coverage of Europe, which often trades on historical references to previous military conflicts (for instance, against the French or the Germans) to help frame coverage of contemporary political issues (Ramsden, 2006: 399–402). Coverage of the asylum seeker issue in some tabloid newspapers at the start of the twenty-first century also played upon cultural stereotypes of the foreigner as alien, untrustworthy and devious. In addition, the personification of good and evil in some news stories may be explained in terms of a cultural approach, with the media helping to maintain and reinforce 'symbolic templates of heroes and villains' (Swanson and Mancini, 1996: 9). The judgemental negative representation of Saddam Hussein in the two Gulf wars (Morrison, 1992) and Slobodan Milosovic in the Kosovo conflict owed much to fictional genres of story-telling, from fairy tales to western movies: Saddam and Milosovic were the recognizable villains of the dramatic plot. More generally, television news items are often called 'stories', composed to hold the audience's attention. These often play on the audience's emotions as in 'disaster stories' or features on feats of extraordinary human endurance, with recognizable 'characters' and 'plots' embedded in news forms and narratives which serve to sustain deeply rooted cultural myths in society (Cottle, 2003: 15).

Source-related variables

Attention to source-related variables complements the focus on the news media as economic and bureaucratic organizations, while also shifting the focus to 'influence exerted by outside interests rather than control directed from editorial or proprietorial authority' (Tumber, 1999: p. xvii). Here we are concerned with the strategies of sources in winning access to the media, an objective they strive to attain because the greater the access the more the likelihood of sources gaining scope to shape the news agenda and influence the framing of issue coverage. A wide range of social, economic and political actors compete to gain access to news media organizations whose journalists enjoy a degree of relative autonomy in their work practices.

Fishman has pointed out that the world is bureaucratically organized for journalists, emphasizing that reporters can depend on the bureaucratic reporting apparatus of officials and authorities for their raw materials (Fishman, 1980). Thus, journalists cover certain news 'beats' – such as the courts for a crime reporter or Westminster for a political correspondent – in the knowledge that reliable quantities of information will usually be made available (Tuchman, 1978). As a result, 'journalism, on a day-to-day basis, is the story of the interaction of reporters and government officials, both politicians and bureaucrats' (Schudson, 2000: 184). The relationship between sources and journalists has been described as resembling a dance, with more often than not sources doing the leading (Gans, 1980). Gans also uses the metaphor of a tug of war as sources and journalists seek to manage each other in pursuit of their respective interests. The two metaphors underline the aspects of cooperation *and* competition which infuse the relationship between sources and journalists.

A classic way of theorizing the power of official sources uses the concept of primary definition. This places the media in a subordinate and secondary role to major power holders in society in the task of agenda construction. According to this account, the organizational demands and professional values of the news production process 'combine to produce a systematically structured *over-accessing* to the media of those in powerful and privileged institutional positions' (Hall et al., 1978: 58, emphasis in original). These actors enjoy privileged access to the media as authoritative sources because of their institutional power, representative status and expert knowledge.

While the model of primary definition has informed a considerable body of academic analysis on source–media relations, it has also been subjected to important criticisms, notably by Schlesinger and Tumber who make six specific points in their detailed critique (Schlesinger and Tumber, 1994: 17–21). First, the model 'does not take account of contention between official sources in trying to influence the construction of a story'. Second, the model 'fails to register the well-established fact that official sources often attempt to influence the construction of a story by using "off-the-record" briefings – in which case the primary definers do not appear directly, as such, in unveiled and attributable form' (ibid.: 18).

Third, do the boundaries of primary definition shift, and if so, why? Access to the media is plainly not equally open to all members of the political class. Schlesinger and Tumber argue that there is 'nothing in the formulation of primary defining that permits us to deal with such inequalities of access amongst the privileged themselves'. Fourth, there is the question of longer-term shifts in the structure of access. The model has the 'tacit assumption that certain forces are permanently present in the power structure'. However, these may be displaced by new forces and in these circumstances it is essential to explain their emergence. Schlesinger and Tumber point, for example, to the decline of the CBI and TUC as major institutional voices with the disappearance of corporatism during the Conservative governments of the 1980s and 90s (ibid.: 19).

Fifth, the concept tends to 'overstate the passivity of the media as recipients of information from news sources . . . Within this conceptual logic, there is no space to account for occasions on which the media may themselves take the initiative in the definitional process by challenging the so-called primary definers and forcing them to respond' (ibid.: 19). Such occasions would include cases of investigative journalism (for example, into political scandals) or whistleblowing leaks. Primary definers may be denied media access or given unfavourable coverage. The news management operations of sources necessarily involve political journalists in an active process of selection, interpretation, evaluation and (re)construction of the information presented them. Referring to the work of Ericson, Baranek and Chan (1989), Negrine comments that while the information subsidy provided by the source 'lubricates the supply of, and demand for, information . . . it cannot guarantee that the information will be processed as desired by the source' (Negrine, 1996: 28).

Finally, the notion of 'primary definition' renders largely invisible the activities of sources that attempt to generate 'counter-definitions' (Schlesinger and Tumber, 1994: 20). The concept fails to take account of the possibility of negotiation over issue definition between power-holders and their opponents prior to interaction with the media, while also minimizing the possibility that non-official sources might be able to influence the shaping of the news agenda. The model thus implies that 'the structure of access *necessarily* secures strategic advantages' for official sources and conversely that 'counter definitions can *never dislodge* the primary definition' (Schlesinger, 1990: 66, emphasis in original).

These criticisms lead Schlesinger and Tumber to argue that 'powerful sources still have to pursue goal-oriented action to achieve access, even though their recognition as "legitimate authorities" is already usually inscribed in the rules of the game. This contrasts with the structuralist notion of "automatic", accredited access resulting in primary definition.' (Schlesinger and Tumber, 1994: 26). In short, 'primary definers' have to work to gain media access; they do not just secure it as of right. In their study of the media politics of criminal justice in Britain, for example, the authors consider the perspectives of official sources, but also examine non-official source competition. Schlesinger and Tumber argue that in terms of the institutionalization of sources 'the most advantageous locations in the crime and criminal justice arena are occupied by the apparatuses of the state such as the Home Office and the Metropolitan Police' (ibid.: 39). However, while the Home Office may be the key player in terms of both news management resources and potential command over the media agenda, other actors including professional associations, trades unions and assorted pressure groups are able to acquire credibility, legitimacy and authoritativeness in functioning as sources through the active development of their own media strategies.

Sources, therefore, engage in a variety of activities to gain access to the news media. 'In the interest of maximizing their access while relegating the opposition to mere coverage, political interests expend enormous resources through a variety of proactive media strategies' (Ericson, Baranek and Chan, 1989). These range from low-level routine processes such as press releases and media briefings to selective forms of interaction with favoured journalists. Sources will sometimes stage events – 'pseudo-events' (Boorstin, 1961) – specifically for the purpose of being reported on by the media. A public relations industry has been built up to help sources gain the news media access they crave.

Official sources generally benefit from greater resources and routine links with news media organizations. In contrast, many actors in the political process are poorly resourced to act as sources and this may result in their exclusion or marginalization from the news agenda (see Chapter 8). However, access to the news media is by no means wholly closed off to non-official sources. If a story fits news value criteria and if the source can mobilize its resources effectively, then it can still gain access. Non-official sources have also learnt to play the public relations game. From this perspective, the media 'occupy space which is constantly being contested . . . The changing contours of this space can lead to different patterns of domination and agenda setting and to different degrees of openness and closure, in terms of access . . . types of discourse and range of opinions represented' (Eldridge, 1993: 20). In short, while in the struggle for access official sources start out as favourites, the competition is more open than is allowed for in some accounts of media domination by powerful elites.

News bias

The range of factors involved in the process of news production inevitably raises questions about the nature of the end product. What picture of the world – or version of reality – does news offer? Can news ever be duly impartial as claimed by public service broadcasters or is all news inevitably biased in terms of the construction of the agenda and/or the framing of issues?

The concept of bias

Let us start by unpacking the concept of bias. Street employs a typology first formulated by McQuail (1992), which employs two cross-cutting axes (intended/unintended and overt/covert) to give four different categories of bias (Street, 2001: 20–22). These are:

- Partisan bias (intended and overt) where a cause is explicitly and deliberately promoted
- Propaganda bias (intended and covert) where a story is reported with the deliberate intention of making the case for a particular party or policy, without explicitly stating this. Street gives the example of a news story about social security fraud which is reported in such a way as to make a particular point about welfare 'scrounging'
- Unwitting bias (unintended and overt) whereby explicit decisions are taken about the importance of a story based on a concept of

newsworthiness and where news practices routinely create hierar-
chies of values, but without the judgements made being conscious
or deliberate
• Ideological bias (unintended and covert) where the bias is hidden
and unintended and rooted in hidden assumptions and value
judgements. 'These assumptions are grounded in ideologies
which seek to explain the way the world works, and these are
themselves "biased" ' (ibid.: 22)

Partisan bias is the most apparent to audiences, while ideological bias
is the least. What evidence of these different categories of bias can we
find in the British news media?

Press bias

Partisan bias in terms of support by a newspaper for a particular party
is the most obvious political bias in the press. We shall consider the
issue of newspaper partisanship in detail in Chapter 8 as part of our
examination of the relationship between parties and the news media.
Intended and overt support for a political party is, however, only one
of the more evident forms of press bias.

For example, viewed in the aggregate, Britain's national newspapers have in the past been criticized for favouring conservative over
radical views (Hollingsworth, 1986) or having an upmarket social
bias (Hirsch and Gordon, 1975). They have also stood accused of
having a London-oriented, metropolitan perspective on issues of
national importance. In part this is because of their London production base and the dominance of the capital in the economic, political
and cultural life of the country (Tunstall, 1996: 7–8). It is also in part
because of the social composition of audiences in the south-east of
England:

> Although the London nationals aim at the whole of Britain, they sell espe-
> cially well in the South-East; since this area has the highest number and
> proportion of affluent AB readers as well as the highest proportion of
> people who do not see a local daily, it makes good commercial sense for
> the *Daily Mail*, *Daily Telegraph* and others to focus heavily on the South-
> East. The London nationals thus become even more London and South-
> East oriented than they might otherwise be. (Ibid.: 72)

This London focus may have undesirable consequences for the
quantity and quality of political coverage across the United Kingdom.

For example, it has been argued that while the Scottish public were well informed by the news media based in Scotland about the issues surrounding devolution, 'the radical implications of devolution are not so well understood south of the Border, where media attention has been somewhat sporadic and rather superficial' (Schlesinger, 1998: 71). While for obvious reasons the devolution referendum and the subsequent creation of a Scottish Parliament were bigger news stories in Scotland than in the rest of the UK, the relative inattention given by the London-based newspapers to the importance of these developments for UK (as opposed to simply Scottish) politics may still be regarded as evidence of a 'London bias' in their political coverage.

Crime coverage by newspapers reveals a different form of bias. Schlesinger and Tumber have argued that there is 'a disjuncture between the real incidence of crime (as officially measured) and the pattern of reported crime (as represented by the news media)' (Schlesinger and Tumber, 1994: 186). Moreover, within the category of crime coverage, disproportionate attention is given to violent crime against the person and to sexual offences. In 1987, for example, violence against the person constituted 3.62 per cent of all notifiable offences reported by the police. 'However, such criminal acts comprised 24.7 per cent of crime-related items reported in the quality press, 38.8 per cent in the mid-market press, and 45.9 per cent in the popular press' (ibid.: 185). Furthermore, while 'most murders and rapes in Britain are committed by people known to the victims, the newspapers focus on the atypically dramatic cases, such as mystery rapists and the fairly rare British cases of serial murder' (Tunstall, 1996: 207). This press bias towards disproportionate coverage of violent crime – driven by the operationalization of news values in conditions of competition for readers – may give audiences a skewed picture of the potential threat from crime when applied to conditions in their local neighbourhood.

Much of the UK press can also be characterized as ethnocentric and at times even chauvinistic in its coverage, particularly notable on the issue of Europe. One aspect of newspaper coverage on the European issue during the Major and Blair premierships has been the significant circulation imbalance between the majority of newspapers articulating a Eurosceptic position and the minority adopting a Europhile perspective (Anderson and Weymouth, 1999). In recent years coverage of Europe by several national newspapers, including the *Mail* and *Telegraph* titles, has been framed from a strongly-held Eurosceptic position (Wilkes and Wring, 1998). Moreover, in the case of the Eurosceptic tabloid press, many stories about Europe have been selected and framed in such a way as to be supportive of the paper's general position on the issue, from pieces ridiculing decisions by the European Commission to articles praising the defence of 'British' values and practices in the face of alleged external threats.

At a deeper level, the emphasis on the Eurosceptic versus Europhile dimension in newspaper coverage has itself skewed coverage of the European Union across much of the British press. Other ways of framing coverage about Europe, such as institutional or investigative journalism, have been largely absent from coverage in British newspapers. In this respect, much British newspaper coverage of the European issue has been overwhelmingly framed within the context of *domestic* political debate and has a peculiarly national quality about it, which makes it stand out in comparison with press coverage of Europe in the press of some other member states of the EU (Baisnée, 2002). More generally, whatever the supposed pressures of globalization on the news media, the high-selling tabloid newspapers in Britain pay little attention to foreign news at all, with much of their coverage characterized by an insular parochialism.

Broadcasting bias

Unlike newspapers, broadcasters are under a regulatory obligation to present news with due impartiality. This is both a legacy of the public service tradition and an acknowledgement of the power of the broadcast media as an information provider. These normative standards have not just been externally imposed. They have also been accepted within broadcasting organizations, including private broadcasting companies, as essential to the practice of news reporting, underpinning the professional self-validation of the work of broadcast journalists and so helping the legitimation of their activity and output. The expectations of audiences are also different in the case of broadcast news as compared to the press, with higher standards of honesty and accuracy demanded by the public.

Broadcasters' claims to be providing duly impartial news are constantly subject to scrutiny. For instance, mainstream political parties regularly monitor broadcast news output for the slightest hint of evidence of journalists not being scrupulously fair in their reporting and interviewing. In addition, in the pursuit of their own political and commercial agendas, some newspapers such as the *Daily Telegraph* and *The Sun* have in recent years lambasted the BBC for alleged bias in its coverage of politics, accusing the Corporation's output of being left of centre, pro-Europe and pro-state regulation among other things.

Not surprisingly, academic studies have also addressed the issue of bias in broadcasting. In this regard the seminal studies in Britain were those conducted by the Glasgow University Media Group (GUMG) in the 1970s and 1980s. The GUMG published four studies of British television news – *Bad News* (1976), *More Bad News* (1980), *Really Bad News* (1982) and *War and Peace News* (1985) – which focused on television news coverage of topics such as industrial relations, business and the economy, and defence. The group's systematic analysis of the framing of television news, including the running order, use of visual imagery and the language employed by news readers, amounted to 'a standing critique of the values and operating principles which have governed first radio, and later television, news practically since the birth of broadcasting in Britain' (Harrison, 1985: 11). Stevenson (1995: 26–7) acknowledges that the GUMG were involved in exposing the ideological bias of television news. For him the group's account of ideological bias operates at three levels: first, the media are biased in their representation of social 'reality'; second, television news can be described as biased according to the extent to which it reaffirms or leaves unquestioned the central economic relations of capitalism; third, the news bias involves the exclusion of working-class voices from the media of mass communication. In short, these 'three notions of bias combine to produce a powerful ideology that distorts reality, reaffirms dominant social relations and excludes contradictory perspectives' (ibid.: 27).

The analysis of the GUMG has come in for considerable academic criticism. Some of this concerns their use of concepts and methodology. For example, although they claimed to be engaging in a scientific study of news content, the authors were themselves accused of ideological bias and 'pseudo-scientific objectivity' (Hetherington, 1985: 20). Their allegations that television news supported 'consensus' and the 'status quo' were criticized because their usage of these concepts was held to be vague and imprecise (Harrison, 1985: 17). Harrison's study *TV News: Whose Bias?* also points to alleged factual inaccuracies and errors of interpretation in the group's analysis, although these charges were in turn contested by the GUMG (Philo, 1987: 397–406). More generally, it could be argued that the ideological bias thesis is too comprehensive and undifferentiated to act as a satisfactory analytic framework for a full appreciation of broadcast news content.

For instance, according to Street, the bias detected by the GUMG was 'deliberate only in the sense that it was informed by routinized journalistic practices' (Street, 2001: 27).

The GUMG studies did, however, have the merit of emphasizing the importance of linguistic labelling in news presentation ('terrorist', 'freedom fighter', 'insurgent', 'guerrilla'), something to which audiences in Britain are now particularly sensitive as a result of the contribution to political discourse of feminism and multiculturalism. The group also drew attention to the significance of visual footage and the way in which this might give an unbalanced picture of events. For example, in the 1984–5 miners' strike/coal dispute, television pictures taken from behind the police lines allowed the viewer to witness scenes of violence from the viewpoint of the police. Footage shot from behind the striking miners, which showed the massed ranks of police opposite, gave a quite different perspective to audiences.

An additional layer of complexity in the debate about broadcasting bias is that in their coverage of certain issues broadcasters are *not* required to be impartial. For example, since the BBC is required to uphold the values of parliamentary democracy, its news output is *not* required to treat with due impartiality those who seek to undermine those values. Public service broadcasters 'should not be expected to give equal weight or show an impartiality which cannot be due to those who seek to destroy it [parliamentary democracy] by violent, unparliamentary or illegal means' (Annan Report, 1977: 268).

In the recent past this injunction has raised difficulties for British broadcasters with regard to their news coverage of the conflict in Northern Ireland (Miller, 1994). While in the eyes of the British government the IRA was not engaging in the same kind of activity as, say, the African National Congress in South Africa because the United Kingdom was held to be a democracy, the democratic legitimacy of British rule in Northern Ireland was the precise point contested by Sinn Fein/IRA. Their dual strategy of violence *and* electoral politics also muddied the waters for broadcasting journalists, since much of the political activity of Sinn Fein in Northern Ireland, for example in local government, was clearly legal. At the same time, violent acts, whether against property or persons, were highly newsworthy, especially as their objective was to challenge the constitutional integrity of the UK state. In covering acts of political violence without legitimizing them, television news programmes tended to show violence as both irrational and indefensible: showing pictures of its effects and then having official spokespersons, such as a government minister, church dignitary or community leader, condemn the violence. The further the programme genre departed from a news format (from current affairs through to documentaries), the greater the scope for fuller contextualization of the use of political violence within the UK. In news programmes, however, the perpetrators of violence tended to be routinely presented as 'terrorists'.

The norm of due impartiality also raises difficult issues in broadcast news coverage of military conflict involving British armed forces. In their coverage of the first Gulf war (1990–91), for example, the broadcasting media were largely coopted by the military and political authorities into accepting the official perspective on the central issues of the war – the sovereignty of Kuwait and the upholding of international law – which were used to bestow legitimacy on the allied cause. The importance of secure oil supplies for western economies was given very few mentions in television news coverage (Morrison, 1992: 76). More generally, television news tended to accept uncritically the military aims of the war (ibid.: 77). Because of its short duration very little of the ground war was actually seen on television: 'the tight control of reporting in the Gulf meant . . . very few pictures of fighting, or indeed, of dead or injured' (ibid.: 73). The control on information imposed by the military through its pre-censorship system and the willingness of most of the media passively to accept what they were being fed at the official briefings meant that during the war the media 'were supportive, largely uncritical and generally reflected the official line' (Taylor, 1992: 268).

Bias in the eye of the beholder?

So far in this section we have concentrated on the *encoding* of bias: the skewing of meaning (intended/unintended, overt/covert) by media personnel in the processes of news gathering, production and programming. It is, however, also important to consider the possibility of bias being present in the *decoding* of news by audiences. Two mini case-studies follow. In the first, we look at how television viewers may interpret the same news message in different ways and how they may behave as an empowered audience. In the second, we consider whether the charges levelled by New Labour ministers and officials of bias in BBC coverage of the 2003 Iraq war may have been driven by their commitment to a pro-war policy, as a result of which they were unable to view the coverage dispassionately.

Television viewers as an empowered audience

The first studies by the GUMG were criticized for paying little or no attention to the reception of news content by audiences. Implicit in the group's early assumptions was the view that audiences interpret a given message in a uniform manner. Yet even if, as the group claimed, television's version of events was skewed, it is still an open question whether audiences internalize the 'bias' of news content in a consistent fashion.

Studies in audience reception (see Chapter 9) have frequently argued that the same media text may be open to varying interpretations by different sections of the audience. Thus, different viewers have different responses to the same televised image. The influence of the media may be limited by the ability of audiences to filter content through a prism shaped by personal knowledge and experience, other socializing agencies (notably the family and the educational system) and sociological variables (such as class, gender, ethnicity and age) (Newton, 2006: 214–19). Empowered audiences respond actively to, rather than just passively accept, a particular text or message. As a result, they may accept the dominant meaning encoded in the text, reject it or negotiate with it (Hall, 1992).

In *Seeing and Believing* one of the members of the GUMG, Greg Philo, examines the response to the same television news coverage of the 1984–5 coal dispute by selected audience groups differentiated on the basis of social class, geographical location, occupation, gender and practical knowledge of industrial conflict (Philo, 1990). Philo argues that differences in political culture and class experience were important variables in influencing audience interpretation of news:

> direct experience can have a crucial influence on how new information from the media is understood. Such direct contacts, together with political culture, class experience, processes of logic, and comparisons made between accounts, were the most important factors in the relation between perception and belief. (Ibid.: 154)

As a result, some of the audience clearly negotiated the meaning of what they were told. Audience responses to the news were not only varied, but the variation did not always happen in predictable ways:

> some people who were sympathetic to the striking miners still accepted the news account on issues such as the nature of picketing (and were consequently depressed by what they came to believe); while some others who were *not* sympathetic to the miners were critical of what they saw and

heard on the news . . . there were also cases where the news message was re-negotiated or completely rejected via the subcultural beliefs of groups. (Ibid.: 199, emphasis in original)

Philo thus presents a picture of a relatively empowered audience who may not accept the dominant version of events put across in the news media. Morrison came to a broadly similar conclusion in his audience study of television coverage of the first Gulf war. The official line dutifully transmitted in news media footage, that the first Gulf war was primarily about the liberation of Kuwait, seems to have failed to convince viewers. Instead Morrison found that viewers considered oil to be a major reason for the adoption of an armed response to Iraq's invasion of Kuwait (Morrison, 1992: 76). Interestingly, however, although they did not accept the simplicity of the official line, the public's support for the allies in the conflict did not seem to be affected. Many viewers seemed to have accepted that the information being put out by the authorities via the media regarding the reasons for the conflict was incomplete; yet this did not affect their attitude towards the legitimacy of the allied military action.

Yet while accepting the existing of differentiated audience response to the same output, Philo also stresses that the meaning of the pictures was not infinitely negotiable by audiences (Philo, 1990: 133). Therefore, in the end he returns to emphasizing the encoding power of the media, 'both in limiting what audiences can see and in providing key elements of political consciousness and belief' (ibid.: 205). In so doing he is seeking to counter those who privilege the role of the active audience in the exercise of media power. This point is also made by Deacon and Golding in their study of media coverage of the poll tax issue during the final years of the Thatcher premiership. How the encoding of media news agendas is influenced by institutions and individuals forms part of an analysis of strategic power, which 'is very different from the tactical power of audiences to select and re-appropriate meaning from individual texts' (Deacon and Golding, 1994: 12).

The New Labour government and the 2003 Iraq war

The idea that bias is involved in the process of decoding broadcast news stories does not just apply to 'ordinary' listeners and viewers. It also includes representatives of a whole range of political organizations, many of which interact with the news media as sources. If an aspect of broadcast news content is not to the source's liking, then it is tempting for the source to accuse the news media outlet of bias. It is possible, however, that the alleged bias may originate less with the news media organization and more with the source itself.

In this context the New Labour government's charge of bias against the BBC in its coverage of the 2003 Iraq war is pertinent. How convincing was the government's case? It was certainly true that the Corporation did not simply act as an apologist for the conflict; nor did it serve as a mere transmission belt for government views; nor did it act as a cheerleader for the authorities as Rupert Murdoch's Fox News did for the Bush administration in the United States. However, the argument that the BBC was somehow institutionally opposed to the war and that this stance was evident in its news coverage is not supported by the evidence. For example, an academic study conducted at Cardiff University of British television coverage of the war in Iraq examined 1,534 news reports during the war on all weekdays from 20 March to 11 April inclusive from the evening news bulletins on BBC1 (6pm), ITV News (6.30 pm), *Channel 4 News* (7 pm) and Sky News (10 pm) (Lewis and Brookes, 2004: 132–43). On the basis of their detailed research, the authors of this study concluded:

> our research suggests that the wartime coverage was generally sympathetic to the government's case. This manifested itself in various ways, notably: the focus on the progress of war to the exclusion of other issues and non-military or governmental sources; the tendency to portray the Iraqi people as liberated rather than invaded; the failure to question the claim that Iraq possessed weapons of mass destruction; and the focus on the brutality or decadence of the regime without putting this evidence in context. (Ibid.: 142)

The authors' conclusion, therefore, suggests that the BBC was far from anti-war. Indeed, based on this study, 'the government's complaints would have been better directed against Channel 4, which emerges as significantly more unfavourable to coalition policy than the BBC' (Tumber and Palmer, 2004: 98).

A second academic study, this time comparing a sample of German television news with the BBC's main evening bulletins and the US ABC news, showed that in comparative terms across a range of indicators including information and commentary the BBC was *relatively* impartial and even-handed in its coverage of the war (ibid.: 96–8). Where the BBC was out of line was in giving *less* coverage to the anti-war movement in Britain; this can hardly be

interpreted as unhelpful to the official position of the UK government. Finally, a third study which among other media coverage
examined BBC1 News (6 pm) and ITV News (6.30 pm) between 20
March and 17 April 2003 concluded that there was 'substantial
homogeneity between the two main terrestrial channels' bulletins'
(ibid.: 111).

Two additional points need to be borne in mind in any evaluation
of New Labour's attack on BBC coverage of the Iraq conflict. First,
some of the particular targets of government criticism of the BBC –
the *Today* programme (Radio 4), *The World at One* (Radio 4) and
Newsnight (BBC2) with their interview formats and, at times,
highly adversarial style of questioning – were not included in the
academic studies of the Corporation's war coverage mentioned
above. Second, these studies focused on television coverage during
the period of the war itself, not in the long run-up phase when there
was heated public and political debate about the legitimacy of military conflict in the absence of a second United Nations resolution.
Yet even allowing for these caveats, it is clear that these academic
studies furnish no evidence that BBC television news had an explicit
anti-government agenda in its reporting of the Iraq war. Nor do the
studies support the view that BBC television news coverage was
even inadvertently skewed in an anti-government direction on a
systematic basis.

Can news be unbiased?

The prevalence of different forms of bias in press and broadcast news
coverage raises the question of whether news can ever be unbiased. It
can be argued that the notion of unbiased news is a myth. Since, it is
claimed, there is no objective reality for the news media to cover,
there is no reliable account of the real that is independent of interpretation. From this perspective, notions of impartiality and objectivity
are simply part of the professional apparatus of news media professionals, helping to legitimize their work and validate the status of their
product for audiences while at the same time masking what is, in
effect, a particular and partial version of events (which nonetheless
may still be reasonably accurate).

This relativistic viewpoint has been challenged. For instance, some
commentators have tried to put up a case in defence of objectivity,
contending that it is possible and meaningful to make objective truth
claims about television news content (Lichtenberg, 2000). Lichtenberg

tries to show that 'in so far as we aim to understand the world we cannot get along without assuming both the possibility and value of objectivity. That the questions reporters ask have answers to which people of goodwill and good sense would, after adequate investigation, agree is the presupposition that we make, and must make, in taking journalism seriously' (ibid.: 252).

Yet even if one were to accept the theoretical possibility of unbiased news, it is possible to argue that in practice there are too many hurdles to its achievement. Even impartiality – a potentially more realizable goal than objectivity – is made difficult by the impact of the different variables involved in the process of news production. Moreover, while impartiality in, say, the treatment of the mainstream political parties may be achievable, much of contemporary political debate spills out from within the constraints of party political competition. Issues such as global warming, the 'war on terror', faith schools or the Middle East conflict are not necessarily amenable to a dualistic adversarial framework in which one view is 'balanced' by an opposing one. The heterogeneous nature of Britain's multicultural society and the complexity of many contemporary political issues may make due impartiality extremely difficult, if not impossible, to achieve with any sense of conviction.

Where then does this leave audiences seeking to inform themselves about politics through the British news media? First, not all political information is open to dispute: for instance, the number of seats held by each party in the House of Commons at a given moment is open to objective verification. Second, however, much of what might seem to be factual information is highly contestable: 'In an era of electronic glut, "facts", more than ever, are manufactured, and they never speak for themselves' (Seymour-Ure, 2003: 14). For example, official crime statistics are open to manipulation by sources such as the police (as well as, of course, to differing interpretations by the media and by audiences) who may have a vested interest in playing up or down incidences of reported crime. Thus, in political debate statistics easily become part of 'spin' and 'counter-spin' on the part of different interested parties.

Third, the 'spin' may come from the news media themselves. Different news outlets, for example, may give different figures for the number of people attending a protest demonstration, influenced among other things by their partisanship and use of sources. Not only are some events deemed more newsworthy than others by journalists, but the selection of material and their framing in a particular news story package introduce notions of judgement, perspective and, therefore, potentially of bias. For example, even if one accepts that the attendance figures for the Millennium Dome in 2000, which were given extensive coverage in the news media, were wholly accurate, they were frequently used within a wider political debate about the utility of the exhibition and the amount of public money devoted to the Dome. Moreover, in a vicious circle of self-fulfilling prophecy, media reporting of the low attendance figures and general negative coverage of the Dome may well have had an influence by dissuading potential visitors.

It could be argued that while normative values such as balance, impartiality and objectivity may not be achievable, they still provide media professionals and the public with certain principles the abandonment of which 'would leave journalists and citizens alike with very little to appeal to in open democratic information exchange' (Stevenson, 1995: 31). Lichtenberg sees them as 'regulative principles', ideals 'that we must suppose to apply, even if at the limit they do not, if we are to possess the will and the ways to understand the world' (Lichtenberg, 2000: 249). Perhaps they are best regarded as aspirations, imperfectly realized in an imperfect world.

Meanwhile, audiences need to recognize that whatever outlets they use for their news provision, none of them can be the purveyor of 'the truth, the whole truth and nothing but the truth'. There is an onus, therefore, on audiences to try to evaluate the reliability and quality of their news providers and to be aware of the power of owners, advertisers and sources among others to influence the news product. Indeed, audiences need to understand that *all* news on *all* media is the product of a process of selection and construction and that the version of events provided by any particular outlet may be reasonably accurate and at the same time biased.

The news environment in the digital age

With the routinization of the use of new technologies, the news environment in the digital age offers fresh challenges and opportunities to sources, journalists and audiences. More news than ever before is now available, including the output of rolling news channels, global news organizations and online providers. Different types of information are also on offer, particularly via the internet, including the websites of non-official sources, newsgroups and individual weblogs ('blogs'), which together profoundly affect the ways in which some sections of the public access news. The mediating role of professional journalists is changing, while the traditional broadcasting norms of balance and due impartiality are no longer necessarily regarded as relevant or even desirable.

The first feature of the digital news environment has been the impact of new technology on the processes of news gathering, production and distribution. Mobile satellite feeds, videophones, lightweight cameras and sound equipment have revolutionized news gathering. Reporters can now send back their reports in real time from the most geographically isolated parts of the globe, while live two-ways between the news anchor in the studio (usually in London) and the reporter in the field have become commonplace in television news programmes. In the newsroom the editing of news has been improved by electronic news systems, while on-screen presentation has been enhanced by computerized graphics. The impact of new technology is also evident in news distribution and consumption. In addition to the traditional outlets of press, radio and television, news can now be accessed through a range of technological devices, including the computer and mobile phone.

A second feature is the huge increase in the amount of news available, especially on broadcast media and the worldwide web. Television viewers, for instance, now have far greater choice not only about which news programmes to watch, but when to watch them, thanks to the advent and increasing availability of 24-hour news channels. These include not just the rolling news channels of national broadcasters such as the BBC and Sky, but also international news providers including CNN International and Euronews. These international news channels may be directly accessed by British audiences, while their impact is sometimes indirect, as when a national news provider uses their output as part of one of its own news packages – for example, a BBC1 news programme showing a clip taken from Al Jazeera. Rolling news channels are the first media source accessed by many viewers when big news stories, such as the war in Iraq (2003) or the terrorist bombs in London (2005), are breaking. In addition, the internet provides users with a wide range of online news from national and international providers.

Third, it is not just quantitatively more news that is now on tap, but qualitatively different sorts of news. With established broadcasters finding it harder to attract audiences to traditional news bulletins, especially among the young, their websites give them the opportunity to provide more background coverage of running news stories. To this must be added the websites of a host of political actors – government, political parties, pressure groups and new social movements – all of whom can now distribute information to audiences without the filtering, gate-keeping intervention of journalists. Other types of 'news' are also available on the web, including blogs – the personal online diaries of journalists and politicians among others. Blogs, discussion boards and online communities are an early signal of how content generated by audiences may come to revolutionize media (BBC, 2005: 17). In terms of form, websites allow for 'layered' news, allowing users to delve further into a story as their interest takes them.

The result – and this is the fourth feature of the digital news environment – is that at least some sections of the public access news in different ways than before. Audiences are now invited to respond to news items via e-mail and text messages, and to sign up to receive the weekly newsletter of the news presenter, while polls soliciting the opinions of listeners and viewers on issues in the news have become an integral part of some radio and television news programmes. Sky News pioneered the use of interactivity in Britain: alternative screens showing different elements, such as headlines, sport or weather and interactive voting; on-screen banners giving breaking news and latest headlines; and new presentation techniques such as the 'news wall' (Ofcom, 2003). The aim of the news organization is to maintain brand loyalty on the part of users by converting them from passive recipients of news to a more active engagement with the news provider. The option of a more personalized news service, customized to meet the needs and interests of the user, further changes the traditional producer–audience relationship. It may also be that the different structure and form of contemporary web-based news gives the user more power than before to reshape the news frame and so impose their own reading on what is being proffered by journalists (Campbell, 2004: 251).

What do these changes mean for professional journalists? The fifth feature is that news is now produced and disseminated faster than ever before, reducing the time gap between an event happening in the real world and its coverage by the news media. It has been argued that news is being redefined as what is happening (or even what may happen), rather than what has happened (ibid.: 241). This means that political reporters and correspondents now have even less time to stand back from events, explain them to audiences and analyze their significance. The expansion in news broadcasts also results in some political correspondents having to spend a considerable amount of time actually appearing on news programmes, which further reduces the time available for checking stories and exploring different angles. This may further limit the opportunities for considered explanation and contextualization. A separate but related development is the move on the part of some (but by no means all) journalists away from being an observer of and commentator on events to being a participant in them, a style of news reporting particularly associated with CNN journalism. At the time of the Hutton Inquiry, the BBC Radio 4 *Today* programme was accused of being too concerned with making the news rather than reporting it. Meanwhile more people outside the journalistic profession are becoming involved in the news gathering process, including members of the public who submit photographs and amateur video footage of events (such as the July 2005 terrorist bombings in London) which are used by news organizations as part of their coverage. Blogs may be more important through the impact they have on the framing of stories by journalists working in mainstream media rather than any direct effect they may have on the online general public (Chadwick, 2006: 305).

Finally, do these changes make the traditional journalistic norms of balance and impartiality in the broadcast media redundant? It could be argued that, in an era of extensive supply, broadcasting should be allowed to go the way of the press in terms of news regulation. This would allow national radio stations and television channels openly to provide different and competing versions of 'reality', potentially even to offer radically different accounts of the world, in the manner, say, of the Iraq war coverage of Fox News and Al Jazeera in the global news sphere. It could be argued that the provision by any single broadcast news outlet of a 'duly impartial' account of the world is neither feasible nor necessary. Instead, news content across a range of broadcast (and narrowcast) providers could overtly articulate a diversity of opinion, while each news provider could proclaim its 'bias' explicitly upfront. This would allow niche news providers to target specific politically differentiated sections of society. This would move well beyond the situation where already radio and television news programmes position themselves in the market to target particular socio-economic groups with different levels of informational complexity in their coverage and analysis.

Would such diversity across the range of broadcasting news outlets (external pluralism) rather than an enforced balance and impartiality within each one (internal pluralism) be desirable? Would audiences gain or lose by a liberalization of the regulatory norms on broadcast news? On the one hand, such a step might free up journalists from a restrictive framework in their approach to news, allowing scope for a more committed and campaigning form of journalism. On the other hand, it might also result in broadcast news and commentary becoming as partisan as that of some newspapers, with audiences 'discovering the delight of having their own prejudices confirmed, rather than challenged' (Lloyd, 2004: 199). It may even result in an even greater exclusion or marginalization of some political views in mainstream news media than is currently the case. For the moment it should be noted that a very high proportion of the audience currently value what they regard as the impartiality of British television news (Ofcom, 2003).

Conclusion

News is not a value-free reflection of the world, nor a neutral summary of key events. Rather, it is the result of a process of selection and construction: first, by sources; second, by journalists working in news organizations; and, finally, by audiences. Within the news media the process of construction is shaped less by the personal views or sociological characteristics of journalists than by their professional judgement as to what they consider newsworthy. It is also influenced by organizational variables, including decision-making procedures and corporate norms. In addition, proprietors and advertisers may exert an influence, while some sources secure routine access to the news media, which gives them a privileged opportunity to help shape the parameters of news coverage. Moreover, since the media do not operate in a social vacuum, news production is affected by the cultural values of society. Finally, in a competitive news media environment audience tastes and preferences also play a part, particularly with regard to news formats and presentation. News can thus be simultaneously regarded as a commercial commodity, a manufactured product and a cultural narrative.

The process of news production does not lead to homogeneity in the news agenda or issue coverage, nor does it necessarily end up with the content of news being biased in a party political sense. However, it does seem to result in the news agenda being constructed through the use of dominant frames of reference, with alternative frameworks being excluded or marginalized. This means that the news media tend to treat some issues as unproblematic because they assume a consensus and reproduce this consensus (for example, on the values of parliamentary democracy); some issues are treated as of legitimate controversy (for instance, mainstream party politics) and some are treated as manifestations of deviance (notably, political violence and terrorism) (Hallin, 1986).

Finally, in the digital age the conditions under which news is produced and received have changed: more news is available around the clock from a variety of traditional and new media outlets. This has created an ambient news culture for consumers, who now have more power to select the news that interests them at a time of their choosing. At the same time, the role of the journalist as intermediary between sources and audiences is being modified, as sources further professionalize their activities and also strive to target audiences directly with their messages. The news environment of the digital age may well empower citizens and consumers, but it may also render the boundary between news and public relations ever more indistinct.

7

The Government and News Management

News management has become a central concern for the government in recent years. In a communications environment characterized by the 24-hour news cycle and a glut of competing media outlets, journalists have a voracious appetite for fresh primary material. At the same time, a whole array of political actors have professionalized their activities as sources for the news media. The government, therefore, has to work hard in its attempts to drive and dominate the news agenda. This involves trying to determine which issues do – and just as importantly which do not – feature in media coverage and how these issues are framed.

A useful starting point for analyzing the government's approach to news management is to see it as being influenced by two apparently contradictory sets of values: a historically well-implanted culture of secrecy, which is linked to the development of the 'national security state' (Hallin and Mancini, 2004: 234), and a more recent public relations culture of self-promotion (Wernick, 1991). Thus, the government is often keen to restrict information from entering the public sphere, while at other times it wishes to publicize its policies in the hope of securing a favourable electoral response (Franklin, 1994: 112). This simple dichotomy, however, is not wholly satisfactory, since a government's attempts to withhold information may sometimes be played out in public, while conversely the release of information frequently takes place in private.

A more comprehensive analytic framework views news management activities in terms of two cross-cutting dimensions. The first has enclosure (or restriction) at one end and disclosure at the other, while the second has overt (or visible) behaviour at one end and covert (or invisible) at the other (Ericson, Baranek and Chan, 1989; Negrine, 1996: 29). This two-dimensional matrix gives a typology of four possible ideal-types of governmental news management activities:

- Overt restriction
- Covert restriction
- Overt disclosure
- Covert disclosure

Overt restriction includes censorship of media content, the application of restraining legislation and a range of pressures intended to delimit media coverage – all played out in the public domain. *Covert restriction* is by definition hidden from public view, though instances may come to light after the event, for example when memoirs are written or official documents released. *Overt disclosure* includes on-the-record governmental briefings and the open promotion of government policy. Finally, *covert disclosure* consists of behind-the-scenes leaks and the provision of information to journalists on an off-the-record basis.

Although these categories are analytically separate, in practice the boundaries between them are not rigid. The secrecy/publicity divide is better regarded as a continuum than as a simple dualistic contrast (Seymour-Ure, 2003: 35–6), while in practice the government often uses a combination of techniques in the management of a specific news story – for example, a mix of off-the-record background briefing and on-the-record statements to the media. In addition, and introducing another layer of complexity, it must be remembered that in pursuing its news management objectives a government has to have a reactive as well as a proactive strategy. While no government can control events in the real world, it has to be able to respond to issues coming on to the news agenda in a manner which, at the very least, limits their potential damage.

This chapter analyzes and evaluates governmental news management activities, using examples taken from the premierships of Thatcher, Major and Blair. The chapter is organized in three sections. The first concentrates on the restriction of information. The second focuses largely on promotional activities associated with disclosure, applying the concept of 'primary definer' to the role of the government as an official source. The final section examines news management during the period of the New Labour government.

Restrictive practices

Keeping it secret

Censorship and restraining legislation are used by the government to prevent the media from reporting on certain issues and to delimit the boundaries of coverage where it does take place (Manning, 2001: 123–30). Measures to restrict the media have been employed in recent years in politically sensitive areas, such as national security, the conflict in Northern Ireland and the fight against terrorism. For example, during the first Blair administration the Ministry of Defence used injunctions and gagging orders under the Official Secrets Act against different media outlets, including *The Sunday Times* and Ulster Television, to constrain them from reporting the activities of the British army's covert Force Research Unit in Northern Ireland.

Overt restriction was a notable feature of news management during the Thatcher premiership (Ewing and Gearty, 1990). Specific instances included the Zircon affair in 1987, which involved a raid on BBC Scotland headquarters by the Special Branch and the confiscation of untransmitted television footage of a programme which argued that the government had misled Parliament about the cost of the Zircon spy satellite (Doornaert and Omdal, 1989: 12–13; Thornton, 1987: 7–9). Ironically, the banned programme had been commissioned by the BBC as part of a series on secrecy in Britain. Around the same time British newspapers were prevented from publishing extracts from the controversial book *Spycatcher*. Written by a former British security officer, Peter Wright, *Spycatcher* made a series of critical allegations regarding the functioning of the British security services. For a while, the book could not be purchased in Britain, even though it was widely available abroad and its contents were therefore public knowledge internationally (Rogers, 1989).

The 1988 broadcasting ban was the most spectacularly visible example of government restriction on a particular aspect of the media's political output over the past twenty years. Under the terms of the ban, broadcasters were prohibited from transmitting any words spoken by persons representing specific named organizations connected with the Northern Irish conflict, including Sinn Fein and the Irish Republican Army (IRA) (Curtis and Jempson, 1993). The government's avowed objective was to keep apologists for terrorism off British television screens and to deprive them of what Mrs. Thatcher had famously called the 'oxygen of publicity' in the propaganda battle. Though opposed by many journalists (*Index on*

Censorship, 1993: 4), the ban represented a perfectly legal use of the government's formal power to veto the transmission of a broadcast programme (Annan Report, 1977: 43) and as a result it seemed that broadcasters had no option but to comply with the terms of the official restriction.

Nonetheless, news editors tried with some success to circumvent the ban, first through the insertion of subtitles and then by using actors' voices dubbed to synchronize with the lip movements of the banned spokespersons who were shown 'talking' on screen. As a result, at face value the broadcasting ban was not as effective as the government had intended. Nonetheless, its impact on coverage was far from inconsequential. One effect was 'a dramatic drop in Sinn Fein interviews in the [following] five years' (Miller, 1994: 57), a result which might be interpreted as a significant victory for the authorities. The imposition of the ban indicated the level of direct intervention in broadcasting which the Conservative government was prepared to countenance to prevent oppositional perspectives on the Northern Ireland conflict from being covered on British television. Remaining in place for six years, the ban was lifted only after the announcement of the IRA ceasefire negotiated by Major's government.

In addition to censorship and legal restraint, the government may use intimidation and pressure, some of which is quite overt, to try to constrain media coverage. During the Thatcher premiership, for example, two instances of government intimidation of broadcasters were especially noteworthy, each linked to the transmission of a specific television programme on an aspect of the Northern Ireland conflict. *Real Lives: At the Edge of the Union* [BBC, 1985] was initially withdrawn from transmission by the BBC Board of Governors, who were widely portrayed as having caved in to government pressure. It was broadcast some time later after only minimal editorial changes (Negrine, 1989: 130–6; Schlesinger, 1987: xvi–xxi). *Death on the Rock* [Thames TV, 1989] called into question the British government's official version of events surrounding the killing by the SAS of three members of the IRA on active service in Gibraltar. The programme was transmitted as scheduled, but was then vilified by the government and sections of the pro-Conservative press (Bolton, 1990; Windlesham and Rampton, 1989).

While censorship, legal restrictions and political pressure may enjoy some success in constraining news coverage, their overt use can also be highly problematic. First, specific interventions may be rendered ineffective by judicial review or media resistance. In the *Spycatcher* case, for example, the Law Lords ultimately rejected the government's arguments and overturned its injunction. In the *Death on the Rock* incident, Thames TV management refused to cave in to government pressure.

Second, even where government intervention is legally upheld and technically successful, its overt nature is often controversial and the subsequent media coverage may be counter-productive. In the Zircon case, for instance, critics argued that while the disclosure of information about the spy satellite was certainly embarrassing to the government, it was not harmful to national security. More generally, government-imposed restraints are frequently resented by the news media as an unwarranted infringement in their professional domain. The restriction itself may become the main news story, as in the case of the ban on newspaper publication of extracts from *Spycatcher*. In such circumstances the affair may generate unfavourable publicity for the authorities. Both the *Real Lives* and *Death on the Rock* episodes became matters of intense media controversy which focused on not just the content of coverage, but also the behaviour and rights of the different players involved – government ministers, regulatory authorities, broadcasting management and political journalists.

Finally, the imposition of restrictions on the news media in peace-time contradicts liberal democratic norms regarding their role in a free society. The reputation of the media as independent institutions is undermined. Overt restriction retains its legitimacy and effectiveness when used sparingly; too frequent recourse to it by government as a tool of news management exposes the authorities to criticism from media, other elite political actors and public opinion. Not surprisingly, therefore, if a government wishes to restrict information from coming into the mediated public sphere, it usually prefers to act in secret.

Freedom of information?

Government restriction on information coming into the public domain has not just been challenged on a case by case basis. In addition, there has been pressure to introduce structural changes to open up the process of government by making more information available (Birkinshaw and Parkin, 1999). In this context the New Labour government's Freedom of Information (FOI) Act, broadly welcomed in principle, has been widely criticized for its timidity and restricted scope (Dyer, 2000). When the FOI legislation fully came into force in

2005, it did contribute to some news stories such as the Major government's handling of sterling's withdrawal from the European Exchange Rate Mechanism (ERM) in 1995 – an apparent attempt by New Labour in the run-up to the 2005 general election to use the media to remind the electorate of past Conservative economic failure. A different story sourced from letters released under the FOI legislation – this time embarrassing to New Labour – concerned the Attorney General's apparent initial reluctance to provide legal justification for the 2003 war in Iraq.

Experience from other countries, such as the United States, however, suggests that because of cumbersome administrative implementation the influence of FOI legislation on journalistic practices is marginal (Downing, 1986: 159) and it may well be that this will also prove to be the case in Britain. Certainly some journalists have in the past expressed scepticism about the possible benefits of any FOI legislation for the news media, arguing that 'each opening up of the channels of communication to the principles of freedom of information has been accompanied by a simultaneous retreat of the sensitive material into a new hiding place' (Aitken, 1991: 54) as the culture of secrecy adapts to new legislative provisions.

In any event, governmental restriction forms only part of the story regarding the non-mediatization of information of potential public interest. The news media are also implicated. For instance, Negrine argues that much information is already available in the public domain, but is not publicized through the media because it is not considered sufficiently interesting on news grounds (Negrine, 1996: 31). Using the 'arms to Iraq' affair of the early 1990s as a case study, he argues that 'opening up currently closed institutions, with "freedom of information" provisions for example, may actually have a very limited impact on media coverage of events. It is not that there is not enough information available . . . but that the willingness to sift through it and to get it published is often not present' (ibid.: 33–4). From this viewpoint it is the media's judgement of the newsworthiness of information rather than its initial availability that determines its mediation into the public sphere.

This shifts the focus away from government restriction and on to the media themselves, raising questions about the time and resources that journalists have to access information, their levels of specialist comprehension and their ability to separate the information wheat from the chaff. Moreover, while the spread of media outlets and the advent of the internet have undoubtedly weakened the capacity of the nation-state to restrict the circulation of information in the public domain, the spread of global communications technology does not of itself resolve these questions about journalists' work practices.

The government as a 'primary definer' for the news media?

Ingham and the lobby during the Thatcher premiership

When it comes to the disclosure of information, the government enjoys the benefit of certain key assets in functioning as an official source for the news media. These include: significant organizational and economic resources; extensive insider knowledge and policy expertise across a range of political issues; a high degree of legitimacy conferred through the electoral process; and institutionalized news beats for journalists (Davis, 2002: 174–5). As we have seen in Chapter 6, one way of theorizing governmental power in news management uses the concept of 'primary definer', whereby ministers and their advisers enjoy privileged access on a routine basis in the processes of agenda construction and issue framing.

The practice of mass institutionalized briefings of political journalists by the government's chief press officer was for a long time widely regarded as one of the main linkages in the privileged relationship the government enjoyed with the news media (Ingham, 1991; Tunstall, 1970). These twice daily 'lobby' briefings of newspaper and broadcasting journalists from both national and provincial media were for a long time conducted on a non-attributable basis (Seymour-Ure, 2003: 150–4). This arguably served the government's interests by giving it greater freedom of manoeuvre than if the briefings had been held on the record. Interestingly the arrangement was also supported by a majority of lobby journalists for whom it provided a regular supply of 'insider' information not available to journalists outside the lobby (Jones, 1995: 87).

These rather cosy arrangements came in for considerable criticism (Morgan, 1991). For instance, the secretiveness of the lobby was contrasted with the more open system of press briefings by the executive in the United States. More importantly, it was argued that the practice encouraged a passive response on the part of journalists. From this perspective journalists frequently collaborated with government in the process of news management, with the result that the official managers of the political news were too often allowed to dictate the agenda (Cockerell, Hennessy and Walker, 1984: 11).

Indeed, the lobby system of briefing achieved a mythical status in the eyes of some critics. Franklin, for example, contends that it was 'appropriated by government as a conduit for information and, in this process, metamorphosed from an active and critical observer of political affairs into a passive purveyor of government messages' (Franklin, 1994: 86). Franklin presents the lobby as it functioned up until the early 1990s as an integral part of a process whereby those political journalists given accredited status effectively became part of the government's news management apparatus.

Such criticisms seemed particularly appropriate during the Thatcher premiership when Bernard Ingham, the Number 10 Press Secretary, was accused by his detractors of manipulating lobby journalists unmercifully. Ingham's tenure of the office was longer than any of his postwar predecessors, virtually coterminous with Mrs Thatcher's eleven and a half years in power. Moreover, Ingham enjoyed a particularly close professional relationship with the Prime Minister, based on an admiration of her views across a range of issues (Kavanagh and Seldon, 2000: 161). In his dealings with the media, he used lobby briefings as much to promote the Prime Minister personally as the government collectively. He could browbeat media professionals, for example on the occasion of Mrs Thatcher's surprise visit to the Falklands in 1983 when he compelled the BBC to pool its television footage of the event with its rival news broadcaster ITN (Harris, 1990: 100–2).

On occasions Ingham also used the lobby as a forum in which to brief against government ministers who were out of favour with the Prime Minister, acting on her behalf in a way in which she could not be seen to do. One of the ministerial victims of this tactic, John Biffen, famously remarked that in this respect Ingham was 'the sewer rather than the sewage' (quoted in Harris, 1990: 148). The abrasive way in which Ingham handled the lobby persuaded *The Independent*, *The Guardian* and *The Scotsman* to boycott the briefings in 1986 and they returned only after Ingham was replaced by a new press secretary in the wake of Thatcher's fall from power. Ingham's hands-on approach to news management set a standard which was matched – and indeed surpassed – in government only when New Labour came to power in 1997.

Constraints on the government's definitional power

Yet notwithstanding its considerable advantages in terms of organizational resources, expert knowledge and political legitimacy, the government is far from simply being able to impose its official version of events on the news media. Several studies of government–media relations – on issues such as the Falklands conflict, Northern Ireland and the poll tax – have called into question some of the key assumptions regarding the former's power as a primary definer, demonstrating that the capacity of ministers and their special advisers to shape the news agenda is frequently highly constrained (Deacon and Golding, 1994; Miller, 1993; Morrison and Tumber, 1988).

Three main weaknesses in the concept of primary definition are particularly relevant (Schlesinger, 1990). First, the notion of primary definer assumes that the government is not subject to internal division and so speaks to journalists with one voice. The model thus suggests that there is a significant level of agreement within the executive when it comes to influencing the framing of a particular news story. Yet it is clear that no British government is a monolithic entity, acting with a unified will and a single sense of purpose. Rather it is a divided and fragmented apparatus, characterized by inter-departmental conflicts, ideological disputes, policy disagreements and personality clashes. For instance, during the Thatcher premiership there were significant disagreements between ministers on the question of state intervention in the economy, and the conflict between the ideological 'drys' and the pragamatic 'wets' was a running media story for much of her premiership. Briefing of journalists and selective leaking of information by ministerial advisers often reveal the extent and intensity of the divisions at the heart of the executive, with the result that 'keenly fought rivalries between departments of government seeking to secure particular understandings of problems or particular "ways of thinking" . . . frequently stimulate new information flows, or "leaks", to the benefit of journalists operating within particular specialisms' (Manning, 1999: 316).

Second, the model implies that the government occupies a dominant structural position in its capacity as an official source with the result that alternative definitions are routinely swept aside by the primary defining power of the executive. Yet the counter-definitional impact on the media of non-governmental sources needs to be borne in mind (Manning, 2001: 137–201). Government actors have no monopoly of resources or credibility. In addition to parties and pressure groups (see Chapter 8), a range of actors including parliamentary select committees, leading members of the judiciary, independent regulatory authorities and devolved assemblies in Scotland and Wales have among others established themselves as legitimate news sources for journalists (Riddell, 1998: 14), partly because of their acknowledged expertise on an issue and partly because they have organized themselves to gain routine access to the media. The news media regularly make use of such sources from a professional concern to cover an issue from different angles and, in the case of public service broadcasters, because they are also subject to regulations regarding due impartiality. These developments have ensured that 'every Lobby journalist develops sources against which he can test material from the centre' (Roth, 1999: 24). While this does not mean that in general journalists actively seek out a large variety of alternative sources, evidence for which seems scant (Negrine, 1996: 27), it does suggest that they routinely access information from a range of sources, both within and outside government.

As a result, government actors often find themselves competing against other sources in their attempt to impose their official perspective (McLaughlin and Miller, 1996). Some sources may challenge the government's attempt to frame an issue in a particular way and may generate counter-definitions to try to displace the government's preferred primary definition. On the poll tax issue, for example, 'the full weight of Mrs Thatcher's authority and government, the concerted efforts of the government's public relations machinery and the considerable resources of the public purse were brought to bear to persuade the citizens of the UK that the poll tax was what the country needed' (Newton, 2001: 162). Local and national media were given 'information subsidies' in the form of publicity material and press releases, designed to reduce the cost to journalists of obtaining information they needed to construct news (Gandy, 1982). Yet the results in terms of media coverage were disappointing for the government. The high level of media antipathy can be explained in part by the fact that 'the policy attracted a swathe of criticism from both private and public sectors, voluntary agencies and all the opposition parties', as well as local government associations and anti-poll tax organizations (Deacon and Golding, 1994: 188). Local authorities were key sources for the provincial media which were particularly critical of the government's plans. As a result, with regard to framing the issue for the media, the Conservative government's status changed from an 'accredited' to a 'discredited' source (ibid.: 201).

Finally, the concept of primary definition tends to place the news media in a passive and responsive mode in their interrelationship with the government as an official source. Instead the media may

themselves take the initiative in subjecting the government's definition of events to their own critical scrutiny, challenging the official
version as put forward by ministers and frequently putting the latter
on the defensive in the process of news framing. Moreover, the notion
of primary definition also downplays variations between news media,
both across and within media sectors of press, radio and television.
For example, on the issue of television coverage of 'terrorism' it has
been shown that different programme genres (news, current affairs,
documentaries) can be distinguished by their degree of openness to a
variety of source perspectives (Schlesinger, Murdock and Elliott,
1983).

The example of the Major premiership illustrates the extent to
which a government can fail to act as an effective primary definer for
the media, even at the minimal level of damage limitation (Seymour-
Ure, 2003: 52–3). In part this was the result of poor organization, a
lack of a strategic approach to government communication and inappropriate personnel. None of Major's three successive press secretaries – Gus O'Donnell, Christopher Meyer and Jonathan Haslam –
enjoyed high status within the government apparatus. Nor were they
given effective control over the media activities of the Conservative
party (as opposed to the government). This led to difficulties in liaison
between the Downing Street press office and Conservative party
headquarters (Jones, 1995: 96). Under Major there was also also a
lack of central control over information coming out of the press
offices of the various government departments (ibid.: 93, 95). In addition, all three press secretaries came from the civil service, with none
having a professional background in journalism. O'Donnell, for
example, was primarily an economist, 'who became a press secretary
only by accident' and 'never entirely settled into the press mould'
(Seldon, 1997: 144). In the light of Major's leadership problems,
press secretaries with stronger political instincts and media experience would have been invaluable (Seymour-Ure, 1994: 413).
Certainly, none of them was able to manage the media, especially the
tabloid newspapers, as effectively as Ingham had done for Thatcher or
Alastair Campbell would do for Blair.

The Major government was also unable to mobilize its structural
resources of authority and legitimacy in managing the news media. The
events of 'Black Wednesday' in September 1992, when the pound was
forced out of the ERM, blew apart the government's reputation for
economic competence (Seldon, 1997: 707–8). Britain's role in Europe,
brought to a head on the issue of the ratification of the Maastricht

Treaty, exposed faultlines within the government and Conservative party, with various news media providing ministerial and party critics of Major's policies and leadership style a platform for their views. These included party dissidents who were able to exploit those sections of the press that were 'Eurosceptic' and take advantage of the government's small and eroding parliamentary majority to increase their political importance and media profile. In addition, the Major government was prone to insider hostile leaking from ministerial heavyweights, such as Kenneth Clarke at the Treasury (Kavanagh and Seldon, 2000: 216), while on some key domestic policy issues, such as the proposal to privatize the Post Office, the government was profoundly split (Davis, 2002: 155). Furthermore, the immensely damaging stories of sleaze, sexual scandal and financial impropriety which dogged the second half of the Major premiership did not just bring into ridicule the moralistic 'back to basics' campaign launched by the Prime Minister in early 1994. By presenting an image of an accident-prone Prime Minister at the mercy of events rather than controlling them, the coverage presented a picture of a Prime Minister who was clearly unable to impose his leadership and authority over either the Conservative party or government (Jones, 1995: 91–121; 189–219).

The New Labour government and news management

The adoption of a strategic approach under Campbell

After its 1997 election victory New Labour placed significant emphasis on news management, which it regarded as an integral part of contemporary government, not an optional extra. As a result, ministers and their special advisers were constantly engaged in seeking to harness the media in the task of promoting the government's achievements to the electorate through positive imagery generation and symbolic management (O'Shaughnessy, 2004: 172–89). Until the resignation of Campbell, the Number 10 communications supremo, in the summer of 2003 the New Labour government's strategic approach to news management was characterized by three key features: centralization, professionalization and politicization (Franklin, 2001b).

First, Campbell put in place a highly centralized organization which sought to coordinate governmental communications and impose a single message from the top down. For example, government ministers who did not adhere to the centrally imposed rules whereby major interviews and media appearances had to be agreed in

advance with the Number 10 Press Office found themselves repri-
manded by Campbell. In addition, any minister or adviser he regarded
as being 'off message' was viewed with suspicion. For instance,
Gordon Brown's press officer at the Treasury, Charlie Wheelan, who
briefed the media on his own initiative to promote Brown's interests,
was regarded by Campbell with considerable hostility right up until
Wheelan was forced to resign at the start of 1999 over his role in leaking information about Peter Mandelson's loan from Geoffrey
Robinson (Jones, 1999: 259–80; Rawnsley, 2000: 210–34).

Second, a highly professional engagement with news management
was evident in the various innovations introduced by Campbell at
Number 10. These included the establishment of a Strategic
Communications Unit to coordinate government news announce-
ments across departments so that a clear, focused policy message was
distributed to the media on any particular day. Former journalists were
employed to ensure that a media rather than bureaucratic mindset
informed the process. The techniques employed by the New Labour
government to try to ensure favourable news coverage included the
following (Barnett and Gaber, 2001: 106–13):

- Firebreaking, whereby a diversion is deliberately constructed to
  take journalists off the scent of an embarrassing story
- Pre-empting, as in the case of the government minister Nick
  Brown, who in late 1998 admitted that he was gay to minimize the
  impact of revelations to this effect which were about to appear in
  the *News of the World*
- Milking a story, whereby advance notice of a governmental initiative is trailed in various media in a drip-by-drip fashion in
  advance of the official announcement so as to obtain the maximum amount of favourable coverage
- Kite-flying, where controversial proposals are floated via the
  media to test public reaction
- Managing expectations, which is particularly evident around the
  time of the Budget, when public expectations may be reduced via
  media briefings in advance of the Chancellor's speech, thus
  giving the Chancellor more favourable publicity if the formal
  announcement contains an unanticipated tax or spend bonus
- Rapid rebuttal to close down the negative impact of the original
  story by immediately adopting an offensive position
- 'Pre-buttal' of opposition criticisms not yet disseminated in the
  public sphere.

Campbell was in many respects the personification of the professionalization of governmental news management. As a former journalist and political editor at the two *Mirror* titles and *Today*, Campbell knew the world of the news media, and particularly tabloid journalism, from the inside. He did not have to second guess what journalists might do with a lead; he knew from his own experience how a story would play in different media outlets. Campbell's attention to detail became legendary, as did his facility for the appropriate soundbite, such as the 'people's princess' used by Blair on the occasion of Princess Diana's death in 1997. Moreover, Campbell was highly valued by journalists as a source because of his well-known proximity to Blair in the inner circle of key ministers and top advisers (Hennessy, 2000). He was the first Number 10 press secretary to attend Cabinet meetings on a regular basis and he acquired the reputation of having more influence in decision-making than some policy advisers (Oborne, 1999: 161; Roth, 1999: 22).

Finally, politicization of news management was evidenced by three important developments. First, Campbell was allowed give orders to civil servants. This meant that he could adopt a more overtly partisan approach in his relationship with the media than had formally been the case with his predecessors. Second, Campbell's belief that the non-partisan civil servants acting as ministerial press officers in the Government Information Service (renamed the Government Information and Communications Service) would be insufficiently proactive in pushing the government's case with the news media led to many of them being weeded out and replaced in the early months of Blair's first term. Third and most controversially, the New Labour government significantly increased the number of politically appointed special advisers in government departments, several of whom fulfilled a proactive partisan media relations role which sometimes brought them into conflict with government information officers steeped in a civil service culture of political neutrality (Barnett and Gaber, 2001: 116–24; Scammell, 2001: 520–6).

Government–media interdependence

Well before New Labour came to power the effectiveness of lobby briefings as a tool of governmental news management had already been called into question (Scammell, 1995: 200). The sheer size of the lobby, with well over 200 accredited journalists, militated against any idea of an all powerful Number 10 Press Secretary. Campbell, therefore, exploited the competitive culture of lobby journalists by favouring some at the expense of others (Hagerty, 2000: 13–14; Palmer, 2000: 54). For instance, certain journalists were given advance notice of material that the government wished to bring into the public sphere in the expectation that the government would receive positive coverage (Gaber, 2000: 69). The Murdoch newspapers were a good example of this exchange relationship. On a day to day basis Trevor Kavanagh, the political editor of *The Sun*, was one of the lobby journalists to be offered insider nuggets of information – such as the date of the 2001 election – ahead of their being made available to other parliamentary lobby journalists. In return, the Murdoch press provided a good platform for the New Labour government. For example, Blair had numerous articles published under his byline, especially in *The Sun* (Johnson, 1998: 19). Another tactic employed by Number 10 was to bypass lobby correspondents by targeting regional newspapers, women's magazines and ethnic minority publications so as to get its message across as unfiltered as possible to different sections of the electorate. For much of its first term in office New Labour enjoyed an extended honeymoon period with much of the news media: the 'media coverage that the Labour government has received, sleaze and scandals aside, was for its first three years in power mostly positive' (Barnett and Gaber, 2001: 122).

As the novelty of a New Labour administration wore off, however, the government's approach to news management ran up against a 'media logic' (Altheide and Snow, 1979) whereby in a highly competitive media system, driven by the relentless pursuit of audiences and advertisers, decision-making in newsrooms focuses attention on those stories that satisfy criteria of newsworthiness (Tumber, 1999). News stories increasingly tended to emphasize conflict and disunity, negative events and Labour personalities in trouble. For instance, the persistent in-fighting at the heart of the executive between Blair and Brown and their respective supporters provided good copy for political journalists, several of whom were happy to side with either the Prime Minister or the Chancellor of the Exchequer in their newspaper columns.

Scandal and impropriety make for 'good copy' in terms of news values. Some of the toughest news management tests for the New Labour government were in this area, hardly surprising in the light of New Labour's attacks on Conservative sleaze during the final years of the Major premiership. Sometimes the government's exercise in damage limitation was successful. For instance, potentially explosive stories, such as Robin Cook's affair with his secretary or the resignation of Ron Davies following his nocturnal wandering on Clapham Common (Jones, 1999: 244–52), were skilfully dealt with by New Labour's media handlers to minimize any adverse publicity for the government. Other stories proved more difficult to manage. The Ecclestone affair, which concerned large secret donations to the Labour party (Rawnsley, 2000: 89–105), and allegations of impropriety made against a succession of ministers, including Geoffrey Robinson, Peter Mandelson and Keith Vaz, revealed the capacity and willingness of the news media, particularly broadsheet newspaper journalists, to initiate and pursue stories highly critical of leading New Labour figures. Coverage of both Mandelson resignations had all the hallmarks of a media feeding frenzy (see Chapter 10).

From around the beginning of 2000 New Labour's capacity to shape the news agenda and influence the framing of coverage started to run into difficulties, as a series of highly problematic issues came on to the political and policy agendas. The Millennium Dome fiasco, the successful campaign for the mayorship of London by the rebel Ken Livingstone standing as an Independent against the official Labour candidate, the protest against the rise in fuel taxation by lorry drivers and the foot and mouth crisis in the countryside were all issues New Labour found difficult to manage in news terms in the run-up to the 2001 general election.

Jo Moore and 'a good day to bury bad news'

During New Labour's second term (2001–05) one incident in particular appeared to many to exemplify the unacceptable face of the New Labour government's approach to news management: the Jo Moore affair. The possibility of the inherent tension between the partisan role of special adviser and the avowedly neutral function of civil servant communication officer exploding into overt conflict was always present under the news management arrangements introduced by New Labour after 1997. The surprising aspect when conflict did erupt was that it happened not in one of the major ministries such as Health, Education or the Home Office, but in the relative backwater of Transport. The desire of Jo Moore, special adviser to the Transport Secretary Stephen Byers, to use the events of 11 September 2001 as a 'very good day to get out anything we want to bury' can be sympathetically regarded as simply an example of the mindset of the communication professional at work. In Moore's defence it could also be pointed out that at the time she sent the e-mail enjoining her colleagues to make use of the events unfolding in New York and Washington as an opportunity to release 'bad news stories' into the public realm, the full extent of what was taking place on the other side of the Atlantic had not yet been appreciated.

Against the background of a government with a reputation for spinning its way out of trouble, however, Ms Moore's comments – made public via an unauthorized leak to the media – represented an open goal for New Labour's critics, since her remarks could be presented as consummate evidence of the cynicism at the heart of the government's communications machine. For some critics Moore personified everything that was wrong with Labour's approach to communication in government: too much emphasis on presentation and spin; the short circuiting of official channels of communication by non-accountable special advisers, always seeking to secure maximum partisan advantage from every ministerial announcement; and the amorality of the belief that all is fair in news management, with the only criterion of success being the quality of the subsequent media coverage.

In the event, Ms Moore initially managed to survive the first onslaught of media-led disapproval, albeit at the cost of a highly mediatized public apology. However, her unfortunate e-mail came back to haunt her when she later became involved in a dispute with the civil servant in charge of communication at the department, Martin Sixmith (Jones, 2002: 271–343). In a battle for control of the department's links with the news media, Sixmith revealed that Moore was apparently intent on using the occasion of the funeral of Princess Margaret to publish potentially damaging statistics on rail industry performance in the hope that these would not be given prominent media coverage. Sixmith protested and in the ensuing dispute both Moore and Sixmith left their respective posts, while Byers himself later resigned in another media 'feeding frenzy'.

Campbell, the BBC and the Iraq war

The events of 11 September 2001, marked by the searing television pictures of aircraft deliberately flying into the twin towers of the World Trade Center in New York, irrevocably altered the development of Blair's second term. His support for the Bush administration in the subsequent 'war on terror' led to British military involvement in two foreign conflicts: first in Afghanistan in late 2001 to remove the Taliban regime which had given succour to Osama Bin Laden and his al-Qaeda terrorist network and then, more controversially, in Iraq in 2003 to find and destroy Saddam Hussein's weapons of mass destruction.

The major focus of news management during Blair's second term centred on the war in Iraq (O'Shaughnessy, 2004: 210–37). During the prolonged run-up to the outbreak of hostilities in the spring of 2003 the government used the news media to put across its case, albeit with mixed success in terms of influencing public opinion regarding the legitimacy of military action in the absence of a second United Nations resolution. During the pre-war phase, the war itself and the weeks immediately following the downfall of the Saddam Hussein regime, Downing Street pursued a bitter campaign against the BBC regarding the Corporation's alleged anti-government bias on the issue of Iraq. The breakdown in the relationship between Number Ten and the Corporation finally came to a head over allegations made in late May on the Radio 4 *Today* programme by its defence and diplomatic correspondent, Andrew Gilligan, that the government had knowingly misinformed the public in presenting the case for war. This broadcast, which indirectly led a few weeks later to the suicide of the government scientist and former weapons inspector, Dr David Kelly, was at the heart of the inquiry led by Lord Hutton into the circumstances surrounding Kelly's death. The Hutton Report published at the start of 2004 (Hutton, 2004) exculpated the government from responsibility and instead directed its fire at the BBC. Its publication was swiftly followed by the resignation of the Chairman of the BBC Board of Governors, Gavyn Davies, the Director General, Greg Dyke, and Gilligan himself.

In any evaluation of the New Labour government's handling of the news media over the Iraq war it must be remembered that all governments in democratic societies are particularly sensitive to news coverage during periods when their country is engaged in armed conflict and the lives of military personnel are at risk. In such a situation the role of the media in the accompanying propaganda war is inevitably subject to critical scrutiny from across society and the political spectrum. In a liberal democracy the news media have a responsibility to inform their audiences about the stakes involved in war and to hold the government to account for its decisions: these are part of the public sphere functions of information provision and 'watchdog' which the media routinely perform in their 'fourth estate' role.

There is a tendency, however, for governments to believe that at

times of military conflict the media should fulfil the function of mobilizing public opinion in support of the official policy: the tabloid
newspapers' 'back our boys' approach. In particular, the myth that
television coverage was responsible for undermining the US position
during the Vietnam war in the 1960s and 1970s (Hallin, 1986) has
reinforced the perceived importance for the authorities of the media
being kept 'onside' during such politically sensitive periods. This was
perfectly illustrated during the Falklands conflict in 1982, when
certain programmes on the BBC, which sought to be even-handed in
their coverage of the official British and Argentinian positions regarding the issue of the islands' sovereignty and the conduct of the ensuing military conflict, were severely criticized by Prime Minister
Thatcher and her Conservative supporters (Harris, 1983).
Broadcasters' notions of balance and impartiality, which are normally
used to underpin news coverage and thus avoid charges of deliberate
partisan bias, may be seen as irrelevant or even damaging when
applied to coverage of a military conflict in which the nation's armed
forces are involved. Broadcasters know, therefore, that in these
circumstances they have to be especially sensitive to the construction
of the news agenda and the framing of stories.

The war in Iraq brought these concerns to the surface in a particularly acute fashion for the New Labour government and the main
public service broadcaster in Britain. While in the run-up to the war
public opinion was fairly evenly split, the intensity of feeling in the
opposition camp was clearly evidenced by the large anti-war demonstrations held across the country, notably on 15 February 2003 when
the 'Stop the War' rally in London represented the biggest demonstration in British history. The mainstream political parties were also
divided, with the Conservatives supporting the government, the
Liberal Democrats opposed to military intervention and the parliamentary Labour party split, with a massive backbench rebellion of
Labour MPs refusing to support the government in the vote on taking
the country to war. There was, in short, no political or popular consensus for the BBC to reflect in its coverage of the issue of Britain's
participation in a war in Iraq.

The government had sought to prepare public opinion for conflict
through the publication of two dossiers designed to support the
government's position regarding Iraq's possession of weapons of
mass destruction (Phythian, 2005). The first and much weightier
dossier, published in September 2002, argued that Iraq could use
some of its weapons of mass destruction within 45 minutes of an order

being given to deploy them and it was this claim that was given particular prominence in British news media coverage. Jonathan Powell, Head of Policy at Number Ten, sent an e-mail to Campbell during the drafting process in which he asked: 'Alastair – what will be the headline in the *Standard* on day of publication? What do we want it to be?' (Hutton, 2004: 138). In the event the headline could not have been better for the government: '45 Mins From Attack' was the *Evening Standard* front page headline on the day of the dossier's publication. *The Sun* was even more apocalyptic the following day: 'Brits 45 Mins From Doom'. Only the *Daily Mirror* and *The Independent*, both of which were to campaign consistently against the war, were hostile in their coverage (Humphreys, 2005: 163).

The September dossier became the subject of particularly intense scrutiny after end of the war was declared as a result of the infamous two-way exchange between Gilligan and John Humphrys on the *Today* programme at just after 6 am on 29 May 2003, during which the government was accused by Gilligan of having 'sexed up' the dossier. Gilligan's assertion further fuelled Campbell's running feud with the BBC. During the war the relationship between the government and the Corporation had been strained to near breaking point over the latter's coverage of the build-up to the conflict in Iraq and of the war itself. Campbell had written to the BBC's Director of News, Richard Sambrook, on several occasions to complain that the BBC's coverage was skewed – '12 separate complaints before that which he sent on Gilligan' (Lloyd, 2004: 80). Blair himself wrote to both the Corporation's director general and chairman of the board of governors to complain that the BBC had gone too far and that 'he had been shocked by some of the editorializing of our [BBC] interviewers and reporters' (Dyke, 2004: 253).

In terms of his relationship with the BBC Campbell had what in police circles would be called 'form', going public on more than one occasion in criticizing the political output of the BBC, especially its elite radio programmes such as *Today* and *The World at One*. One of the Blair government's favourite means of refusing to engage with broadcasting journalists in the hope of killing off a story had been to decline to provide a spokesperson for interview – a tactic employed, for example, on the elite late evening television news programme, *Newsnight*. On one occasion the programme went so far as to display an empty chair in the studio, with presenter Jeremy Paxman complaining that 'no ministerial bottom' could be found to fill it (Rawnsley, 2000: 101). Campbell's criticisms of BBC reporting were particularly in evidence when Britain was engaged in a military conflict. During the Kosovo crisis in 1999, for instance, he had criticized the reporting from the Serb capital Belgrade of the BBC's foreign correspondent, John Simpson. Campbell's views had been given to the political editor of *The Times*, Philip Webster, and they formed part of a front page story in which 'senior government officials accused [Simpson] of . . . swallowing Serb propaganda' (Oborne and Walters, 2004: 255). During the war in Afghanistan Campbell had also complained about some of the reporting of the BBC correspondent Rageh Omaar as being too sympathetic to the Taliban regime, after the reporter had spoken of 'an alleged blunder by Allied bombers which, according to the Taliban, had caused civilian casualties' (ibid.: 281).

In the immediate aftermath of the overthrow of the Iraqi regime of Saddam Hussein, the government entered into a highly public conflict with the BBC over aspects of the Corporation's reporting of the official case for going to war. In particular, Campbell called on BBC management to apologize for Gilligan's broadcast comments, seeking to throw the Corporation on to the defensive and regain the initiative in the process of framing the story about the conflict in the Gulf. While the government may have chosen to hit out at the BBC in an attempt to divert attention away from other war-related issues, such as the controversy surrounding the failure to find weapons of mass destruction in Iraq, there is little doubt that the government's anger with the Corporation was real and that, in showing its ire in public, one of its aims was to send a warning shot across the BBC's bows. In the eyes of the government the BBC's coverage revealed an abuse of media power.

The Hutton Inquiry

The increasingly conflictual relationship between Campbell and the BBC did not cease with the formal end of hostilities in Iraq. Instead it was to flare up dramatically following the Humphrys/Gilligan *Today* interview and an article a few days later written by Gilligan for *The Mail on Sunday* in which Campbell was accused – this time by name – of having exceeded his presentational remit in the construction of the September dossier. Campbell used his appearance at a meeting of the Foreign Affairs Committee (FAC) on 25 June to launch an attack on BBC journalism, and followed this up on 27 June with an impromptu, highly agitated appearance on *Channel 4 News*. The FAC subsequently cleared Campbell of substantively altering the dossier, but only on the casting vote of the chair, with the committee simply dividing on partisan lines in the relevant votes (Kaye, 2005: 178). It is an open question as to how the relationship between the government and the BBC would have evolved over the summer of 2003 if events had unfolded differently. The suicide in July of Dr Kelly, who had emerged as the source for Gilligan's critical assertions, ensured that the September dossier, the government's case for war and the standards of BBC journalism remained firmly in the news for the following six months.

On 18 July 2003 the government requested Lord Hutton to conduct an investigation into the circumstances surrounding the death of Dr Kelly. The Inquiry was played out as a piece of political theatre during the late summer and autumn, with apparently all the key *dramatis personae* including the Prime Minister appearing before Lord Hutton to give evidence. The proceedings of the Inquiry were published in full on the internet, almost in real time. With evidence from e-mail exchanges, personal diary entries and witness statements, the proceedings laid bare the decision-making procedures at the heart of the Blair administration, as well as the editorial procedures at the BBC.

With regard to the issue of the preparation of the September dossier, Hutton exonerated Campbell from the 'sexing up' charge where 'sexed up' was defined by Hutton as embellishing 'with items of intelligence known or believed to be false or unreliable to make the case against Saddam Hussein stronger' (what one might call substantive sexing-up) rather than an alternative weaker interpretation of the term to suggest that 'the dossier was drafted in such a way as to make the case against Saddam Hussein as strong as the intelligence contained in it permitted' (presentational sexing up). With regard to the conduct of the BBC, Hutton was damning. Gilligan's allegations on the *Today* programme were deemed to be 'unfounded'; the BBC's editorial system was 'defective'; BBC management was at fault 'in failing to investigate properly the Government's complaints' regarding the Gilligan broadcast; and the Governors were criticized 'for themselves failing to make more detailed investigations into whether this allegation reported by Mr Gilligan was properly supported by his notes and for failing to give proper and adequate consideration to whether the BBC should publicly acknowledge that this very grave allegation should not have been broadcast' (Hutton, 2004: 212–14).

The Hutton Report was much criticized at the time of its publication for having delivered a 'whitewash' pro-government verdict (Doig, 2005: 120). One of the sternest critics, not surprisingly, was Dyke who devotes a significant chunk of his autobiography to a critique of Hutton: 'it was Lord Hutton, not the BBC, who got it fundamentally wrong' (Dyke, 2004: 287). Among other things, Dyke condemns Hutton's narrow interpretation of his terms of reference; the Inquiry's failure to call Kevin Marsh, the editor of the *Today* programme as a key witness; the report's blanket condemnation of the BBC's editorial procedures; and its selective interpretation of the evidence (ibid.: 287–317). For others, however, the main culprit was Gilligan and his flawed report of 29 May (Glees, 2005: 145–52). For example, in an excoriating attack on the culture of the media in contemporary Britain, Lloyd argues that Gilligan's broadcast was 'carelessly done' and that 'it was a grave charge, but it was lightly made (Lloyd, 2004: 6 and 7).

Others try to steer a course in between these two opposing views. Kaye argues that '[t]he specific allegation of the BBC broadcast that the government included, or even fabricated, evidence in the dossier against the wishes of the Joint Intelligence Committee was demonstrably false. The wider belief, that the dossier had included unreliable claims against the advice of some members of the intelligence community, seemed to have been borne out. This, and the removal of caveats, clarifications and qualifications, would, for many, amply justify the sobriquet "sexed up".' (Kaye, 2005: 185). In similar vein, the director of BBC News contends that 'we [i.e. the BBC] got some things right and we got one big thing wrong' (Sambrook, 2004: 12).

Certainly the official position of the BBC in the aftermath of Hutton was that mistakes had been made inside the Corporation, notably by Gilligan in the wording of his report: 'a core script was properly prepared and cleared in line with normal production practices in place at the time, but was then not followed by Andrew Gilligan' (Neil Review, 2004: 26). An internal review headed by Ronald Neil, former director of BBC News and Current Affairs, made a variety of recommendations regarding the handling of external complaints, the appropriateness of 'live' two-ways in breaking stories containing serious or potentially defamatory allegations and the usage of material supplied by anonymous single sources. In the run-up to the debate on the renewal of its Charter, it was clear that the BBC was determined not just to put its house in order, but to be seen clearly to be doing so.

The New Labour government and news management post-Campbell

The system of lobby briefings lost much of its mystique after Blair acceded to the premiership. Though the televising of its proceedings continued to be rejected on the grounds that this would give too much publicity to the PMOS, briefings were now carried out on an on-the-record basis and, from March 2000, a selective summary of the briefing has been made available on a government website (http://www.number-10.gov.uk). Yet these initiatives were woefully inadequate in addressing a growing critique of New Labour's news management techniques, and in particular the charge that this was a government obsessed with 'spin'.

In 2002, dissatisfied with much news coverage and conscious of the counter-productive nature of its reputation for 'spin', New Labour introduced a reform of the lobby briefings, opening up the morning sessions to a wider cross-section of journalists, including specialist and foreign correspondents. The Prime Minister also started to hold monthly press conferences. These were 'on the record, televised, accessible to a much wider range of journalists than the lobby (including overseas journalists) and unrestricted in subject matter' (Seymour-Ure, 2003: 170). The government argued that these American-style reforms were a genuine attempt to be more open with the media and less 'buttoned up' about the next day's headlines. However, according to leading lobby journalists such as Trevor Kavanagh, political editor of *The Sun*, and Adam Boulton, political editor of Sky News, the government's aim was to minimize the disruptive potential of the traditional lobby correspondents who were accustomed to 'grilling' a government spokesperson on a particular issue in comparative secrecy. Some lobby correspondents feared that the new media briefings would become more orchestrated by government, for example through the choice of journalists invited to ask questions and in the lack of opportunity to engage in sustained interrogation, and so give ministers more power to shape the news agenda.

In any event these changes were overtaken by the fallout from the Jo Moore affair: a critical parliamentary investigation into the role of special advisers in government followed by an Independent Review of Government Communications. The Review Group was chaired by Bob Phillis, Chief Executive of the Guardian Media Group and initially consisted of thirteen members, representing communications experience within government, across the media and in advertising and public relations. Its terms of reference were:

to conduct a radical review of government communications. This will
include the examination of different models for organising and managing
the government's communication effort, the effectiveness of the current
model based on the Government Information and Communication
Service, and the roles played by other civil servants, including those
special advisers who have a responsibility for communications. (Phillis,
2004: 1)

The final report of the review was published almost contempora-
neously with that of Lord Hutton in January 2004. The Phillis
Report argued that there had been a three-way breakdown in trust
between government and politicians, the media and the general
public, which had led to popular disillusionment and voter disengagement from the democratic process. In particular, the aggressive
approach of Labour and 'their increased use of selective briefing of
media outlets, in which government information was seen to be
being used to political advantage, led to a reaction from the media
that has produced a far more adversarial relationship with government' (ibid.: 7). On the particular issue of the use of special advisers
by New Labour, the report commented that many of them 'concentrate their limited time on the political reporters in the "lobby" and
on a handful of specialists. . . . this has created an "inner circle" of
reporters who have good access, but a disenfranchised majority who
do not' (ibid.: 10).

Among the twelve specific recommendations of the Phillis Report
was one for a stronger communications structure at the centre, headed
by a new Permanent Secretary, and a clearer definition of the roles of
the Prime Minister's official spokesperson – a Civil Service appointment – and that of his politically appointed Communication Director.
Phillis thus supported two separate but complementary communications teams at the centre of government: one a strong Civil Service-led
communications unit, based in the Cabinet Office, and the second a
well-resourced communications team supporting the Prime Minister,
based at Number 10 and including both civil servants and political
appointees (ibid.: 13). Phillis also recommended that the Prime
Minister's Director of Communication should not have Order in
Council powers that enable special advisers to manage civil servants
(ibid.: 21).

With regard to the system of lobby briefings, Phillis argued that
the system was no longer working for either the government or the
media, with ministers and officials complaining about media distortion and deliberate misrepresentation while journalists complained

about information 'being used as the currency in a system of favouritism, selective release and partisan spinning' (ibid.: 25). Phillis recommended that the lobby briefings should be televised, with full transcripts made available promptly online and with proceedings webcast. The Review also recommended that goverment ministers should play a bigger part in the daily briefings rather than official spokespersons, thus bringing the daily meetings 'closer to the model of the Prime Minister's monthly press briefings' (ibid.: 26).

Blair had already accepted the break-up of Campbell's role into its constituent parts when Phillis had published an interim report in September 2003, just a few weeks after Campbell's resignation. Because of the special nature of the relationship Campbell had enjoyed with Blair, nobody could in any case have convincingly stepped into the former's shoes once he had left. In that sense the style of New Labour media management after Campbell was always going to be different. In addition, however, the circumstances surrounding Campbell's departure and the widespread feeling that he had become too public and controversial a figure meant that the debate about his succession was not just confined to a question of individuals but also covered appropriate structures, norms and procedures. Campbell's replacement in the new slimmed down post of Director of Communication at Number 10 was David Hill, who had previously been head of communications at Labour party headquarters. Hill was regarded as a dedicated and intelligent professional, trusted by journalists, and a less keen advocate of pre-emptive 'spin' than his predecessor. However, he was also seen as not nearly so close to Blair.

The bigger question is whether the structural changes proposed by Phillis make sense. While the recommendations in reaction to the perceived excesses of the Campbell era are understandable, some have argued that the distinction between partisan and non-partisan information is fundamentally flawed. Sir Bernard Ingham, for example, contends that it is possible to have only one spokesperson at Number 10, either a civil servant or a party political appointee. Gaber not only agrees with this criticism, but also argues that the Phillis recommendations simply strengthen the communication power of Downing Street: 'Phillis has based many of its recommendations on the unsustainable assumption that this Government's communication effort is weak and uncoordinated and that the remedy lies in the path of greater centralisation' (Gaber, 2003).

Conclusion

In its news management activities, the government is routinely involved in both the restriction and promotion of information. Since it enjoys privileged access as an official source and can provide important information subsidies to political journalists, the government may reasonably hope to act as a 'primary definer' for the news media. However, the power of ministers and their advisers to shape the news agenda and frame issues is frequently constrained by divisions at the heart of the executive, competition from other institutional sources and the critical, even oppositional, stance adopted by some media outlets. The power relationship between the government and news media, therefore, is based not so much on top-down control, but rather on mutual dependence. This incorporates elements of cooperation, negotiation and bargaining as ministers and advisers engage in strategic and tactical deals with media actors – proprietors, editors and journalists – in an exchange of resources, with no advance guarantee of success.

8

Parties, Pressure Groups and the Media

The central role played by the news media in the process of political communication ensures that a range of political actors seek to use them for their own ends: to communicate with the public, recruit members, mobilize support, raise issues on the political agenda and influence policy-making. As a result, contemporary British politics is heavily influenced by the promotional culture of a 'public relations democracy' (Davis, 2002). The objective of this chapter is to examine key features of the inter-relationship between the news media and two sets of political actors: parties, traditionally seen as aggregators of interests in electoral politics, and pressure groups, which represent and articulate more segmented interests.

The media and political parties

This section examines two aspects of the interdependence between political parties and the media. The first is the professionalization of parties' political communication activities. The second is the changing nature of national newspaper partisanship.

The professionalization of parties' political communication activities

The professionalization of political advocacy was highlighted by Blumler and Gurevitch in the mid-1990s as 'arguably the most formative development in the political communication process of present-day democracies' (Blumler and Gurevitch, 1995: 207). In the case of political parties this phenomenon – also described in terms of 'packaging politics' (Franklin, 1994), 'designer politics'

(Scammell, 1995) and 'the new marketing of politics' (Kavanagh, 1995) – was originally confined to the short period of election campaigns. However, with electoral popularity now measured on a constant basis via opinion polls, the main political parties have become involved in a permanent campaign involving image projection, news management and strategies of symbolic construction. The following analysis covers three features of this professionalization of parties' public communication activities: the mediatization of political leadership, the portrayal of party unity and the adoption of political marketing techniques.

The mediatization of political leadership

Television in particular has a tendency to personalize political debate and its prominence as a medium of political communication has helped elevate the status of party leaders at the expense of their immediate colleagues. This is the phenomenon Foley calls 'leadership stretch'; that is, the way that 'party leaders have increasingly stretched away from their senior colleagues in terms of media attention and popular awareness' (Foley, 2000: 205). The mediatization of political leadership requires parties to have a single designated leadership figure. The Social Democratic–Liberal Alliance had real difficulty in the late 1980s with their dual leadership of David Owen and David Steel, since the news media were always prone to look for any expression of difference between the two and play this up as evidence of conflict at the top. The lack of a single leader of the Green party detracted from its public communication activities, since it was not always clear who spoke authoritatively on behalf of the organization.

Some adaptations by leaders to the age of mediatized politics are largely matters of presentation: from the correct tone of voice to appropriate style of dress. For instance, when Thatcher took over as leader of the Conservative party in 1975, she was a poor television performer. Tutored by her media guru, Gordon Reece, she learnt to modulate her voice and soften her hair style to come across better on television. Michael Foot, leader of the Labour party in the early 1980s, was pilloried by sections of the pro-Conservative media for his rather unkempt appearance, famously turning up at the Remembrance ceremony at the Cenotaph one year in what was – wrongly – described by sections of the press as a donkey jacket. His successor, Neil Kinnock, kept his hair short and wore dark blue suits to project a statesmanlike look. In general, a leader's capacity to come over well on television is considered an electoral asset for a party, as was recognized by many Labour members who supported Blair in the 1994 leadership contest (Jones, 1995: 157) and by those Conservative activists who backed David Cameron in their party's leadership election in 2005.

More important than a leader's personal telegenic skills is the ability to convey through the media an image of leadership that is consonant with public expectations: the personification of values such as competence, integrity and firmness. Party leaders now spend a considerable amount of time appearing in the media – communicating their policies to the electorate and trying to win over public support. Since symbolically they embody the values of their party, party leaders need to pay close attention to their media image. The description of Thatcher as the 'Iron Lady' conveyed precisely the public image she wished to project as the tough, no-nonsense 'Maggie' willing to 'handbag' her opponents in defence of the national interest abroad (for example, at European summit meetings) and Thatcherite values at home. Yet at times Thatcher also sought to soften her image: for instance, during the 1979 general election campaign she was photographed cuddling a calf on a farm, a photo opportunity skilfully staged to play up the caring side of the Conservative leader. After Blair's election as party leader in 1994 his advisers moved quickly and effectively to shake off the initial representation of him by some media outlets as the Disney character 'Bambi', which they correctly regarded as an electorally damaging label if it were allowed to stick.

Blair was a prime example of highly mediatized leadership. For some politicians and commentators, Blair was instrumental in providing a presidential dimension to Labour in power (Foley, 2000). Whatever the substantive validity of this claim, there is no doubt that in media terms Blair strongly personified New Labour. His high profile leadership style was not confined to election campaigns, nor was the apparent presidentialization of his public role attributable merely to the impact of television on political presentation. Rather, Blair actively and consciously sought to focus media attention on his own role as a strong leader by deliberately associating himself with high-profile policy proposals. For example, in a memo leaked to the media in the spring of 2000, during a period when the government was going through a bad news trough, 'he asked his aides to provide him with "headline grabbing initiatives" on touchstone issues that would change public perceptions of the government' (Butler and Kavanagh, 2002: 27).

Blair tried with considerable success to portray himself as a combination of decisive political leader and everyday family man, and through media management 'to define the private so as to fit a public image' (Seymour-Ure, 2003: 45). This constructed image thus combined both 'formal authority and the ordinary "blokeishness" that is so central to his style' (Finlayson, 2002: 593). During his first term as Prime Minister one commentator argued that a crucial part of the success of Blair's style was 'his capacity to, as it were, "anchor" the public politician in the "normal person" – the necessary posturing and evasions of politics are it seems at least partially redeemed by Blair's capacity to reassert constantly his normal, decent, likeable personality' (Fairclough, 2000: 7).

Blair's highly proactive stance during the war in Kosovo in 1999 and his unflinching 'shoulder to shoulder' support for President Bush's 'war on terror' in the aftermath of the events of 11 September 2001 were eloquent media manifestations of Blair playing the role of international statesman. Television news footage of the Prime Minister talking to British troops on active duty in the Balkans or visiting 'ground zero' in New York can be seen as created media-events where good pictures are the principal object of the exercise. In addition, Blair was not averse to displaying a tough side to his medi-ated persona in statements on domestic policy issues such as crime and anti-social behaviour.

Yet Blair also cultivated a concerned, emotional side to his image, evident when he talked about the 'caring' issues of educa-tion and health as well as his feelings as a father. A complex mix of values, including competence, pragmatism and personal integrity, was fused in a coherent media image where the notion that Blair was a politician the voter could trust was central. The aftermath to the 2003 Iraq war threatened to tarnish this constructed image as Downing Street's role in preparing the case for war was called into question by some media outlets, including most contro-versially the BBC, and the question of whether Blair had know-ingly misled the British public became a topic of public debate. These events were a reminder that the media may help undermine a leader's carefully crafted image just as effectively as they can rein-force it.

For instance, almost exactly a year before the 2001 general elec-tion Blair was slow hand-clapped by sections of the audience as he was giving a speech at the annual conference of the Women's

Institute. Television news coverage that evening showed an obviously embarrassed Prime Minister failing miserably to get his message across to the representatives in the conference centre. The story in the next day's newspapers concentrated not on the government's proposed policy initiatives – the formal substance of the speech, but rather on this very public failure of prime ministerial communication, the resonance of which was hugely amplified by being shown on television. Two years later, stories in the *Spectator* magazine, the *Evening Standard* and *The Mail on Sunday* that Number 10 had intervened to try to enhance the Prime Minister's role at the funeral ceremony for the Queen Mother conveyed the impression of an arrogant Blair trying to hijack the occasion for his own purposes. The fallout from the episode was damaging to the Prime Minister's reputation (Oborne and Walters, 2004: 303–12).

While there is no single template for a successful mediatized image, one which is weak or incoherent, such as that of William Hague as Conservative party leader, is potentially highly damaging. Between the 1997 and 2001 elections Hague projected a confused image: for example, attending the Notting Hill carnival at the start of his leadership conveyed a message of multicultural social inclusiveness which was at odds with the controversial speech in the spring of 2001 where he claimed that a second term of Labour government would turn Britain 'into a foreign land'. While the Conservative leadership claimed that this speech was about Britain's relations with Europe, rather than race, this was not how it was spun by party advisers and subsequently covered in the media (Butler and Kavanagh, 2002: 62). By the end of his four years as party leader, Hague had failed to project a positive, integrated media image. His successor, Iain Duncan-Smith, was no more successful. In his case the problem was not so much a contradictory media image as a non-existent one – which the Conservatives desperately tried to turn to their advantage by labelling their leader 'the quiet man' – to no avail (Lloyd, 2004: 103–6).

It is undeniable that the role of the media in leadership projection has contributed to, though not been the sole cause of, the emergence of a clear 'leadership dimension in contemporary British politics' which 'has established the meaning and value of leadership as a political issue in its own right' (Foley, 2002: 5). For instance, Prime Minister's Question Time in the House of Commons is an occasion for the two main party leaders to go head-to-head in a competitive contest in front of the television cameras, with an edited version of the exchange being served up on the main evening news programmes. Journalists frequently evaluate the performance of the two 'heavy-weights' as they would boxers in a prize fight, determining if either managed to land a 'knockout blow'. More importantly, many substantive policy issues are now presented and interpreted by the media to a significant extent in terms of their impact on the party leader's authority and popularity in opinion polls. The media's unremitting focus on leadership may possibly have created public expectations of 'interventionist or directive leadership' and rendered a more 'consensus-managing collectivist' approach difficult to sustain, especially in the case of the Prime Minister (Seymour-Ure, 2003: 64).

The portrayal of party unity

An important test for the three main party leaders is their ability to control the party so that it presents a picture of unity and fitness for government to the electorate. Instantaneous nationwide coverage of political events by national media outlets underlines the importance of a single coherent party message, and party leaders will go to great lengths to prevent the media from portraying an image of a divided party.

Nowhere is the concern with the image of unity more apparent than at the annual party conferences, which are now rigorously packaged for media consumption (Stanyer, 2001). For McNair, contemporary party conferences have become 'spectacles designed for the maximisation of positive press coverage' (McNair, 2003: 141), a process that he argues began with the Conservatives in the 1980s and which was then taken up by Labour in the 1990s. Media advisers have a considerable input into the staging of the conference, from the colour of the backdrop to the use by speakers of the transparent autocue, the so-called 'sincerity machine'. However, they are not just concerned with presenting the party to the television cameras in as friendly a manner as possible and letting the media get on with reporting the proceedings. They are also proactive in seeking to control media coverage by helping to set the conference agenda and putting a favourable 'spin' on stories, whereby they try to ensure that the official line is played up and any possible dissent played down.

In general, divisions within parties are not just reported, but ruthlessly exploited and amplified as the media feed off intra-party conflict. Dissenters may be given extensive media coverage, as in the case of those Conservative MPs who had the whip withdrawn by the party leadership in 1994–95 over the issue of Europe (Seldon, 1997: 511–2) and of the rebel Labour MP Ken Livingstone when he stood as an Independent candidate for the post of Mayor of London in 2000. After his resignation from the government in 2003 over his opposition to the war in Iraq, Robin Cook was able to put across his forceful and articulate case in various newspaper articles and broadcast interviews. Stories about internal splits, dissension and division conform to news value criteria regarding 'good copy' which are by no means unique to the British media (Hallin and Mancini, 2004: 290; McCurry, 1996: 5). Party conflict is more entertaining and attention-grabbing than party unity. As one leading political editor, Michael White of *The Guardian*, argued:

> I sometimes get a fear that it is impossible to have a civilised and reason-
> able debate about, let us say, the merits of the Euro within a political party
> . . . because people like us cry 'Split'. The reason we cry split is because it
> is one way of getting things into print in an adversarial media culture. The
> word 'split' will get you into a newspaper more quickly than the words
> 'total agreement', so it tends to feed a slightly vicious circle there which
> accentuates even mild disagreement between colleagues. (House of
> Commons Select Committee on Public Administration, 1998: 19)

Journalists argue that coverage of party division is a legitimate part of their news gathering activities. In this way they claim to bring to the attention of the public differences of policy within parties which the leadership of the latter will naturally try to conceal. At the same time, in a highly competitive media environment there may be the commercial temptation to give undue weight to a viewpoint that is held by only a minority of a party. In addition, the desire for superficial balance in a story may push broadcasters to play up the minority viewpoint, 'balancing' a majority-held view with one that has little support. Leaders have to walk a fine line between appearing weak and indecisive in dealing with differences of opinion within the party or of being accused of suppressing dissent through heavy-handed management. Sometimes it must seem a 'no win' situation for party leaders: they are presented either as 'ineffective' (for example, Major) because they cannot impose their authority or as 'control freaks' (for instance, Blair) because of their obsession with imposing a united front.

The marketing of parties

The mediatization of leadership and the portrayal of unity may be combined with a third feature of party behaviour: the adoption of political marketing strategies, in which the media are implicated even if they are by no means the sole (or even necessarily the most important) factor underpinning this development in party strategy and behaviour (Scammell, 1999). Lees-Marshment argues that parties can broadly adopt three approaches in seeking to win electoral support. The first is that of the Product-Oriented Party, which 'argues for what it stands for and believes in' (Lees-Marshment, 2001: 28) and does not design its policies (the product) in response to voter concerns (consumers). Voters have to move towards the party, not the other way round. For Lees-Marshment, the Labour party in the early 1980s was a classic example of a Product-Oriented Party (ibid.:120–31).

The second approach is that of the Sales-Oriented Party, which 'focuses on selling its argument to voters' (ibid.: 29). A Sales-Oriented Party focuses on presentation and communication as it strives to persuade the electorate of the strengths of its product. In this approach the professionalization of communications activities can be quite marked, as with Labour in the 1987 general election. The product itself, however, remains largely unaltered.

The third approach is that of the Market-Oriented Party, which 'designs its behaviour to provide voter satisfaction' (ibid.: 30). A Market-Oriented Party is prepared to change the product and not just its presentation or packaging to achieve electoral success. For Lees-Marshment, the Conservatives under Thatcher, first in opposition and then in government, were pioneers in the British context in applying the techniques of political marketing to the party's product, at least until the final years of her premiership (ibid.: 49–94). The author argues that the classic Market-Oriented Party was New Labour in opposition under Blair in the run-up to the 1997 general election victory (ibid.: 181–210).

What then were the key changes in the professionalization of the Labour party's approach to political communication from the early 1980s up to 1997? The process began during Neil Kinnock's leadership (Shaw, 1994). The 1983 general election campaign and the landslide defeat acted as a wake-up call for the party. After 1983 the Labour party determined to embrace a positive approach to political communication as part of a broader process of modernization. It entered the era of political marketing (Wring, 2005a), incorporating into its policy manifesto a 'strategic concern with what the market (electorate) wants and what it will bear' (Scammell, 1995: 8). A key figure on the communications side was the party's Director of

Campaigns and Communications, Peter Mandelson, who master-minded Labour's professionally presented 1987 election campaign which saw the party's image projection move in the space of a few years from 'red flag' to 'red rose'.

Yet despite media-friendly campaigns in 1987 and 1992, Labour under Kinnock was unable to make the final breakthrough and win power. The party's fourth consecutive general election defeat in 1992 seemed convincing evidence that the changes in presentation intro-duced since the mid-1980s were insufficient to mobilize many voters who remained sceptical of Labour: the transition from a Product-Oriented to a Sales-Oriented Party was not sufficient. There was a recognition that some policies could not be sold to the electorate, however they were presented in communication terms; skilful pack-aging could not disguise what a majority of the electorate consistently regarded as an unattractive product. For example, attempts by the Labour party in the 1980s to persuade the electorate of the merits of its unilateralist nuclear defence policy were unsuccessful, not because the audience misunderstood the message but because a majority of them rejected it. The electoral failures of Labour up to and including the 1992 campaign illustrate that image projection goes beyond simply good advertising and public relations to embrace marketing and branding.

The professionalism of New Labour's news management activities after Blair took over the party leadership in 1994 culminated in the 1997 general election landslide (Esser, Reinemann and Fan, 2000). New Labour's success with the media was much commented on, not least by political journalists who contrasted it with the failed efforts of the Conservatives during the Major premiership (Johnson, 1999; Jones, 1995, 1999 and 2002; Oborne, 1999). More importantly, this professionalization of communication activities formed an integral part of a broader process of party reform which embraced ideological repositioning, new policy proposals, a rebranding of Labour's image and internal constitutional change to strengthen the power of the lead-ership (Heffernan and Marqusee, 1992; Hughes and Wintour, 1990; Shaw, 1994; Wring, 2005a). For instance, Blair built on reforms intro-duced by his immediate predecessors to strengthen the power of an inner core party elite based around the dominant position of the party leader to make policy and take charge of the party's strategic commu-nications with the media. This leadership core argued that policy formulation and communication were not distinct activities but had to be dealt with in an integrated fashion.

Changes in organization to improve the party's communication with the electorate were accompanied by a cultural shift whereby such activities were regarded as central to the way in which New Labour functioned: the Millbank model. The successful rebranding of Labour was illustrated in the change of name to 'New Labour' as an appropriate label to describe the reconciliation of the party's core values with the needs of a modern society and economy. From this marketing perspective, media management activities go beyond trying to obtain favourable coverage on isolated issues or even dominating the news agenda. More fundamentally, the Labour party sought to use the media to promote the 'New Labour' brand in the electoral marketplace, just as private companies such as Nike and Benetton do in the commercial sphere (Klein, 2000). As Prime Minister, Blair emulated practices from the commercial model of 'relationship marketing' that 'emphasises sustained interaction between producer and consumer' (Needham, 2005: 347) in his efforts to maintain an effective leadership brand and retain voter loyalty during the period between elections. In an electoral marketplace where brand integrity is regarded as crucial, the great fear is that the brand may take on negative associations and so become 'contaminated', as the party's marketing guru, Philip Gould, contended New Labour's had become in the summer of 2000.

Supporters of the marketing approach to political competition argue from a business analogy: if a product is not selling and no amount of changes in the packaging can persuade consumers to buy, then a commercial company would examine the product and make appropriate modifications. The modernization of Labour after 1983 certainly involved substantial policy changes as well as improvements in presentation. This process was largely electorally driven (Scammell, 1999: 735) and one aspect of the media's role was to act as a conduit between the electorate and the party, for example reflecting the unpopularity of certain policy proposals. In this the media were just one part of a huge feedback exercise to the party which included its own private polls and focus groups.

Yet it could also be argued that the media did not confine themselves to a neutral transmission function. Some media outlets actively undermined certain policy options, for example by designating them as 'extreme'. This media framing may be reflected in opinion polls, the findings of which are then highlighted by the media to confirm proprietorial views and editorial positions. Proponents of the market-oriented approach tend to take the electorate's views as given and concentrate on the need for party adaptation. It has thus been argued that 'marketing may actually democratise politics by making parties more responsive to voters' wishes and by contributing to the design of more voter-friendly communications' (Scammell, 1999: 738; see also Scammell 2003). Yet in at least some instances the media may play a critical role in forming and even mobilizing public opinion as opposed to simply reflecting it. Critics of the desirability of parties' adopting a marketing approach tend to ascribe considerable significance to the media in the tasks of setting the agenda and framing issues for the electorate. The downside of political marketing may thus include 'the deliberate narrowing of the political agenda, an emphasis on message discipline, repetition of messages rather than engagement in argument and an increasing reliance on negative campaigning' (Scammell, 1999: 739).

Newspaper partisanship

In examining the issue of newspaper partisanship, the model first outlined by Seymour-Ure in the 1970s remains a useful starting point. He argues that the connection between individual parties and newspapers can be measured by reference to three characteristics of parties: (i) organization; (ii) goals (programmes and tactics); and (iii) members and supporters. A newspaper is defined as 'paralleling' a party if it is closely linked to that party by organization, loyalty to party goals and the party allegiances of its readers (Seymour-Ure, 1974: 160 and 173).

Applying this model to national newspapers in contemporary Britain, it is clear that none has close organizational links with any of the major parties. The demise in 1964 of the *Daily Herald*, which had retained a formal connection with the Labour party and the Trades Union Congress into the postwar years (ibid.: 161), marked the end of the era of this type of party political press. Nor do newspapers have a readership that is drawn exclusively from supporters of a single political party (see Table 8.1). During the Thatcher premiership, for instance, *The Sun* was read by many Labour voters despite the paper's pro-Conservative stance. The case for national newspapers being politically partisan rests therefore on Seymour-Ure's second variable – the fit between party goals and newspaper content.

Table 8.1 Party preference of daily newspaper readers

Newspaper	Year	Party supported by readers		
		Con %	*Lab* %	*Lib dem* %
Daily Telegraph	2004	61	15	17
	2001	65	16	14
	1997	57	20	17
	1992	72	11	16
Express	2004	41	29	19
	2001	43	33	19
	1997	49	29	16
	1992	67	15	14
Daily Mail	2004	53	21	17
	2001	55	24	17
	1997	49	29	14
	1992	65	15	18
Financial Times	2004	45	23	24
	2001	48	30	21
	1997	48	29	19
	1992	65	17	16
The Times	2004	40	26	29
	2001	40	28	26
	1997	42	28	25
	1992	64	16	19
Sun	2004	31	41	13
	2001	29	52	11
	1997	30	52	12
	1992	45	36	14
Daily Star	2004	17	53	16
	2001	21	56	17
	1997	17	66	12
	1992	31	54	12
Independent	2004	12	36	39
	2001	12	38	44
	1997	16	47	30
	1992	25	37	34
Mirror	2004	15	60	18
	2001	11	71	13
	1997	14	72	11
	1992	20	64	14
Guardian	2004	5	44	37
	2001	6	52	34
	1997	8	67	22
	1992	15	55	24

Sources: Data from Scammell and Harrop, 1997: 161; 2002: 180; 2005: 139.

A pro-Conservative press: 1945–92

It is not so much the links between any *individual* newspaper title and a particular party that have traditionally provoked controversy, as the extent of parallelism between the national press *as a whole* and electoral support across the party system. There is widespread acceptance in a free market of the inevitability and even desirability of newspaper titles openly proclaiming their support for a specific political party. In contrast, the imbalance between newspaper partisanship across the range of national titles on the one hand and the spread of public opinion as measured by electoral behaviour on the other has often been a cause of concern, especially to Labour supporters.

This was because for much of the postwar period there was a relative lack of newspaper support for Labour and an over-representation of pro-Conservative views (though it is also worth noting that the Liberal Democrats have suffered even more than the Labour party from the skewed nature of newspaper partisanship) (see Table 8.2). Prior to the 1997 contest, at every postwar general election a higher percentage of national newspapers (as measured by circulation figures) than voters supported the Conservative party. This situation became particularly acute following the switch of *The Sun* to supporting the Conservatives in 1974. By 1987 'the Conservative Party had the support of 72 per cent of national daily circulation but only 43 per cent of the vote' (Curran and Seaton, 1991: 124), while in the 1992 contest the figures were 64 per cent and 42 per cent respectively (Seymour-Ure 1996: 219).

Moreover, throughout the Thatcher premiership the majority of national newspapers were strongly, indeed stridently, supportive of the government's policy mix of economic neo-liberalism and social populism (Gamble, 1988; Goodman 1990: 3), especially at critical moments such as the Falklands conflict and the miners' strike and on major reforms such as trade union legislation and privatization. The *intensity* of partisanship, especially among the tabloids, was thus a notable feature of newspaper coverage during the 1980s (Seymour-Ure, 1992: 52). So too was the tabloid emphasis on negative stories and 'knocking copy'. For example, the most infamous headline of the 1992 general election campaign appeared in *The Sun* on polling day. It showed the Labour leader's head in a light bulb with the caption: 'If Kinnock wins today will the last person to leave Britain please turn out the lights'.

The sympathy of most of the national press towards the

Table 8.2   Newspaper partisanship at general elections 1945–2005

	Conservative		Labour		Liberal	
	% circulation	% votes	% circulation	% votes	% circulation	% votes
1945	52	40	35	48	13	9
1950	50	43	50	46	10	9
1951	52	48	39	49	10	2
1955	52	50	40	46	9	3
1959	54	49	38	44	9	6
1964	57	43	42	44	–	11
1966	55	42	42	48	3	8
1970	57	46	43	43	5	7
1974	71	38	32	37	5	19
1974	69	36	50	39	26	18
1979	67	44	27	37	–	14
1983	78	42	22	28	–	25
1987	74	42	26	31	2	23
1992	64	42	27	34	5	18
1997	33	31	62	44	–	17
2001	26	32	74	41	–	18
2005	41	33	54	36	2	23

Note: Circulation percentages include papers with divided support. Percentages may therefore add up to more than 100.
Sources: Data from Seymour-Ure, 1996: 218–19; 1997: 82–3; and author's own figures for 2001 and 2005.

Conservative party continued during the early period of the Major premiership. Soon after the 1992 election, however, the relationship between the Major government and much of the traditional Conservative press disintegrated. Indeed, a striking feature of national newspaper content between 1992 and 1997 was the way in which several traditionally pro-Conservative papers (such as the *Daily Mail*, *The Sun*, *The Times*, *The Sunday Times* and the two *Telegraph* titles) launched a frequently vicious offensive against what were presented as failures of government policy and the allegedly ineffectual leadership of the Prime Minister. Much of the national press in the early 1990s was not so much functioning as a conduit for the views of the Labour and Liberal Democrat parties as adopting its own pro-active oppositional stance to Major's premiership (Jay, 1994; Jones, 1995: 91–121, 189–219; Seldon, 1997: 708).

Blair's New Labour party and newspaper partisanship

The disenchantment of many newspapers with the Conservatives opened up the possibility of a realignment of newspaper support in favour of the Labour party. Neutralizing traditional press opponents or, even better, bringing them round to supporting the New Labour project were more realistic options for the party leadership than hoping for the entry of new pro-Labour papers into the market. An attempt to launch a popular pro-Labour paper in the late 1980s, for example, had combined elements of tragedy and farce, with the *News on Sunday* closing after the publication of only a few issues (Chippindale and Horrie, 1988).

In the run-up to the 1997 general election New Labour was incredibly successful in disarming the guns of the Tory press and even winning some national newspapers over to its cause. In addition to disillusionment with the perceived failures of the Major premiership, four factors help to explain the apparently remarkable change in newspaper partisanship between the 1992 and 1997 elections (McNair, 2000: 146–55). First, Labour's ideological repositioning to appeal to the electoral centre ground made it a more acceptable alternative party of government for some newspaper proprietors and editors. As a result, little remained of the 'loony Left' type story which had been such a feature of tabloid coverage in the 1980s (Curran, Gaber and Petley, 2005). Moreover, Blair personally was regarded as a strong and effective leader who was playing a key part in strengthening the party's appeal to the electorate of 'Middle England'. Murdoch's former editor of *The Sunday Times*, Andrew Neil, argues that 'Blair was saying many of the right neo-Thatcherite things on the economy, tax, the family and welfare' (Neil, 1997: xxii). On the first anniversary of Blair's election as party leader, *The Sun* editorial wrote that 'he has vision, he has purpose and he speaks our language on morality and family life' (21 July 1995). This combination of forceful leadership in the service of ideological moderation was a winning combination in the eyes of many newspaper proprietors and editors.

Second, under Blair's leadership New Labour in opposition actively set out to curry favour with sections of the national press, especially the Murdoch papers (Hagerty, 2000: 15; Johnson, 1998; Neil, 1997). This was in marked contrast to the late 1980s when Labour boycotted News International titles following the company's prolonged dispute with its workforce over the introduction of new technology. As part of the charm offensive, Blair flew halfway around the world to give a speech to News International executives. In addition, New Labour seemed prepared not to attack the commercial power of leading media companies. For instance, speculation was rife that in return for support from Murdoch's newspapers, an incoming Labour government would not introduce tough cross-media ownership legislation. While there may not have been an explicit deal between Murdoch and Blair that *The Sun* would support Labour 'in return for promises that a Labour government would leave Rupert's British media empire alone' (Neil, 1997: xxv), at the very least a tacit understanding emerged between Blair and Murdoch on this issue.

Third, a more sophisticated approach to news management ensured that New Labour's attacks on Conservative government policy were skilfully prepared for journalists across a whole range of issues. These included the running of the Health Service, rail privatization, the huge salary increases and perks of the heads of private utilities, and the Conservative government's record on tax and sleaze.

Finally, as New Labour's electoral fortunes improved and opinion polls showed them pulling well ahead of the Conservatives, newspapers had good commercial reasons for modifying their attitudes towards the party so as to stay in tune with the views of their readers. In a competitive market, refusing to support a popular party in newspaper columns would have done little to boost circulation figures among voters, many of whom were eager for a change of government.

The 1997 election campaign witnessed an apparent sea-change in the partisan allegiances of several leading newspapers (Scammell and Harrop, 1997). Overall six out of ten national dailies supported Labour in 1997, compared with only three out of eleven in 1992 (see Table 8.3). So too did five of the nine national Sunday titles, as against a mere three five years earlier (see Table 8.4). Indeed, 'the support in 1997 placed Labour for the first time in a position of disproportionately high circulation compared to its share of the vote: 62% of circulation and 44% of the vote, compared with the Conservatives' 33% of circulation and 31% of the vote' (Seymour-Ure, 1997: 80–1). The single most important contributory factor to this change was the decision by *The Sun* to overturn more than twenty years of pro-Conservative sympathies and move straight across into the pro-Labour camp. Because of its huge circulation and its unbridled hostility to Labour since the mid-1970s, the support for New Labour expressed by *The Sun* in 1997 had immense symbolic significance, even if its impact on voting behaviour was negligible (see Chapter 9).

Table 8.3   National daily newspaper partisanship by title

Newspaper	Year	Party support
Sun	2005	Labour
	2001	Labour
	1997	Labour
	1992	Conservative
Mirror	2005	Labour
	2001	Labour
	1997	Labour
	1992	Labour
Mail	2005	Not a Labour victory
	2001	Conservative
	1997	Conservative
	1992	Conservative
Express	2005	Conservative
	2001	Labour
	1997	Conservative
	1992	Conservative
Star	2005	No preference declared
	2001	Labour
	1997	Labour
	1992	Conservative
Telegraph	2005	Conservative
	2001	Conservative
	1997	Conservative
	1992	Conservative
Times	2005	Labour
	2001	Labour
	1997	Eurosceptic
	1992	Conservative
Guardian	2005	Labour
	2001	Qualified Labour
	1997	Labour
	1992	Qualified Labour
Independent	2005	More Liberal Democrats
	2001	Not Conservative
	1997	Labour
	1992	Independent
Financial Times	2005	Labour
	2001	Labour
	1997	Labour
	1992	Labour

Sources: Data from Newton 1993: 153; Scammell and Harrop, 1997: 157–8;
2002: 158–9; 2005: 120–1.

220

Table 8.4   National Sunday newspaper partisanship by title

Newspaper	Year	Party support
News of the World	2005	Labour
	2001	Labour
	1997	Labour
	1992	Conservative
Sunday Mirror	2005	Labour
	2001	Labour
	1997	Labour
	1992	Labour
Sunday People	2005	Labour
	2001	Labour
	1997	Labour
	1992	Labour
Mail on Sunday	2005	Not Labour
	2001	Conservative
	1997	Conservative
	1992	Conservative
Sunday Express	2005	Conservative
	2001	Labour
	1997	Conservative
	1992	Conservative
Sunday Telegraph	2005	Conservative
	2001	Conservative
	1997	Conservative
	1992	Conservative
Sunday Times	2005	Conservative
	2001	Labour
	1997	Conservative
	1992	Conservative
Observer	2005	Labour
	2001	Qualified Labour
	1997	Qualified Labour
	1992	Labour
Independent on Sunday	2005	Liberal Democrat
	2001	Qualified Labour
	1997	Labour
	1992	Not Conservative
Sunday Business	2005	–
	2001	Labour
	1997	–
	1992	–

Sources: Data from Scammell and Harrop, 1997: 172; 2002: 160; 2005: 121.

Yet the qualitative nature of the shift in newspaper partisanship should not be overstated. *The Sun* was the only national daily that moved straight across from openly supporting the Conservatives in 1992 to calling for a Labour victory five years later. Compared with the altered partisanship of *The Sun*, other changes in daily newspaper support were more modest, as in the case of *The Independent* which moved from an independent stance to supporting Labour. Thus, Deacon *et al*. argue that the 1997 election did not see such a radical change in newspaper partisanship as might appear at first sight. Rather than merely listing the party support of newspapers, they try to evaluate the intensity of partisan commitment as expressed in editorial opinion. They conceive of 'national press editorial opinion as falling at different points on a continuum between the two main parties, rather than categorizing support on an "either/or" basis', with the continuum ranging from staunch Labour at one end through what the authors call 'the corridor of uncertainty' to staunch Conservative at the other. By this assessment, no newspaper title (including *The Sun*) made the complete journey from one end of the continuum to the other between 1992 and 1997. As a result, they conclude that in editorial terms between these two elections, 'press opinion shifted rather than completely reversed' (Deacon, Golding and Billig, 1998: 147):

> Although the majority of editorial opinion, whether measured in terms of titles or readership, backed the Labour party, a large portion of this support was conditional and cautionary in nature. Certainly, while the Tories may have received a bad press from many of their previous cheer-leaders in 1997, in no way can it be said to have approached the level of vitriol heaped on Labour in 1992. Labour's achievement in this election was in decommissioning the big guns of the Tory press rather than in turning their fire on their previous masters. (Ibid.: 148)

They call this phenomenon 'hollow-centred partisanship'. Other commentators also emphasize what they regard as the partisan dealignment rather than realignment of the press in the 1997 election (Scammell and Harrop, 1997: 184). Scammell and Harrop, for example, support their assessment with reference to the critical stance of some traditional pro-Conservative newspapers which opted to continue to support the Conservatives in 1997 through their editorial columns, but were also critical of the leadership and the party's stance on Europe (McKie, 1998: 125; Scammell and Harrop, 1997: 168; Seldon, 1997: 709). Among those papers that supported the

Conservatives, the intensity of support was in general considerably less marked than before. The two *Express* titles, for example, both supported the Conservatives, but 'only tepidly, as if they were giving a speech at a farewell party for someone they disliked' (Seldon, 1997: 713).

Norris goes further in arguing the case for press dealignment (rather than realignment) in the late 1990s. She contends that it is not sufficient just to examine the stated editorial opinions of the newspapers, but that their news coverage, especially front page stories, also needs to be assessed. Her view is that front page stories have become more similar across all the papers, 'driven by news values irrespective of any paper's ostensible partisanship' (Norris, 1998: 123). Political coverage, she argues, is 'now driven more strongly by an autonomous "media logic" in the fierce competition for readers than by traditional allegiances or the proprietor's politics' (ibid.: 124). Thus, in her view partisan dealignment among newspapers is largely the result of media factors as newspapers struggle for readers in a more competitive market.

The partisan dealignment thesis continued to apply to newspaper preferences in the 2001 election campaign. Even more national titles supported Labour than in 1997, giving the impression that press support leant heavily towards Labour to the detriment of the Conservatives (Deacon, Golding and Billig, 2001) (see Tables 8.2, 8.3 and 8.4). However, despite the massive quantitative advantage Labour enjoyed in terms of both number of titles and circulation figures, in qualitative terms newspaper support for Labour during the 2001 campaign 'was generally subdued, often qualified and sometimes critical' (Scammell and Harrop, 2002: 156).

By the time of the 2005 general election, Labour's support in the press had declined, with the two *Express* titles and the *Sunday Times* returning to back the Conservatives. The complexity of newspaper partisanship remained evident with traditional newspaper party loyalties being subjected to strain in the wake of Blair's handling of the Iraq war issue. There was strong evidence of negative partisanship, often expressed in highly personalized terms of anti-Blair (for instance the *Daily Mail*) or anti-Howard (the *Daily Mirror*), while criticism of the Prime Minister by several newspapers did not necessarily persuade them to support the Conservative alternative. In the opinion of one commentator on the 2005 election, press dealignment 'has produced mixed (but largely negative) messages about all the parties' (Bartle, 2005: 706).

The end of newspaper partisanship?

Five features of press partisanship since New Labour first came to power are worthy of emphasis. First, while some national newspapers still tend to have a natural affinity with a particular party (such as the *Mirror* titles for Labour, and the *Mail* and *Telegraph* titles for the Conservatives), partisanship is more *conditional* than in the past. For example, the support given by *The Sun* to the Blair government after 1997, evidenced by the paper again backing Labour in the 2001 and 2005 general elections, cannot be compared with the unconditional adulation the same newspaper accorded the Conservative government and party during the 1980s. Whereas Mrs. Thatcher could largely rely on allegiance from a phalanx of sympathetic press owners and their editors, New Labour has had to bargain hard to obtain newspaper support. It looks likely that all parties in future will have to court newspapers on a continual basis for the latter's sympathy. *The Sun* may have declared that 'the Tory party . . . has passed away. Cause of death: Suicide . . . Like Monty Python's parrot, it has fallen off its perch' (*The Sun*, 6 October 1998). However, it is by no means impossible for the Conservatives to win back the support – albeit conditional – of the Murdoch press in the future.

Second, national newspaper partisanship has become more *volatile*. A newspaper's proclaimed editorial partisanship does not determine the nature or tone of journalistic coverage on a daily basis. For instance, newspapers supportive of New Labour in the 1997 and 2001 campaigns frequently adopted a hostile attitude in their coverage on certain issues and at particular times in the subsequent electoral cycle. A leading media correspondent on *The Times*, for example, pointed to evidence of journalists turning on the party and government at the start of 2000. 'What has been surprising as Blair marked his first thousand days has been *the criticism from the papers that are sympathetic to him*' (MacArthur, 2000, my emphasis). Though by no means a wholly new development in British politics – witness the critical coverage given by the *Daily Mirror* to Labour Prime Minister Harold Wilson in the late 1960s (Pimlott, 1992: 505–6) – for the media-sensitive New Labour leadership newspaper volatility is a particularly unwelcome state of affairs.

Third, partisanship has become more *personalized*. In general, the newspaper support given Blair has been greater than that accorded New Labour as a whole. In the 1997 campaign, for example, *The Sun* was more supportive of Blair than of the Labour party. This personalization of newspaper support is not a wholly new phenomenon. In the 1980s pro-Conservative newspapers were more supportive of Thatcher than of the party; similarly, but in a reverse direction, in the mid-1990s newspapers were frequently more hostile to Major personally than to the Conservatives. 'WHAT FOOLS WE ALL WERE', *The Sun* headlined early in 1994: John Major had 'all the leadership qualities of a lemming' (Seymour-Ure, 1994: 415). This tendency towards distinguishing between the party and its leader, however, became even more marked during the Blair premiership.

Fourth, newspaper support has become more *issue-oriented* than party-based (Seymour-Ure, 1998). For instance, on the issue of British involvement in the war against Iraq in 2003 the *The Mirror* and *The Independent* opposed the war, while *The Sun* and the other Murdoch titles backed Blair's stance. Newspaper positions on the issue of Europe, including the possibility of British adoption of the single European currency, also illustrate the general point about issue partisanship. Of the newspapers that supported Labour in 2001, many were later strongly opposed to the government's policy on the Euro. In circulation terms the pro-Europe newspapers are far outsold by a fiercely Eurosceptic press which has participated actively as advocates against closer European integration in editorial columns, commentary and news coverage (Anderson and Weymouth, 1999; Wilkes and Wring, 1998). *The Sun*, for instance, has remained wary of Labour on the issue of Europe, portraying Blair as 'the most dangerous man in Britain' because of his stance on the single currency (*The Sun*, 24 June 1998) and leading on its front page with the headline 'Blair surrenders Britain to Europe' with regard to his stance on the EU Constitution (*The Sun*, 15 May 2003).

Finally, individual newspaper partisanship has become more *pluralistic* and multi-faceted. Coverage of – and even support for – different political options is now evident within a single newspaper. This phenomenon of internal pluralism is particularly marked among the broadsheets, which have seen 'the decline of the single editorial voice' (Seymour-Ure, 1998: 43). Sometimes this development may be explained with reference to a particular electoral context. For instance, in the London mayoral elections of 2000 *The Mirror* supported the Conservative candidate, calling on its readers to vote Conservative for the first time since 1929, but urged readers beyond London to vote Labour. More generally, broadsheet newspapers have magnified their tendency to incorporate different partisan viewpoints in their political coverage: 'Papers make a virtue out of a variety of opinion. Where they have a party tendency, they license some discordant voices' (ibid.: 47).

This manifestation of internal pluralism is linked to the increased importance of columnist journalism. In providing commentary on events and interpretation of issues, political columnists are less restricted than lobby correspondents or leader writers by hierarchical controls or corporate constraints. The genre of columnist journalism lends itself both to a critical approach and a policy focus (Tunstall, 1996: 281–96). Columnists can engage more easily in a highly personalized, opinionated and literary form of political journalism which does not necessarily conform with the editorial stance of the newspaper. According to one political journalist, during the first Blair government this was the case at *The Times* where

> readers of the top people's paper were presented with a schizophrenic menu. The political news pages endeavoured to place the best possible construction on [Labour] government policy, while on the comment pages Gove, Kaletsky, Rees-Mogg, Parris and others . . . were all capable of placing the worst. (Oborne, 1999: 175)

Tabloid newspapers can also exhibit the same tendency. For example, Richard Littlejohn's forceful column in *The Sun* was often highly critical of Blair's premiership. While this form of internal pluralism is not synonymous with a simple rejection of party political endorsement, it is clear that editorial opinion as expressed in a paper's leader column no longer defines the framework for a newspaper's political coverage as a whole.

The media and pressure groups

Pressure groups are also heavily involved in the promotional culture of mediatized politics. However, unlike the government and the major political parties, which routinely enjoy privileged status as official sources, pressure groups have to plan carefully and work hard to gain media access. This section begins with a survey of some examples of pressure group media activity. Although not designed to be representative in any scientific sense, the examples given illustrate the diversity of pressure groups and some of their contrasting approaches to media relations. This is followed by an analysis of the factors that may influence the process whereby a pressure group secures media access. Finally, we consider whether there is any correlation between a pressure group's media profile and its political influence.

A range of pressure group media activity

One group well-known for its media activities is the environmentalist organization, Greenpeace, which regularly provides stories and images that journalists and television cameras appear to find irresistible. Whether exposing alleged leakages of toxic substances, alerting the public to raw sewage disposal around Britain's coastline or interfering with whale hunting at sea, Greenpeace is a master of the constructed media event, geared to satisfying news value criteria (Hansen, 1993). More generally, Greenpeace has often been able to act as a 'definer' of environmental issues for the news media in the agenda-building process (Anderson, 1997: 161–6), frequently making a major impact on the way in which environmental issues are framed by journalists. The organization's investment in media-related material resources, facilities and staff make it one of the most media-savvy and communications-oriented pressure groups, highly skilled in running professional public relations campaigns at both national and transnational levels.

A highly focused single-issue group which was relatively successful in obtaining favourable media coverage was the Campaign for Lead-free Air (CLEAR), which lobbied in the 1980s to persuade the government to ban the use of lead in petrol (Wilson, 1984). Negrine shows how the director of CLEAR, Des Wilson, established privileged links with some newspapers, especially *The Times*, and used a copy of a letter written by the Chief Medical Officer at the Department of Health and Social Security to help structure the media agenda on the issue (Negrine, 1994: 145–51). Several newspapers, especially the broadsheets, gave the campaign supportive coverage.

A more loosely organized group than either Greenpeace or CLEAR, but one which nonetheless gained considerable favourable publicity in the mid-1990s, was made up of animal welfare protestors campaigning against the export of live veal calves to the continent of Europe (McLeod, 1998). Footage of demonstrations against the lorries carrying the calves at British ports and airports became a regular feature of the nightly television news, while the protest was also carried on the front pages of newspapers. Spokespersons for the protestors were regularly interviewed by the media, and the government was obliged to make a public response on the issue. Media coverage was largely sympathetic to the protestors' cause. The issue was non-party political; the protestors made apparently reasonable arguments in an articulate fashion; the pictures of animals packed together in lorries produced emotive television images; and the issue could be presented within an established media paradigm of a common-sense British viewpoint being contested by a combination of continental farmers and European bureaucrats.

Another media success story was the Snowdrop Appeal which campaigned in favour of tighter gun control in the wake of the Dunblane massacre in 1996 when 16 young pupils and their teacher were killed in a shooting at the local primary school (Thomson, Stancich and Dickson, 1998). Thomson *et al.* argue that the 'role played by the media, in particular the press, was a vital factor in the campaign for tighter gun controls' (ibid.: 338), with the Snowdrop campaign being 'adopted' by sections of the press, especially tabloid newspapers. They argue that there was a reciprocity of interests at work on this occasion: 'the media used the Snowdrop appeal to sell newspapers, but Snowdrop also used the press in order to gain publicity for its campaign' (ibid.: 343).

In contrast to Snowdrop, an organization that is frequently campaigning *against* the dominant framing of issues by the mainstream news media is the civil liberties group, Liberty. This organization not only lacks funds to support intensive media-related activities, but is also faced with the problem that, for example, its concern with the rights of asylum seekers or 'terrorist' suspects frequently does not fit with the newsframes imposed by several proprietors, editors and journalists. According to Smith, in the late 1990s Liberty had set out three strategic priorities to manage its scarce resources: first, no issue surfing – that is, a refusal to spread its message thinly; second, the identification of specific issues on which media coverage would be both obtainable and desirable by taking issues already on the news agenda and emphasizing the human rights aspects; and, third, seeking outlets other than the mainstream media, such as the specialist press (Smith, 1999: 25). Liberty thus concentrated its communication activities in terms of issue selection, message framing and media distribution.

The experience of many trade unions shows how difficult it can be for some pressure groups to gain media access and favourable publicity. Trade unions have desperately sought to improve their relationship with the media since the low point of the 1970s, when they were frequently presented as bearing the responsibility of all Britain's economic and political ills, culminating in the 'Winter of Discontent' of 1978–79 which helped provide a platform for Thatcher's first general election victory. The coal dispute of the mid-1980s illustrated many of the difficulties frequently faced by unions at this time: an overwhelmingly hostile press; a well-resourced government communications operation; an iconic 'media hate figure' in the leader of the National Union of Mineworkers, Arthur Scargill; and a lamentable lack of attention to public relations activities on the part of the union (Jones, 1986).

Since the 1990s trade unions have recognized the need to professionalize their communication activities. Union leaders are trained on how to project a positive image on television and put their case across succinctly and effectively. Trade unions also engage in a range of media-friendly initiatives in an attempt to obtain access and influence the framing of coverage. Partly as a result of accommodative news media strategies, whereby the unions adapt their attitudes, behaviour and organization to meet the needs of the news media, some unions have scored notable 'media successes' in support of their industrial action. These include the 1989 Ambulance dispute in which 'news editors abandoned "the militant public sector" news frame in favour of an approach that highlighted "mercy men" and "angels with blue flashing lights"' (Manning, 1998: 316–57) and the 1997 British Airways dispute where the union managed successfully to 'establish a news framework in which the cabin crews were characterised as the underdogs locked in a battle with a giant corporation behaving like a "nineteenth-century mill owner", bullying workers and denying workplace rights' (Manning, 2001: 181). In contrast, trade unions have been criticized in recent years for their reluctance to make full use of the internet to mobilize support for their campaigns (Ward and Lusoli, 2003).

The corporate sector, including big business and financial institutions, has also developed its public relations activities over a number of years, particularly since the 1980s. Davis argues that its activities are geared to influencing not so much the output of mainstream news to the general public as the content of specialist magazines and news sections that offer business, financial and economic news (Davis, 2002: 45–59). The result is the 'capture' of business news by financial elite news sources, operating within what Davis calls 'closed elite discourse networks', to the exclusion of non-financial elites. These networks can be seen as analogous to 'policy communities' in the general literature on policy-making. In terms of news content:

> business, financial and economic news coverage has been shaped to the
> needs of corporate elites, thus bringing more technical and pro-business

news rather than debate and critical analysis . . . an unchallenged business consensus has developed that promotes policy-making and regulation which naturally supports City institutions, large multinationals and City elites. (Ibid.: 77)

This does not mean that business and financial elites are always successful in influencing the news agenda and the framing of business stories. Despite their organizational and resource power, they are often unable to prevent 'bad news' ranging from financial scandal to the perks of 'fat cats' in mainstream coverage (Tumber, 1993). There are various reasons for this. First, the operationalization of news values makes stories about scandal and corruption attractive to editors and journalists. Second, there has been an increase in consumer issues as newsworthy stories, exemplified in television programmes such as BBC1's *Watchdog* (Manning, 2001: 162). Third, companies are frequently quite poor at mobilizing their resources, often being unable to respond quickly to breaking news because of their top-heavy managerial structures. Finally, businesses are in competition with other sources (including trade unions, environmental groups and consumer associations) in seeking to shape the mainstream news agenda and influence the framing of issue coverage. The distinction between generalist and specialist news outlets/content thus helps to explain the paradox that 'whereas companies are often reported as negative, scandalous and self-interested in mainstream news, they appear positive, respectable and objective in business news' (Davis, 2002: 79).

Pressure group resources

It is clear from even these few examples that the complexity of pressure group interaction with the media makes simple categorization difficult. Certainly, the conventional distinction between promotional groups, which represent some belief or principle and seek to act in the interests of that cause (such as animal welfare), and sectional interest groups, which represent a section of the community and look after its common interests (such as a trade union or professional body), is not particularly useful in an analysis of groups' public relations and communication strategies. Grant's original typology (1989) of insider groups, which enjoy regular access to government, and outsider groups, which are denied such routine access, is potentially more helpful in that the former may influence policy formulation in advance of media publicity and also 'may secure a stronger position in the struggle to primarily define news events' (Manning, 2001: 141). Schlesinger and Tumber give the example of the Law Society as one such 'insider' group in the Home Office, emphasizing its role in helping to shape criminal justice policy (Schlesinger and Tumber, 1994: 62). Yet at the same time, a strategy incorporating a low media profile is now considered old-fashioned by most groups. Several 'insider' groups have shifted to the high profile category, as they have found it necessary 'to try and create a favourable public image to reinforce their contacts with civil servants and politicians' (Grant, 1989: 80).

Deacon proposes yet another distinction: between 'advocates', 'who are seen to represent a particular view or constituency', and 'arbiters', who are used as expert sources 'to assess the views of protagonists in a political debate' (Deacon, 1996: 179). He argues that because they are often defending clear vested interests, trade unions and professional organizations are more likely to appear as 'advocates' in media coverage. Conversely, pressure groups which have no overt party political or professional allegiances benefit from greater flexibility. Deacon gives the example of voluntary organizations which may gain media access as 'advocates', pushing their particular cause, but also as 'arbiters', whose 'practical knowledge of the issues under debate' and 'charitable ideals and credentials were seen to place them above selfish factionalism' (ibid.: 18).

Of the various factors that influence the capacity of a group to gain access as a source for the news media and thereby to increase its chances of obtaining beneficial coverage (Davis, 2002: 173–4), three are particularly important. The first is *economic capital*. This refers to the financial power of a group, whereby significant resources can be allocated to public relations and media-oriented activities. With news media outlets under severe pressure to control costs in a competitive market, journalists have become more dependent on information supplied by sources. Economically well-resourced groups are clearly in a better position than their resource-poor counterparts to provide news-gatherers with 'information subsidies' to help in the compilation of a story. By the standards of protest groups, Greenpeace, for instance, is resource-rich. It can afford to provide the media with well-packaged material, such as video news releases, and maintains a high quality website. In contrast, resource-poor groups may find it difficult to make sufficient investment on a routinized basis to maintain an active presence in a political communications environment of multiple media outlets and competing sources.

The second asset is *media capital*. This refers to the legitimacy, authority and expertise of the group concerned. Many groups may be able to present themselves as reliable and authoritative sources in particular policy fields, such as the Police Federation, the Law Society and the National Association for the Care and Resettlement of Offenders in the related fields of criminal justice and prison reform (Schlesinger and Tumber, 1994: 43–105). Conversely, some groups are regarded by the media as either unrepresentative and/or operating outside the parameters of legitimate socio-political behaviour. For example, the Animal Liberation Front rarely secures mainstream media coverage for its cause, because its methods, including the destruction of property, are generally regarded as extreme. However, the use of violence against property (and even more so against persons) may well secure news coverage for a group through the media's application of routine news values. Groups such as anti-globalization protestors may therefore have to decide between using violence and possibly securing media coverage, albeit critical, or employing peaceful campaigning methods at the risk of securing little or no publicity.

The third factor is a source's *natural affinities with news producers*. Two aspects are noteworthy in this context. The first is bureaucratic compatibility between journalist and source. This refers to the ease with which journalists may practically report sources, influenced by factors such as organizational structures and physical proximity (Davis, 2002: 174). For instance, it is easier for a group to gain access if there are specialist correspondents working in the area of its concerns. Even economically resource-poor groups can foster 'exchange relationships' with journalists, by providing valuable background briefing to a story (Manning, 2001: 178). The second aspect is the group's recognition of what journalists consider to be newsworthy. Events that are likely to have a major impact on the public, such as strike action in a key economic sector, may thrust a group into the media spotlight. A national rail strike, for instance, will guarantee media access to the rail unions. A group may also stage pseudo-events to exploit different media outlets' application of news values, though some stunts may risk diminishing their political credibility. Finally, a group may find it easier to obtain coverage if their area of concern is already an issue on the media agenda, especially if the group can provide a new angle. Relief agencies such as Oxfam depend in large part on media coverage for publicity. The problem they face is that famine and droughts are often not considered sufficiently newsworthy in themselves (Negrine, 1994: 141–2).

No single factor trumps the others. The capacity for a group to gain access to the media is not determined solely by, say, possession of significant economic resources or journalists' recognition of its legitimacy as an authoritative voice on a particular issue. Two further points are worthy of note (Manning, 2001: 151). First, the interaction of these variables produces a highly complex set of possibilities and opportunities for groups in terms of their relations with the media as sources. It is, therefore, quite inappropriate to divide pressure groups into two opposing camps: those with and those without media power. Instead it is more appropriate to view them as occupying positions along a continuum that covers a variety of possible pressure group-news media interdependencies, which themselves are influenced by the interplay of different factors at any particular moment in time. A well-resourced company regarded as possessing legitimacy in its sphere of competence and with a coherent media strategy may still come unstuck in the media management of a particular issue, such as the laying off of staff. Conversely, a poorly resourced group, generally considered as politically marginal, may secure favourable media attention if its activities conform to news values on a specific issue.

Second, the interaction between pressure groups and news media is dynamic rather than static. Pressure groups may become better (or less well) organized and resourced, thereby giving the potential for their media coverage to improve (or deteriorate). Social norms may change and this may affect the media's attitude to groups. For example, violence against property no longer appears to preclude *favourable* media coverage for a group. In the mid-1990s, for instance, public opinion in Britain seemed more accepting of civil disobedience tactics in environmental protests. This was reflected in media coverage, for example of the protests against the construction of an urban motorway in East London and of the M3 extension across Twyford Down. In addition, the organizational structure of media institutions may undergo transformation. The status of specialist correspondents may alter in response to changing social, political and economic conditions and the resources of the media organization. The media may establish (or abandon) specialist correspondents in a group's field of interest.

Furthermore, the media's assessment of the political importance of a group may change over time. A sectional group's political influence may be judged to have increased (or declined), while the issue on which a cause group is campaigning may be perceived to have grown in importance (or vice versa). Trade unions, for example, have become less important political actors in British politics since the advent of the Thatcher government in 1979. The reduction in their political influence and 'industrial muscle' has been reflected in less prominent media attention to their activities, including the abandonment of 'live' mainstream television coverage of the annual Trades Union Congress (TUC) conference. The public furore in the early 1990s surrounding the activities of the Child Support Agency highlighted the issue of single parent families and maintenance support, which in turn raised the media profile of groups speaking on behalf of single parents. Conversely, in the post-cold war era the role of the Campaign for Nuclear Disarmament (CND) has diminished in importance and this has been reflected in much less media coverage in the 1990s than in the previous decade.

Nonetheless, while the media may be more open to a greater diversity of non-official sources than some deterministic analyses allowed for in the past, this does not mean that there is a level playing-field. Depending in part on their resources, legitimacy, expertise and public relations professionalism, some pressure groups are more likely than others to obtain media access. In addition, the

> processes of news production, and the ideological structures and political-economic forces which provide the context both for political activity and media representation, ensure that the politics of news sources is also characterised by relative stability. Politically marginal news sources may struggle to improve their position through effective news media work and the skilful mobilisation of resources but their prospects of moving further along the continuum towards the powerful may be limited and their command of an improved position always precarious. In contrast, powerful non-official news sources, by virtue of their position in relation to ideological structures and political-economic forces are far more (although never entirely) secure. (Manning, 2001: 151)

Media access and political influence

Is there any link between media access and publicity on the one hand and political influence on the other? This is a complex question, riddled with conceptual and methodological difficulties such as how one defines 'influence' and measures its exercise, what time frame is being employed and whether – and, if so, how precisely – one can isolate the effects of the media from other non-media variables (Negrine, 1994: 142–5). Moreover, it must always be remembered that frequently groups engage in restrictive media management activities, expressly designed to keep issues out of the media. For some groups at least some of the time the absence of media coverage may be politically advantageous. Certainly groups may be prepared to eschew certain types of media activities in return for privileged access to policy-making and the accumulation of greater political capital. Media publicity may certainly help a pressure group achieve political results. One example is the campaign undertaken by the Union of Communication Workers in its opposition to the privatization of the Post Office in 1994. Despite lack of resources and limited institutional authority the union was able to use the media to its own advantage (Davis, 2002: 150–70). It did so not just by exploiting divisions within government and Post Office management, but also by a positive approach to communications which included the use of public relations expertise, media contacts and the union membership; third party endorsement of its case through the use of public opinion polls, outside experts, supportive politicians and consumer groups; and positive image projection, agenda-setting and targeted attacks on the proponents of the privatization case. The union's campaign would appear to have been a determining factor in the collapse of the government's proposals.

Another apparently successful use of the media by a pressure group for political ends was Greenpeace's opposition in 1995 to the disposal at sea of a Shell oil platform, the Brent Spar (Bennie, 1998). On this occasion Greenpeace linked their media activities with political lobbying and a call for a public boycott of Shell products, particularly effective in Germany and the Netherlands. Despite both a response by Shell using scientific research which supported the company's decision and the British government's backing for the oil giant's chosen option, the company crumbled in the face of mounting public opposition as Shell lost the image battle. On this particular issue Greenpeace had apparently succeeded in using the media to mobilize public opinion to good effect and defeat the combined power of a major multinational company, the British government and a body of scientific expertise. Yet the Brent Spar case can also be viewed from another perspective. Later it emerged that certain claims made by the pressure group were inaccurate and Greenpeace was obliged to apologize. After the event, some media practitioners thought that the media had been insufficiently dispassionate in their coverage of Greenpeace's activities and the credibility of the environmental organization with the news media – and arguably its political influence – was reduced, at least in the short term (Palmer, 2000: 97–118).

Conversely, an emphasis on media activity may indicate a reduction in, or even the absence of, political influence. The British Medical Association (BMA), for instance, is one professional group that has stepped up its media activities in recent years. In part this has been in response to successive government policies which have reduced the power and status of doctors within the National Health Service to the benefit of managers. Therefore, it could be argued that the BMA's higher media profile has in part been driven by the decline of its 'insider' influence in the field of health policy.

In general the link between media coverage and political influence in the short term at least is a tenuous one. Getting an issue on to the media agenda does not guarantee that it will feature on the political agenda or, if it does, that the pressure group will have its viewpoint acceded to. The Greenham Common peace camps obtained considerable media coverage; staged events such as the encircling of the air base by demonstrators holding hands provided great pictures for the media; the issue of nuclear weapons was an important one on both the media and political agendas in the 1980s; and the profile of the anti-nuclear cause was raised. However, faced with the government's sustained efforts to control the framing of the nuclear issue, the peace movement was unable to dominate the media debate at a time of renewed cold war tension in international politics and the group's impact on public policy was nil: 'In the end cruise missiles were installed in Europe, Britain commissioned the Trident submarine system and the US government pursued its desired nuclear weapons programmes' (McNair, 2003: 178). Even the CLEAR campaign, which met with some success in policy terms, fell short of its objectives, while conversely its low media-profile predecessor, the Campaign Against Lead in Petrol, had some policy success (Negrine, 1994: 149–51).

In short, media publicity, especially if it is favourable, is increasingly (but not inevitably) a necessary condition for the exercise of political influence for many pressure groups. However, in any evaluation of pressure group influence on policy, the role of media activities has to be situated in a wider context by being considered alongside non-media variables. In their explanation of the success of the Snowdrop campaign for instance, Thomson *et al.* isolate four factors in addition to the role of the media: the campaign tactics of the group, the tactics of the pro-gun lobby, the intervention of traditional party politics and the moral climate of the time (Thomson, Stancich and Dickson, 1998: 341–3). How much weight to attribute to the media variable in this case as in others must remain a matter of debate.

Conclusion

The age of mediatized politics has seen a growing emphasis placed on communication activities by a range of political actors including parties and pressure groups. The constant competitive struggle for electoral support in an era of permanent campaigning has ensured a high profile for the media activities of the major parties, from leadership projection to news management. Increasingly the mediatization of parties forms part of a broader process of marketing.

Because of their huge variety, the impact of the media on pressure groups is more difficult to generalize. Yet it is clear that most groups now pay greater attention to cultivating the media than in the past. While there is no guarantee of success, in terms of either favourable media publicity or, even more so, political influence, the refusal to engage with the news media is an option few groups can afford to contemplate with equanimity.

9

The Media and Elections

General election campaigns are heavily mediatized events involving three sets of political communication actors: political parties, the news media and the public, with the latter acting in a dual capacity as voters and media users. In this trilateral relationship of interdependence the media fulfil five key functions. They:

- Provide information and comment to audiences
- Act as platforms for party leaders and candidates to communicate their messages to the electorate
- May themselves engage as partisan advocates in support of a particular party or candidate
- Help in the construction of the campaign agenda
- Contribute to the electoral mobilization of voters.

From this list it is clear that the news media do not simply report on an election campaign being fought in constituencies across the country; nor are they simply neutral conduits for the transmission of information from parties to the electorate. Rather, the media are political communication actors in their own right, with the capacity to bring issues on to the campaign agenda, subject the activities of parties and candidates to critical scrutiny and mobilize public opinion in support of (or in opposition to) a particular party. In several important respects, therefore, the media *are* the election campaign.

The objective of this chapter is to examine key aspects of this interdependent relationship between parties, the media and the public, with examples drawn from recent general elections. The chapter is divided into two sections. The first considers the impact of the media on the process of campaigning: campaign effects. The second concentrates on the influence of the media on the electorate: voter effects.

The media and the campaign

From pre-modern to postmodern campaigns?

Norris argues that general election campaigns since 1945 can be analyzed in terms of three consecutive historical phases: premodern, modern and postmodern (Norris, 1998: 114–17). The premodern campaign was characterized by 'the predominance of the partisan press, a loose organisational network of grassroots party volunteers in local constituencies, and a short, ad hoc national campaign run by the party leaders with a few close advisers' (ibid.: 115). Political parties aided by the press were the main agencies of electoral mobilization, supported by local public meetings and party literature. In particular, there was no campaign coverage on television. For most of the 1950s, for instance, the monopoly BBC television service largely ignored general election campaigns and it was only following the path-breaking coverage by ITV of the Rochdale by-election in 1958 that television became actively involved in election coverage, with the 1959 general election generally considered to be the first 'television election' in Britain (Cockerell, 1988: 58–60).

The advent of television coverage marked the transition to the second phase, that of the modern campaign. This saw 'a shift in the central location of electoral communications, from newspapers towards television, from the constituency grassroots to the party leadership and from amateurs towards professionals' (Norris, 1998: 115). More emphasis was given by parties to national politicians, especially party leaders, a coordinated, centrally controlled campaign designed for television consumption and activities staged for the benefit of the cameras.

Finally, in the late twentieth century Norris argues that Britain experienced the rise of the postmodern campaign. This is marked by 'the emergence of a more autonomous and less partisan press, following its own "media logic", the growing fragmentation and diversification of electronic media outlets, programmes and audiences, and, in reaction to all these developments, the attempt by parties to reassert control through strategic communications and media management during the permanent campaign' (ibid.: 117). Even what appeared in 1992 to be a reversion to a previous era of premodern campaigning – Major's use of a soapbox as a platform for his tour speeches – itself became a postmodern media event: the soapbox was the story (Newton, 1993: 154).

In analyzing these historical phases in terms of particular structural and operational features of the interrelationship between political and media developments, Norris's three part framework is a good starting point for an examination of the role of the media in general election campaigns. For instance, the rise of television as the primary means of information for voters was undoubtedly the single most important media development in election campaigns during the second half of the twentieth century, with the medium coming to provide saturation coverage. For instance, Harrison (1992: 156) estimates that in the 1992 campaign the volume of election programming on the free-to-air terrestrial networks (BBC1, BBC2, ITV, TV-AM and Channel 4) amounted to about 200 hours in total or more than seven hours a day.

Since then the advent of a fifth terrestrial network and of rolling news channels has further increased the total amount of election content on television, though of course many voters may not watch very much of it if they so choose. In the main, audiences for the major terrestrial television news broadcasts have fallen with the expansion of channels, with the result that in 2005 it was 'easier than ever to both watch a lot of television and yet avoid all but a passing acquaintance with the election issues' (Bartle, 2005: 709). In the 2005 campaign just over half the electorate thought that television devoted the right amount of time to election coverage, while as many as four in ten considered that there was too much (Ofcom, 2005: 5). In addition, around 40 per cent of voters reported that they paid a lot of attention to television news coverage of the election, no matter which political parties were featured.

At the same time one should remember that in practice the boundaries between the three historical phases are fluid rather than rigid. Practices from a previous phase frequently survive the transition to its successor. For example, some aspects of party campaigning from the premodern era, such as the input of local party volunteers, still survive today, even if constituency campaigns are more controlled from central party headquarters and more targeted on marginal seats than in the past. Moreover, the extent to which Britain has fully entered the phase of the 'postmodern campaign' is questionable. For instance, while the internet first made a contribution in the 1997 election, this was largely at a symbolic level. By 2001 the long-awaited 'internet revolution' had still failed to materialize, with a mere 6–7 per cent of the electorate using websites for election communication during the campaign (Ballinger, 2002: 226).

In the 2005 general election, the opinion poll organization

YouGov adopted the internet as the medium for collecting information about vote intentions, confirming 'that internet polling is as reliable as polling by conventional means' (Crewe, 2005: 696). Yet
despite the BBC website generating 45 million impressions by the
day after the election (Bartle, 2005: 710), 'only 8 per cent of the
public claimed to have paid "a lot" or "some" attention to politics online' (Kavanagh and Butler, 2005: 173). This compared with 72 per
cent who said that they received 'a lot' or 'some' of their news and
information about the election from television, 48 per cent in the case
of newspapers and 27 per cent for radio. In short, as far as voters were
concerned, the 2001 and 2005 campaigns were dominated by the
traditional news media rather than the more interactive new technology channels of communication.

Broadcasting and the campaign

News values and balanced coverage

General election campaigns provide good case study material of the
differences in political journalism between the press and broadcast
media (Denver, 2003: 130–2). While newspapers may adopt partisan
positions in support of particular parties, broadcasting outlets are
required to be impartial. Moreover, because of their perceived non-
partisan status, the broadcasting media are more trusted by voters than
is the press. The issue of newspaper partisanship was discussed at
length in the previous chapter. Therefore, in this section we will
concentrate on broadcasting and, in particular, a key feature of radio
and television output – the question of balance. During election
campaigns broadcasters take their commitment to balanced coverage
very seriously. They do so partly out of a sense of professional responsibility, partly because of regulatory norms and partly because the
parties assiduously monitor radio and television coverage and make
great play in complaining about any alleged transgression of the rules.
Yet the practical application of the notion of balance to broadcast election coverage is fraught with difficulties.

Let us begin with a general point about the overall composition of
the news agenda. Here the question facing news editors is *how much
coverage* to give to election stories; that is, the balance to be struck
between election and non-election news items. Should media personnel treat the election as inherently important and thus deserving of
coverage as a matter of course – a 'sacerdotal attitude' – or should the

election have to compete with other stories on the basis of the application of everyday news values – a 'pragmatic' approach (Blumler and Gurevitch, 2001: 381–2)? In the 1997 campaign Blumler and Gurevitch found that public service broadcasters 'approached the election . . . as if it deserved more attention than news values alone would justify, i.e., sacerdotally' (ibid.: 398). However, while this approach held true for the overall construction of the news agenda, in terms of the framing of coverage they also point to a significantly less sacerdotal approach than in the past.

In 2001, the election campaign occupied a smaller share of total broadcast news coverage than in 1997, perhaps because the contest was perceived by broadcasters to be less interesting in terms of newsworthiness. In a multi-channel environment, broadcast outlets risk losing audiences to competitors if voters suffer from 'campaign fatigue'. Yet public service broadcasters still consider that they have a duty to cover election campaigns in depth. Moreover, any broadcast outlet that has taken the decision in advance to allocate considerable resources to campaign coverage will be obliged to give space in news programmes to election stories in a bid to recoup its investment. In 2005 the main news bulletins of BBC1, ITV1, Channel 4, Five and Radio 4 'devoted 49 per cent of their time to the election' (Harrison, 2005: 97), while 'despite the competition from other stories, the election was usually top on every channel' (ibid.: 99). In short, broadcasters give a general election campaign extensive coverage irrespective of the newsworthiness of particular election items.

Stopwatch balance and tone of coverage

There then follows the question of *how* the election campaign should be covered. Should broadcasters seek to maintain equity of treatment between the main parties, whatever the material made available from the parties as sources and whatever the findings of the opinion polls, or should election coverage be driven by the application of 'normal' news values? It could be argued that 'stopwatch balance' – how much coverage is devoted to each party simply in terms of time allocation – is not the most suitable criterion by which to make editorial judgements regarding the newsworthiness of election issues and events. Yet to abandon equity of treatment between the major parties lays broadcasters open to the charge of not just partisan advocacy but political bias.

In the past there was a tendency to suspend the application of routine news values during coverage of campaigns in favour of equitable (though not strictly equal) treatment of the main parties. This meant that broadcasters were often receptive to what was being offered by the major parties in their campaigns. In 1992 ITN took the decision to approach election coverage from a news value perspective, an approach repeated in 1997. In comparison with the stopwatch approach of BBC news, ITN's news values approach may have led to greater coherence in the coverage of certain topics in the 1997 campaign (Semetko, Scammell and Goddard, 1997: 104–5). BBC guidelines for the 2001 campaign allowed sequences 'to achieve balance over a week rather than on a daily basis' (Harrison, 2002: 133), giving broadcasters greater flexibility in principle. However, these developments did not result in significant disparities between the main parties in share of news coverage. Moreover in terms of news story priorities, in 1997 'BBC1 and ITV led on essentially the same story on at least 38 evenings out of 44' (Harrison, 1997: 137), while in 2001 'essentially the same story topped their election package every evening but two [out of 30]' (Harrison 2002: 137–8).

By the criterion of stopwatch balance the campaign record of broadcasters is in general reasonably good, particularly with regard to the allocation of time between Conservative and Labour parties. In the past there was a ratio of coverage agreed in advance between the three main parties and broadcasters. In 1987, for instance, the Conservatives, Labour and the Liberal/Social Democrat Alliance were supposed to receive an equal allocation of time. In 1992 the ratio changed to 5:5:4 and this was maintained in 1997. Nonetheless, in 1992 the Conservatives obtained more broadcast news coverage than Labour, while the Liberal Democrats were a poor third (Golding *et al.*, 1992: 8). There is also evidence of some stopwatch imbalance to the advantage of the Conservatives in 1997 and to the benefit of Labour in 2001 (see Table 9.1). In these three cases the beneficiary was the governing party with a record to defend.

Despite the statistical imbalance to the detriment of the Liberal Democrats, paradoxically the stopwatch approach is especially valuable to them, since they 'can expect a much higher news profile in a campaign period than when more normal news criteria apply' (Goddard, Scammell and Semetko, 1998: 170). However, from an audience perspective there may be disadvantages to an overriding concern with stopwatch balance. First, 'a strict interpretation of balance *within* stories (as opposed to *between* stories) can have the effect of extending and fragmenting stories, because of the need to

Table 9.1   Parties' share of broadcast news coverage during general election campaigns

	Con	Lab	LibDem	Others
2001	34.3	36.1	21.1	8.6
1997	35.3	31.3	25.0	8.4
1992	36.8	30.8	25.2	7.2

Note: Figures based on cumulative news coverage on BBC1, ITV, Channel 4, Channel 5 (2001 only) and Radio 4.
Sources: Data from Harrison, 1992: 171; 1997: 139; 2002: 134.

include statements, sometimes poorly matched, from the various parties' (ibid.: 170). Second, television's interpretation of stopwatch balance may add to the impression of a negative campaign, as politicians' soundbites are 'balanced' by a counter-attack from rivals (ibid.: 171).

The main defect of the stopwatch approach, however, lies not so much in the difficulties associated with its application, but in its inherent limitations. The concern with time allocation tells us nothing about the tone and style of coverage. This is where the qualitative concept of 'directional balance' comes in. Norris *et al.* argue that 'participant observation studies of British newsrooms during election campaigns have found that editors and producers commonly stress the need for equidistant coverage of the main political parties, balancing favourable and unfavourable stories about each party, as well as even-handedness in commentary interviews with party leaders and reports from the campaign trail' (Norris *et al.*, 1999: 130).

Are these prescriptions carried through into their election coverage? Certainly there seems to be little evidence of consistent gross directional imbalance despite party complaints to this effect. In terms of news headlines, however, the Conservatives had the most negative ones in 1997, losing 'the battle of the headlines in 1997 as decisively as they won it in 1992' (Harrison, 1997: 137). Moreover, while Norris *et al.* found that overall in 1997 the vast majority of television news stories were balanced in tone, they also found the Conservatives receiving more unfavourable than favourable stories (especially on the BBC news), coverage of the Labour party as modestly positive and the Liberal Democrats receiving the most favourable treatment, attracting almost no negative coverage at all (Norris *et al.*, 1999:

31–2). In the 2005 campaign Harrison argues that 'the balance of headlines on both channels [BBC1 and ITV1] arguably ran slightly in the Conservatives' favour', which he attributes to the fact that Labour had been in power for eight years (Harrison, 2005: 99).

This leaves the question of 'agenda balance' – the way in which the broadcast campaign agenda focuses on certain policy issues, perhaps to the benefit of one party over the others. If balanced broadcast coverage between the main parties is to be fully realized, then neither 'stopwatch' nor 'directional' balance is sufficient. In addition, and most importantly, the issues focused on by the broadcasters must not consistently advantage or disadvantage one party over the others. This is by far the most controversial aspect of balance for broadcasters and the most difficult to achieve during an election because the construction of the campaign agenda is not within their sole control. It is, therefore, on the question of the campaign agenda that imbalance in broadcast coverage is most likely to be evident.

The campaign agenda

Who sets the campaign agenda?

This leads to the question of who sets the campaign agenda around which the election is fought. Do the media largely follow the parties' agendas, reflect the concerns of the electorate or form a campaign agenda on their own initiative? Is it possible to regard the major parties as the principal campaign agenda-setters, with the media in a largely subordinate role? Certainly the parties devote considerable efforts to harnessing the media for their own partisan objectives. For instance, they may hold daily press conferences at which they put forward a theme for the day, hoping that media coverage will concentrate on that issue. These events are designed specifically for the party to get its message across and so party spokespersons try to establish tight control of proceedings. In 1992, for example, journalists were collectively given little time in which to pose questions and individually were rarely allowed to ask probing supplementaries (Riddell, 1992: 13).

More generally, during campaigns parties devote even more attention than normal to news management activities, providing the media with stories, photo opportunities and soundbites which the news media may find hard to resist. While it may well be that some television journalists on the ground have become more sceptical of, and even hostile to, their allotted passive role in the parties' staged media events (Golding *et al.*, 1992: 7), it can still be difficult for a television reporter to present a piece that goes against the pictures. As much as possible, parties impose control from the top down so that all their spokespersons stay 'on message'. Leading party figures may be kept away from the media because of the 'dissident' nature of their views or because they are regarded as poor communicators – or both.

A contrasting view directs attention towards the agenda-setting power of the media, with news staff acting more proactively and independently of the parties. This has been called the 'discretionary power' of the media: 'the ability of journalists to tell the campaign story in their own words, scenarios, and assessments (rather than politicians'), to highlight the issues on which they believed the election should turn, and to initiate reports based on their news values and interests' (Blumler and Gurevitch, 2001: 381). One commentator has even argued that it is 'television producers and commentators who decide which campaign issues will be discussed and which events reported' (Denver, 1994: 123). Moreover, with regard to the framing of issues, there is evidence of a more interpretative style of reporting by journalists, providing their own commentary on party policies and campaign strategies. In the 2005 campaign, for instance, Bartle argues that television news bulletins frequently opened with quotes from party leaders, which were 'invariably followed by an exchange between newsreader and political editor, or by further analysis by an expert who would dissect what had been said' (Bartle, 2005: 708). According to Bartle, this represents the continued growth of the trend he calls 'analytical mediation'.

Yet approaching the agenda-setting process from either a party- or media-led perspective is misleading. As Kavanagh argues, the 'politicians disagree among themselves about the main themes and issues, and the mass media, including different television channels, programmes, newspapers and magazines, are hardly homogeneous' (Kavanagh, 1995: 3). As a result, it is best to see the campaign agenda emerging from *both* a process of competition between the main parties *and* a complex dynamic interaction between parties, media and public opinion, which may involve elements of party-media cooperation as well as conflict. The end result is a campaign agenda where some issues are highlighted at the expense of others, while occasionally media attention may even be focused on an issue which no party has chosen to emphasize and to which the public do not attribute high salience.

Parties and issue ownership

Parties tend to consider themselves and be regarded by voters as stronger on some issues than others. The theory of issue ownership suggests that it is easier for parties to secure an electoral advantage on those issues that they 'own' (Budge and Farlie, 1983). For example, 'competence' issues such as law and order, economic management and defence were traditionally 'owned' by the Conservative party, while Labour has traditionally 'owned' health, social welfare and other 'caring' issues. Thus, the Conservatives would usually have preferred the campaign to concentrate on 'competence' issues, with Labour favouring a 'caring' issue agenda. Of course, a party may lose ownership of an issue, at least provisionally, as the Conservatives did with their declining reputation for economic competence in the 1990s in the wake of the events of 'Black Wednesday' in September 1992 (Whiteley, 1997). Conversely, a party may lay claim to ownership of an issue on which it was previously regarded as weak, as with Labour on law and order under Blair's leadership in the run-up to the 1997 election. Finally, parties have to try to project a positive image even on those issues that are not perceived as their natural strengths.

Each of the main parties, therefore, seeks to promote its chosen issues as well as those potentially most harmful for its opponents. A party may prefer an issue to lie dormant because of internal divisions (Labour and defence in 1983, the Conservatives and Europe in 1997), because its policy is not popular (Labour and unilateral nuclear disarmament in 1987) or because its position has not been finalized (Labour and proportional representation in 1992). Conversely, a party may push an issue but fail to have it picked up on by the media. In 1987, for example, the Liberal/Social Democrat Alliance failed to get the media to focus on the constitutional issue which it had placed at the centre of its manifesto. All the parties now use mediated images as visual supports for the policy issues they wish to emphasize. Thatcher and Major appeared in factories producing high technology goods to give an impression of economic success, while Kinnock was shown in hospitals as part of Labour's focus on the health service (Riddell, 1992: 13). The need for good visuals to support coverage of an issue has been well understood by party advisers as parties try to engineer the pictures they want to come across on screen in television news programmes.

In the 1992 election, fought against the backcloth of an economic recession, the Conservatives were largely successful in having the campaign focus on their chosen 'competence' issues of the economy and taxation, while 'caring' issues featured remarkably little (Harrison, 1992: 162–6; Harrop and Scammell, 1992: 200; Newton, 1993: 145). Labour's attempt to make health a major campaign issue largely failed, because of the way in which the media covered the story. The Labour party election broadcast (PEB) designed to highlight the health issue (the 'Jennifer's ear' broadcast – see Harrison, 1992: 177 for a summary) was picked up on by the press and dominated newspaper coverage for three days. This emotional PEB, centring on the problem of National Health Service waiting lists, aroused controversy in the media regarding the acceptability of using a real case to make a political point and specifically over the question of who released the girl's identity to the media (ibid.: 163–5; Newton, 1993: 147–8). In the ensuing debate, television news bulletins and newspaper articles tended to concentrate on the ethics of the broadcast and as a result, Labour's initial message about health was lost (Riddell, 1992: 16). The failure of Labour to control the framing of the health issue in 1992 was a notable example of the press helping to shape the campaign agenda (Harrop and Scammell, 1992: 203), as pro-Conservative newspapers neutralized what should have been a Labour strength.

The role of the media in helping to set the campaign agenda was also evident in 1987 when defence became a central issue due to responses by the Labour leader, Neil Kinnock, to questions put by David Frost in an interview on the latter's Sunday morning television programme. Kinnock's support for the unilateralist position in nuclear defence opened the way for the Conservative party and the pro-Conservative press to present Labour's defence policy in terms of surrender, and to place Labour on the back foot on an issue not of its choosing for several days in the middle of the campaign. This media focus on defence and security issues helped construct an agenda favourable to the Conservatives (Miller, 1991). Here was an example of the press taking an issue from television coverage and then running with it, to the detriment of the Labour party:

> It was journalists who spotted the potential in Kinnock's answer to a question about pitting British soldiers against the nuclear weapons of an enemy. In truth, Kinnock's waffled answer was far from clear but in three of the following day's papers – the *Express*, *Telegraph*, *Today* – it was construed as a 'dad's army' faith in guerilla warfare to beat the enemy. The story ran for most of the week, spurred on by Kinnock's replies to follow-up questions. Arguably this story helped pin defence more firmly in the headlines than any of the campaign tactics and techniques employed by CCO [Conservative Central Office]. (Scammell, 1995: 141)

'Media logic'

The news media may not just undermine the issue campaign of a specific party, but may even pursue a largely different agenda from the main parties as a whole. In 1997, for example, the media failed to follow the lead set by the parties, whether in focusing on the economy as the Conservatives would have wished, or on social welfare issues as Labour would have preferred (Norris *et al.*, 1999: 80–1). Of course, this is a generalization covering a wide range of news media. Some media outlets were willing to play a subordinate and supportive role to parties in the transmission of their agendas to the electorate. For example, the coverage by *The Mirror* in 1997 'was clearly coordinated with Labour's campaign headquarters at Millbank' (Scammell and Harrop, 1997: 166). Nonetheless, the central point remains. 'The general election of 1997 was . . . one in which . . . the political media – especially the press – were at the centre of campaigning as agenda-setting actors in their own right' (McNair, 2000: 163).

Sleaze and Europe were the two issues that dominated the campaign agenda in 1997. Both were largely media-driven. Sleaze featured prominently in press coverage, especially in the tabloids, in the early part of the campaign. Europe – in particular Britain's possible membership of the single currency and the divisions within the Conservative party over this question – was the single most important policy issue for newspapers, dominating coverage in the second half of the campaign, while in broadcast coverage it was the most time-consuming single substantive issue overall (Goddard, Scammell and Semetko, 1998: 158). However, it was also the case that the 1997 election saw a decline in media-initiated stories and an increase in party-initiated subjects on British television compared with the 1992 contest (ibid.: 168–9) and so one should be cautious about making wide-sweeping generalizations about the independent agenda-setting power of the media.

In the party battle to set the campaign agenda in 1997, the Conservatives were the clear losers (Deacon, Golding and Billig, 1998: 141). The style and tone of much of the media coverage on sleaze and Europe were critical, while on the latter issue the party could not keep its Euro-rebels out of the media spotlight. Interestingly, in terms of issue prominence, party partisanship did not affect newspaper agendas. Pro-Conservative newspapers such as the *Daily Express* and the *Daily Mail* paid considerable attention to the sleaze issue and played a key role in putting Europe on the campaign agenda.

Thus, while in terms of editorial opinion these newspapers may have supported a Conservative victory, with regard to news coverage they gave prominence to issues that were not favourable to the Conservative party – an example of Norris's 'media logic' at work and yet another illustration of the complexity of newspaper partisanship.

The 2005 campaign was dominated in the case of the broadcast media by the issues of Iraq, taxation, health and immigration/asylum and, in the case of newspapers, by the election process, Iraq, immigration/asylum and Blair's leadership. The press agenda was 'firmly anti-Labour' and 'far closer to the Tory wish-list than to Labour's' (Scammell and Harrop, 2005: 130). Indeed, the importance accorded the immigration issue by sections of the news media overstated the emphasis placed on it in the Conservative campaign. Neither the Labour nor Conservative party wanted Iraq as an election issue; nor was Iraq particularly high on the public's agenda. That it featured so prominently in the campaign can be attributed to media coverage of the partial disclosure of the Attorney-General's March 2003 advice to the Cabinet on the legality of going to war without a further United Nations resolution. This was leaked on 23 April and covered initially by *Channel 4 News*. Iraq was an issue, therefore, brought on to the election agenda by the news media acting independently from the two main parties and the public.

Whatever the respective input of parties and media in the battle to set the campaign agenda, the result is frequently an agenda dominated by a remarkably narrow range of issues. Many issues either do not feature on the campaign agenda or are so marginalized as to be of minimal significance. In 1997 a range of issues including social security, Northern Ireland, employment, housing and defence among others received scant coverage (Deacon, Golding and Billig, 1998: 138). In 2005 neither Europe nor the environment featured prominently, despite the proposed EU constitution and climate problems associated with global warming. Moreover, the lack of attention paid to certain issues during an election campaign may underestimate their subsequent political importance. In 1987, for example, the poll tax was not a major election topic, though in the subsequent Parliament the issue made a huge contribution to the enforced departure of Thatcher as Prime Minister. Similarly, in the 1992 campaign Europe scarcely featured, yet the government's policy on Europe was to dominate the Major premiership in the following five years.

During election campaigns a varying amount of media coverage is not about issues at all (policy coverage), but focuses on the conduct of the campaign, party strategies and the activities of party leaders (process coverage) and on opinion poll findings ('horse-race' coverage). Even stories that appear to be issue-based may be part of media coverage that focuses on party strategies. For example, in the 1997 campaign many media stories with a focus on Europe were in reality more about divisions within the Conservative party on the issue of European integration. In 1992 the media gave extensive coverage to opinion poll surveys of electoral opinion. The failure of the polls to get the result right in 1992 contributed to a downgrading of their media salience in the two subsequent contests, as did the consistently large projected lead of Labour over the Conservatives. In 1997 well over half of media coverage was given over to covering the process of the campaign, while in 2001 the 'largest single element was the reports from the correspondents accompanying the leaders' (Harrison, 2002: 143), although the most memorable single incident was undoubtedly John Prescott's punch directed against a member of the public.

The Americanization of British election campaigns?

Several features of contemporary electoral communication in Britain have led commentators to ask whether it has undergone (or is undergoing) a process of 'Americanization' (Kavanagh, 1995: 218–27; Negrine, 1996: 146–66; Scammell, 1995: 288–94). The notion of 'Americanization' is not without its problems when applied to British election campaigns. First, the term lacks precision. As Blumler and Gurevitch remind us: 'It can imply direct *imitation* of American styles and practices; it can be based on a selective *importation* and *adoption* of such practices; or it can involve adaptation of American practices to an existing set of practices, assimilating new modes of operation into older ones' (Blumler and Gurevitch, 2001: 400). The term may also suffer from being too static, conveying a false impression of an unchanging US system (ibid.: 400). Finally, 'Americanization' comes laden with pejorative connotations and negative overtones for some observers. Yet despite these difficulties with the operationalization of the concept, Blumler and Gurevitch point to some evidence in support of the 'Americanization' thesis (ibid.: 385–90). First, there is the professionalization of party campaigning. Second, there is growing cynicism on the part of the electorate to politicians and political institutions. Third, they note a greater independent attitude on the part of the media towards coverage of campaigns (see above).

The general professionalization of parties' communication activities has already been examined (see Chapter 8). During election campaigns the professional model of campaigning is particularly in evidence (Blumler, Kavanagh and Nossiter, 1996). The image-driven campaign with its soundbites and photo opportunities, the focus on personalities, particularly party leaders, the important role accorded communication consultants and opinion pollsters, the use of marketing techniques by the major parties, the recourse to negative campaigning and the recognition of the importance of the 'long' campaign prior to the official campaign of only a few weeks may all seem to be imports into British practice from the United States where there is a long tradition of image-oriented electoral politics (McGinniss, 1969).

There is, for instance, a presidential style focus in British election campaigns as both the main parties and the media, particularly television, give increasingly prominent exposure to party leaders (and increasingly to their wives as well). In 1987 Kinnock fought his first election as leader of the Labour party against a Prime Minister whose image as the 'Iron Lady' was by then well established in public opinion. Labour used a PEB to emphasize Kinnock's personal qualities, his strengths as a leader and his capacity to become Prime Minister. The PEB concluded on a highly presidentialized note by urging the electorate to vote for 'Kinnock'. In 1992 the roles were reversed and it was now the turn of the Conservatives to project their new leader as a competent, caring Prime Minister. A Conservative PEB showing Major returning to his roots in Brixton was designed to present to the electorate a carefully orchestrated and mediatized image of Major as both 'a nice man' and someone who was capable of governing Britain (Harrison, 1992: 175). Five years later the caption in a Labour PEB asked voters to give Tony Blair their vote (Harrison, 1997: 152) in what was generally a highly presidential-style Labour campaign.

The presidential focus of the media reflects the parties' campaign strategies which are increasingly built around leader appearances on television, whether on the campaign trail or in formal interviews. In the 2001 campaign, for example, Blair was quoted in free-to-air national television and Radio 4 news programmes almost five times more frequently than the next Labour politician, Gordon Brown. Indeed, Blair was quoted more often than *all* other Labour politicians put together (Harrison, 2002: 140). In similar fashion Hague for the Conservatives and, even more so, Kennedy for the Liberals dominated their party's campaign news coverage. In 2005 Michael Howard monopolized the Conservative campaign, while in television and radio news Blair was quoted over four times more than Brown. 'During the campaign Blair appeared in an unprecedented range of broadcast formats in a bid to reach the widest possible audience' as part of the so-called 'masochism' strategy (Wring, 2005b: 720). However, with his personal opinion poll ratings on the decline in the wake of the Iraq war and the issue of 'trust' firmly on the campaign agenda, Blair also made several public appearances with Gordon Brown at his side in what was clearly an attempt to present a united dual leadership of Labour to the country. Labour's first PEB specifically focused on the apparently positive and harmonious nature of the Blair–Brown relationship. Yet despite the media's unrelenting focus on the party leaders, astonishingly less than half the electorate claimed to have seen any of them on television during the 2005 campaign (Kavanagh and Butler, 2005: 169).

The importation of American campaign practices into Britain is neither new nor accidental. In the 1950s they influenced British parties struggling to adjust to the demands of the new medium of television (Negrine, 1996: 151). In the 1980s the Conservative party consciously borrowed from the campaigns run by Ronald Reagan and the Republicans. The Conservative party rallies of the 1980s can be seen as an attempt to import the 'feel-good' atmosphere of a US convention into British electoral politics. In the 1990s the Labour campaign team learnt lessons from Clinton's campaigning approach, including a rapid rebuttal unit using a computerized database (Excalibur) which would allow the party to make a quick response to opposition attacks that might be potentially damaging.

Yet one should be wary of extrapolating from these instances of the adoption of American practices or the apparent 'presidentialization' of party campaigns to a generalization about the Americanization of British general elections. One counter-argument is that this is not simply one-way traffic (Negrine and Papathanossopoulos, 1996). For example, in the 2000 US congressional elections the Democratic Party copied the idea of pledge cards, modelled on those deployed by New Labour in 1997 (*The Guardian*, 25 July 2000). Two other sets of counter-arguments need to be examined.

First, despite certain similarities in campaign communications, the national contexts pertaining to British and American elections differ in several important respects. One contrast is the nature of the two political systems. Britain has a parliamentary system of government, while the United States has a presidential system. Political leaders in

Britain operate within the parliamentary system and the Prime Minister is usually the leader of the majority party in Parliament. It is not possible to construct a British prime ministerial candidacy simply through a media-based campaign. In addition, despite the apparent presidentialization of British campaigns, there is no tradition of head-to-head televised leadership debates as take place in the United States. In the 1997 campaign the parties considered the prospect, but ultimately failed to reach agreement among themselves and with the broadcasters (Butler and Kavanagh, 1997: 85–90; Tait, 1998). In 2005 the three main party leaders did appear successively in a special edition of *Question Time Leaders Special* but this still fell far short of a head-to-head US presidential style debate.

Moreover, the impact of leadership on voter choice in Britain is open to debate. Up until relatively recently there was considerable evidence that the influence of the leadership variable on voter preferences was marginal: the electorate tended to vote for a party rather than a leader. Some election analysts are still keen to downplay the impact of the leadership variable. For instance, King argues that party leaders' characteristics are 'only very seldom *both* on such a large scale *and* so skewed in their direction as to determine which party actually wins' (King, 2002: 29, emphasis in the original). This may well be generally true, although when a result is very close, as in 1992, it might be the case that voter perception of leadership attributes does make a significant difference.

In any event, it is likely that as voters have become less aligned with political parties, the role of the party leader in influencing voter perceptions, attitudes and even behaviour has grown and that this is likely to continue (Denver, 2003: 121). A popular leader, like Blair in 1997, attracts voters to the party, while an unpopular one, like Blair in 2005, repels them. Certainly parties increasingly seem to regard their leaders as an important electoral asset or liability, as is clear from debates surrounding leadership contests in all three main parties after the 2005 general election. Yet while the leadership variable has become more important in recent years, it would still be a mistake to accord it too much independent influence on electoral behaviour. A variety of factors such as policy preferences, the salience of campaign issues and perceptions of economic performance influence voters' decisions, alongside their evaluations of the party leaders.

Finally, party structures are also different in the two countries. In Britain the parties are 'more disciplined, programmatic and the national leadership has more control over local nominations and campaigns' (Kavanagh, 1995: 220). In the United States the lack of party cues in primary contests and of collective party discipline, combined with weak national organization, make the party label less significant. One possible consequence is that the 'candidate-centered nature of the U.S. party system has made it much more open to being reconfigured by the Internet' (Chadwick, 2006: 151). In contrast, the impact of the internet on party campaigning in Britain has been significantly less in evidence (ibid.: 157–62). In the 2001 general election, for example, fewer than 10 per cent of constituencies had candidates operating websites, compared with 65 per cent in the United States in the 2002 mid-term elections (Gibson and Römmele, 2005: 279). In seeking to explain this comparatively low level of supply, Gibson and Römmele emphasize the 'opportunity structure' that has so far mitigated against significant web campaigning in Britain: the centralized nature of the British polity, the nature of party competition, party organization and tight campaign finance regulations (ibid.: 281–2).

There are also important differences in the structures, functioning and regulation of the media systems of the two countries. Blumler and Gurevitch (2001) give five main media elements of contrast between the UK and US which put the UK system outside the Americanization thesis. First, there are no paid-for political commercials on British television. Instead, election broadcasts are provided as of right to parties, subject to certain conditions. Second, while the commercialization of the media is certainly not absent in Britain, it has not achieved the same levels as in the USA, especially in broadcasting. The US media system is also more fragmented and localized, while the British media are more national and, in the case of broadcasting, subject to stricter regulation. The regulatory tradition in British broadcasting means that election coverage remains strongly marked by a public service ethos, while the combined strength of parties and media at the national level mean that election campaigns in Britain are fought largely on national issues. Third, British broadcasting takes elections more seriously than its American counterpart, with more coverage on mainstream television news. Moreover, in Britain the media agendas have not gone nearly as far in decoupling themselves from the party agendas as is the case in the USA. Fourth, there are more populist 'talk-show' type programmes in the USA. In contrast, in Britain audience participation programmes are still based on the idea of 'rationalistic civic discourse'. Finally, in Britain campaign coverage is still dominated by mainstream journalism rather than alternative media.

The second set of counter-arguments to the Americanization thesis accepts that British election campaigns have changed over time but argues that this is part of a wider process of modernization rather than simply Americanization. For example, Negrine argues that the changes in British election campaigning may be more the result of the rise of television as a mass medium of communication and wider social changes (such as social fragmentation and the decline in class-based structures) connected with social modernization. The changes in British election campaigning are thus seen as largely media-driven and, while media changes tend to originate in the USA, it is the combination of technological and social change rather than simply the adoption of US practices which is more significant (Negrine, 1996: 146–66). Thus, Americanization may be an unhelpful concept because it underestimates the extent to which changes in British election campaigns have been driven by national circumstances combined with the development of new communications technology (Scammell, 1995: 291). While it is possible to see future alignment of the British case along the US model, perhaps driven by communication factors (including the development of the internet), it is more likely that national variations and particularities will continue to exist. In short, evidence of the adoption and adaptation of American campaign practices by British politicians and media do not of themselves amount to an Americanization of election campaigns in Britain.

The media and voters

Three waves of audience research

Parties pour resources into their campaigns, highlight the qualities of their leaders and strive to impose their favoured issues on the media agenda in the hope that all this activity will have an impact on voters and, in particular, influence their preferences at the ballot box. Yet is there any evidence of the media playing a significant role in influencing voter knowledge, attitudes and behaviour during the relatively short period of an official general election campaign?

To help address this question it is important, first of all, to have some understanding of the results of decades of academic research on the general effects of the media on audiences. It is possible to point to three successive waves of research findings (Miller, 1991: 1–4; Norris *et al.*, 1999: 1–19). The first was the propaganda model, popular in the inter-war period, which argued that the mass public was easily swayed by media messages. This model thus ascribed considerable power to the media. It 'assumed a very passive and uncritical audience, which was highly receptive to media messages, with little or no ability to select, reject, choose or make judgements about media messages. In this sense the model was highly deterministic' (Franklin, 1994: 206). The propaganda model was based on little empirical investigation and therefore tended to assume rather than establish that the media exercised significant power over audiences.

The second wave of audience research was the minimal effects or partisan reinforcement model, which owed much to early postwar election studies undertaken by social science researchers in the USA. Empirical research undertaken on the impact of the media in US presidential campaigns in the 1940s and early 1950s tended to downplay the influence of the media on voters. It was argued that, first, the media tended to have little direct effect on electoral choice during campaigns and, second, inasmuch as the media did have an impact, they tended to 'act as reinforcers of beliefs already held, rather than as forces which develop new opinions' (Gunter, Svennevig and Wober, 1986: 8–9). With regard to the British experience, early studies by Trenaman and McQuail (1961) and Blumler and McQuail (1968) on the role of television in British elections lent support to the reinforcement thesis. Yet whether the reinforcement model was historically valid or not, it should be noted that it still allows for audiences being influenced by the media: to put it another way, even media reinforcement of audience attitudes and behaviour is evidence of a media effect.

The third wave of audience research has treated the media user as an active and empowered participant rather than a passive receiver. Audiences filter media messages, engaging in a selective process in terms of *exposure* (which media outlets and what content they access), *perception* (what aspects of accessed content they pay attention to and how they interpret it) and *retention* (what they remember from their media usage) (Denver, 1994: 120). Moreover, audiences do not use the media as an undifferentiated mass. Instead the audience is heterogeneous. For instance, a study of the press and its political impact during the first New Labour administration (1997–2001) found that coverage of economic news in the broadsheet and 'black top' titles (but not the tabloid 'red tops') exerted a modest influence on the economic and political attitudes 'of particular *parts* of the electorate' (Gavin and Sanders, 2003: 589, emphasis in the original). The authors argue that 'we need to be wary of looking at the impact of media content on the whole population. We must not lose sight of the fact that the audience is variegated' (ibid.: 589).

The possibility that the media may exercise a more important influence than allowed for by the minimal effects model has been boosted over the past quarter century by evidence such as the decline in the mobilization function of political parties, partisan dealignment among the electorate, electoral volatility and a marked reluctance on the part of some sections of the electorate to vote at all. In these circumstances, the media may play an important role in influencing voter attitudes and behaviour, with even the validity of the filter model of media effects being called into question in an era where voters' opinions seem more amenable to media influence (Denver, 2003: 132–4).

The media and voter preferences

Let us begin by examining the possible impact of the media on voters' choice at the ballot box. Clearly many electoral preferences are fixed before the campaign begins. It would be naïve to expect the official campaign to have a radical effect on all or even the majority of voter preferences, most of which are formed in the lengthy period between elections rather than during the short campaign period itself. Media coverage of the 'winter of discontent' may have played a part in undermining the credibility of the Labour government in 1978–79 and contributed to the Conservative electoral success in 1979. Similarly, media coverage of the victory in the Falklands conflict may have played a part in preparing the electorate for Mrs. Thatcher's second electoral victory in 1983. Overall the media undoubtedly have an impact on voter preferences over the longer term. But do they exert any influence during the official campaign?

In their study of the role of the media in the 1997 general election, for example, Norris *et al.* found that television news during the official campaign had little impact at the aggregate level on changes in party support and the same was also true of newspapers. But was this because a large Labour victory was anticipated well before the official campaign started? Does the same hold true if the election looks to be a close run race? This was exactly what happened in the 1992 general election, which sparked a debate about the impact of the Tory tabloid press in securing the re-election of a Conservative government. In his resignation speech as Labour party leader Kinnock drew attention to the allegedly crucial influence of the pro-Conservative tabloids (a position he later moved away from), while in what became an infamous post-election headline *The Sun* claimed that 'It's the *Sun* wot won it' (11 April 1992). In contrast, much academic research on this question tends to downplay or even dismiss the notion that in 1992 the Conservative tabloid press had a major influence on voting behaviour during the campaign period and in particular that it was responsible for any late swing towards the Conservatives (Curtice and Semetko, 1994; Harrop and Scammell, 1992: 207–9; Newton, 1993: 158).

More recent research into the possible impact of national newspapers on voting behaviour with reference to the 1992 and 1997 elections has, however, called the minimal effects findings into question. Newton and Brynin (2001) accept that many newspaper-reading voters select the paper 'that fits their political inclinations, and that papers reflect rather than create voting behaviour. For this large group of self-selecting readers in the population, newspapers *reinforce* the basic political inclinations of their readers, rather than moulding or shaping them' (ibid.: 268, emphasis in the original). In particular, 'Labour papers are comparatively more important in reinforcing the Labour Party vote than Conservative papers are for the Conservative cause' (ibid.: 278).

At the same time, they argue that 'the evidence generally suggests that among those with no party identification there is a significant tendency for newspaper readers to vote for the party their paper supports' (ibid.: 278). Nor is this a tendency confined to readers of *The Sun*. Newton and Brynin conclude that the evidence they present is consistent with the argument that pro-Conservative newspapers 'did indeed help to win the 1992 election for the Conservatives' (ibid.: 280). Their overall conclusion is that 'newspapers do matter, and that Conservatives election results have benefited to a statistically significant degree from a pronounced and growing advantage in the circulation of national daily papers' (ibid.: 280). They argue that this might well have affected the result of various closely contested postwar elections, including 1992, which might well have been different if newspaper partisanship between the two main parties had been more equally divided. In short, there is a newspaper effect on voting behaviour. It may be small and variable (e.g. between elections; between party identifiers and non-party identifiers; between broadsheet and tabloid readers), but it is still evident and can in the circumstances of a close electoral contest have significant consequences for the overall result.

More generally with regard to the 1992 contest it has been argued that the extensive media attention to the opinion polls – which got the result so badly wrong – may have helped the Conservatives to victory. Since the majority of the polls showed a Labour lead in voting intentions (Butler and Kavanagh, 1992: 136; Newton, 1993: 160), the polls 'certainly contributed to the impression that Labour was winning the campaign' (Butler and Kavanagh, 1992: 146). If this had the effect of strengthening the resolve of undecided voters or lukewarm Conservatives to vote Conservative, then 'perhaps for the first time in a British general election – a strong case can be made for saying that the message of the polls materially affected the outcome of the election: and the message was wrong' (Butler and Kavanagh, 1992: 146; Kellner, 1992: 8).

In the 2005 general election about 60 per cent of voters had decided how they would cast their vote before the official campaign began. However, a significant proportion of voters – roughly 25 per cent – decided how they would vote during the later stages of the campaign (Ofcom, 2005: 4). During the five week campaign voter preferences for the main parties tracked by opinion polls showed a decline in the Conservative share (–2.6 per cent), an increase for the Liberal Democrats (+2.1 per cent) and relative stability for Labour (–0.7 per cent). On the basis of these shifts in voter preferences, Wlezien and Norris (2005) argue that while the official campaign in 2005 did 'not alter party control of Parliament or even the rank ordering of the parties' (ibid.: 877) it did influence the size of Labour's overall majority in the House of Commons. Had preferences not changed during the campaign, they argue that 'Labour's majority would have been a mere 18 seats or so' (ibid.: 877).

There was, therefore, a campaign effect on voter preferences in 2005. Of course, the existence of a campaign effect on voter preferences is not synonymous with an independent media effect. Kavanagh and Butler argue that in 2005 Labour lost the media agenda but 'comprehensively won the campaign agenda, measured by surveys of the major concerns of voters' (Kavanagh and Butler, 2005: 192), while for the Conservatives it was the other way round. Without the media attention on the issue of Iraq in the second half of the official campaign, the Labour vote might well have been higher and their margin of victory in terms of parliamentary seats larger than it was. Paradoxically, therefore, the campaign helped Labour in its fight against the Conservatives as 'the Government succeeded in mobilising some of its natural supporters' (Crewe, 2005: 693) as the campaign progressed, while the contribution of the media in terms of the issue agenda and the critical coverage of Blair's leadership harmed Labour to the benefit of the Liberal Democrats in the final days of the campaign. In short, both the campaign and the media had an impact on voter preferences in 2005, even if neither affected the outcome in terms of the winning party.

Other media effects

In addition to pursuing the question of the media's power to reinforce or change voting behaviour, recent effects research has also widened its field of inquiry. Academic research into media effects on voters in election campaigns now adopts a broader perspective which includes the evaluation of parties, candidates and the political system (attitudinal effects), the decision to vote (mobilization effects), knowledge about the issues, the parties and the candidates (cognitive effects), perceptions of the salience of issues (agenda-setting effects), changes in the criteria used to assess politicians (priming effects) and media influence on the conceptualization of issues by audiences (framing effects) (Aarts and Semetko, 2000: 1). Rather than asking the broad question 'Do the media influence voters?', researchers are now more likely to ask 'Which media sectors (press, broadcasting, online) and outlets (for example, "red tops", "black tops" and "quality" newspapers) and what types of media coverage (for instance, news, party election broadcasts, newspaper advertising) affect what sections of the electorate (committed/uncommitted party identifiers; politically interested/uninterested; regular/infrequent media users) in what ways (voting preferences, priming, mobilization) under what sets of circumstances (close election/predicted easy victory) over what periods of time (long campaign/official campaign)?'

It is within the context of this broader research perspective that Norris *et al.* studied the effects of the media on voters in the run-up to and during the 1997 election campaign (Norris *et al.*, 1999). As well as the capacity of the media to influence voting behaviour (see above), they examined the impact of the media in two main areas of inquiry: civic engagement and agenda-setting. Civic engagement embraces cognitive and mobilization aspects: the political knowledge of voters, their interest in the election and the likelihood of their voting. Agenda-setting in this context refers to the capacity of the media to set the agenda for the public: the media may influence the issues that the electorate considers to be important.

With regard to the media's impact on civic engagement, their study showed that in the long term 'levels of political knowledge and participation are significantly associated with patterns of media consumption' (ibid.: 113). 'Those most attentive to news on television and in the press, and regular viewers and readers, were significantly more knowledgeable than the average citizen about party policies, civics and the parliamentary candidates standing in their constituency. They were also more likely to turn out' (ibid.: 113). In short, there was a virtuous circle of long term effects (ibid.: 182). This finding is in line with subsequent research which argues that attention to newspapers and television news on the part of voters is positively linked with greater than average propensity to political activism (Norris, 2000b).

However, the evidence from short-term media effects based on changes in knowledge and attitudes during the long and short campaign showed a different pattern. 'Patterns of media use and attention had little significant impact, positive or negative, on *changes* in levels of political knowledge, efficacy, and participation during the 1997 election' (Norris *et al.*, 1999: 113). The short-term impact of campaign information on civic engagement was nil; specifically, different patterns of media use and attention were not associated with changes in political learning, trust, efficacy, or turnout (Aarts and Semetko, 2000: 2).

With reference to the media's impact on the public's agenda, the Norris *et al.* study argued that previous studies had failed to detect direct evidence that television coverage affected voters' policy priorities (Norris *et al.*, 1999: 115). For example, a study by Miller focusing on the 1987 election found a gap in the issues dominating the television agenda and those prioritized by the public (Miller, 1991). Television in 1987 gave significant prominence to defence and security issues, while the public emphasized unemployment and social welfare issues. Miller argues that the media's concentration on the defence issue did not reflect electoral concern with this topic and did not persuade the public that it was an issue of key importance. He concludes, therefore, that in the 1987 campaign there were two parallel agendas: the media agenda controlled by the parties – and in particular by the Conservatives – and the popular agenda which was concerned with unemployment, health and education. In 1992 there was also some evidence that the media's agenda did not accurately reflect the concerns of the electorate. Unemployment was rated a key concern by voters, yet it hardly featured on the media agenda. Conversely, taxation was an important media issue, but not a highly salient one for the electorate.

The Norris *et al.* study also found a gap between the media campaign agenda and the public agenda in the 1997 election. For example, while the media focused on sleaze and Europe as prominent issues, these were not the most important issues in the eyes of the electorate (Norris *et al.*, 1999: 128): 'despite extensive coverage in the news headlines the issue of Britain's role within Europe, a matter of heated passion to editorial writers, and a matter which publicly split the Conservative leadership, did not rise on the public's agenda during the official campaign' (ibid.: 128). A similar disjuncture was evident in 2005. The issues that the media considered important, such as Iraq and immigration/asylum, did not feature nearly so prominently as salient issues on the public's agenda. This may show two things. First, that the media agenda does not reflect voter concerns. Secondly, that the media do not determine what the electorate consider to be the key issues facing the country.

Conclusion

Elections are an integral part of the ritual of British representative democracy. Not only do they have substantive importance because the result has a direct effect on the governance of the country, but they also have a symbolic significance for the legitimacy of the political system. The impact of the media on elections is essentially twofold. First, they have profoundly influenced the substance and style of the campaign, contributing to the professionalization of party campaigning and helping to set the issue agenda. Second, the media have had an impact on the public. This is not just confined to reinforcing voters' pre-established electoral choice, but also includes expanding voters' political knowledge, mobilizing voters to turn out at the polls and, in the case of at least some voters, changing their party preferences.

10

The Media and Democracy

The significant role played by the media in contemporary British politics raises key questions about their relationship to the institutions, practices and values of representative democracy. Two debates are particularly important in this regard. The first focuses on media performance and, in particular, examines whether a combination of factors has resulted in an ongoing crisis of public communication in Britain. The second debate is normative in character, asking how the media ought to be organized and regulated to enable them to function as an effective public sphere. These two debates are closely inter-linked. Empirical research on political communication is often laden with normative assumptions, sometimes more implicit than explicit, as to how the media ought to perform. Similarly, normative-based theories on the desired contribution of the media to fostering a healthy democratic polity frequently derive from a critique of the perceived defects of existing practices. This chapter examines each of these debates in turn.

Crisis of public communication?

In simple terms, there are two antithetical assessments regarding the contribution of the media to politics in advanced societies such as Britain. The first is essentially pessimistic. It argues that the commercialization of the media has turned politics into another branch of the entertainment industry by personalizing and trivializing political debate. At the same time, the media have become overly critical and adversarial, while also abusing their agenda-setting power for public opinion. Specific media defects include: the 'dumbing down' of political content, the rise of 'infotainment' and the tabloidization of news in increasingly competitive media markets; an overload of political information; disproportionate media focus on the process of political competition and not enough on policy substance; a glut of interpretative journalism at the expense of straight reportage; and excessive media emphasis on hyperadversarialism with journalists undermining the integrity of public life (McNair, 2000: 3–7). The result is a conflictual and frequently hostile relationship between the media and politicians, which does little to foster public understanding of key issues. As a result, the media are not satisfactorily performing a variety of their functions (such as information provision, watchdog and electoral mobilization) as effectively as they could do, should do and – in the eyes of some critics – have done in the recent past.

The contrasting evaluation is essentially optimistic. It argues that the growth of the media has opened up new channels of communication between elites and the public, expanding the sources of information, widening access and increasing the diversity of content. The media perform important information, communication and agenda-setting functions, acting as a platform for competitive political elites to present their policies for scrutiny to the electorate and raising issues of public concern. The media also fulfil a key watchdog function, exposing corruption and malpractice. Not only do audiences have access to more and better information about politics than ever before and can pragmatically adapt their political values, attitudes and behaviour accordingly, but they are also more semiologically sophisticated than previous generations in decoding media messages. The media have helped demystify the political process and empower citizens. Moreover, this empowerment is set to continue as technological change increases the range and diversity of media provision and content, making it more difficult for politicians to manipulate the supply and presentation of information and hugely increasing citizen choice.

Dumbed down journalism and switched off voters?

Blumler and Gurevitch are leading proponents of the view that there is a crisis of public (or civic) communication in liberal democratic societies such as Britain. In their opinion, this undesirable state of affairs can be seen in the way the 'political communication process now tends to strain against, rather than with, the grain of citizenship' (Blumler and Gurevitch, 1995: 203). Aspects of this crisis are described by them as follows:

Thus, confidence in the norms of citizenship is waning. Tactics of political campaigning appear ever less savoury. The watchdog role of journalism is often shunted into channels of personalization, dramatization, witch-huntery, soap-operatics and sundry trivialities. It is difficult for unconventional opinions to break into the established 'marketplace of ideas', and political arguments are often reduced to slogans and taunts. Suspicion of manipulation is rife, and cynicism is growing. The public interest in constructive civic communication has been short-changed. (Ibid., 1995: 1)

More specifically, they identify four major trends in the organization of public communication which together contribute to this sense of crisis (ibid.: 207–12).

First, there has been a thoroughgoing professionalization of political advocacy, with an emphasis on proactive strategies of media control, negative campaigning, political marketing, and the use of image projection, soundbites and political events with high visual or symbolic appeal, resulting in the transformation of politics into a sort of virtual reality. This adaptation by politicians to the age of mediatized politics has been covered elsewhere in this book (see Chapters 7, 8 and 9).

Second, Blumler and Gurevitch point to the journalistic fight-back whereby the media have become fixated on the process rather than the policy substance of political debate. Process journalism refers to stories that comment on and evaluate the behaviour of political actors (party strategies, leadership tactics, personality rivalries) in contrast to policy journalism which explains issues and assesses policy proposals (McNair, 2000: 42–60). Moreover, as part of their coverage of politics as process, journalists have learnt to disdain the communicative efforts of politicians, presenting these as public relations exercises, contrived for media coverage. For example, during the period when Campbell was Chief Press Secretary at Number 10 'spin' provided the narrative frame for much of the news coverage of the New Labour government, as journalists 'unpacked' the government's news management activities. With media attention on the attempted official 'spin' played up in some journalistic coverage, the presentation by ministers rather than the substance of policy frequently dominated the news frame.

There are several reasons for the place accorded process journalism in the media's coverage of politics. First, since political actors pay considerably more attention to public relations and promotional strategies than ever before, this development is a legitimate matter of public interest for journalistic commentary. Second, journalists enjoy an 'insider' position in the political communications environment. They can write about a political game in which they are perfectly familiar with the players, rules, strategies and tactics, and can communicate that 'insider information' to their audiences. Third, writing about process is often easier than writing about policy. Process journalism can focus on human interest stories – who's in and who's out of favour in the governmental entourage. In contrast, a focus on policy may require technical knowledge and skills which many political journalists quite simply lack. Fourth, process journalism covers information audiences can easily assimilate. Conversely, in an age of increasingly technical debates – for example, on the issues of climate change, genetically modified food and currency convergence – and a more complex decision-making process involving largely remote and unfamiliar supranational and global actors such as the European Union and the World Trade Organization, it is more difficult and time-consuming for audiences to grasp the essential features, far less the details, of many policy issues. Finally, the focus on spin allows journalists to reassert their own power in the interdependent relationship with politicians and demonstrate this publicly to their audiences. In commenting on the political 'game' journalists seek to show that they cannot be fooled by the news management tricks of politicians. Building up the power of political spin helps in this self-legitimation exercise by journalists.

Process journalism is frequently characterized by a highly adversarial stance on the part of the news media. In this context journalists ascribe to themselves the role not of mere reporters of – or commentators on – the political process, but rather that of critics willing to condemn aspects of its functioning and prepared to engage in highly personalized attacks against politicians, both individually and as a group. In an excoriating attack on the British media's standards of political coverage, for instance, Lloyd argues that broadcasters have become 'openly abrasive and cynical' and that they have assumed 'the position of the opposition' (Lloyd, 2004: 126). For Lloyd, too much news media coverage of politics is what he calls 'laser-guided journalism', which

> depends on a pervasive contempt for the governing classes, especially for politicians; a definition of all official or corporate public relations and briefings as 'spin'; a concentration on process at the expense – often to the complete obliteration – of policy and outcomes; a privileging of conflict and complaint and a dramatization of ordinary conflict, such as within

government, as crises, irrespective of any tendency to contain the conflict with compromise. (Ibid.: 195)

A notable example of the 'journalistic fight-back' is the phenomenon known as 'attack journalism' whereby journalists engage in ritualistic 'feeding frenzies', when a politician is named and shamed and the media pack move in for the metaphorical political kill (Sabato, 1991). Recent examples include the resignations of Mandelson (twice), Byers and Blunkett (twice) from New Labour Cabinets. *The Sun's* leader column on the occasion of Mandelson's second resignation was particularly blunt: 'He is out on his ear again because he is a lying, manipulative, oily, two-faced, nasty piece of work who should never have been allowed near the Government in the first place' (*The Sun*, 25 January 2001).

The third component of Blumler and Gurevitch's critique is that there exists normative uncertainty about the ethical rules of the new publicity game. This doubt has arisen 'from shifting roles, increased conflict and intensified competition – among politicians for electoral support and among media outlets for audience patronage' (Blumler and Gurevitch, 1995: 211). Politicians, for instance, now appear not just on traditional news programmes, but also on television chat shows such as *Richard and Judy* and *Parkinson*. In early 2003 Blair went on MTV as part of his campaign to make the case for the war against Iraq. Politicians argue that these sorts of media appearances are necessary to reach out to those sections of the electorate who do not regularly access more traditional political formats. This may well be true. It is also the case that there is significant media and audience interest in the private lives of leading politicians, which the latter seek to satisfy, albeit under conditions they wish to control. At the same time, in the eyes of critics such media appearances may allow politicians to by-pass interviews on serious policy issues and to escape tough questions from professional political journalists.

With regard to changes in the media, Franklin (1997) examines how developments in the organization, financial structures and regulation of news media, combined with changes in journalism's composition and news-gathering practices, have resulted in shifting editorial standards in newspapers, radio and television. A competitive media environment, government media policy, the development of new technologies and changes within journalism itself are together responsible for what he regards as the downgrading of journalistic product (ibid.: 15–21). In particular, in an increasingly competitive media market, Franklin argues, the pressures on news media have resulted in news becoming part of the entertainment industry. He contends that the media in Britain have in general embraced tabloid journalistic values, including an emphasis on scandal and sensationalism, to produce a product which he calls 'newszak' whereby news is 'a product designed and "processed" for a particular market and delivered in increasingly homogeneous "snippets" which make only modest demands on the audience. Newszak is news converted into entertainment' (ibid.: 4–5):

> Entertainment has superseded the provision of information; human interest has supplanted the public interest; measured judgement has succumbed to sensationalism; the trivial has triumphed over the weighty; the intimate relationships of celebrities from soap operas, the world of sport or the royal family are judged more 'newsworthy' than the reporting of significant issues and events of international consequence. Traditional news values have been undermined by new values; 'infotainment' is rampant. (Ibid.: 4)

With specific reference to BBC current affairs output, Lloyd refers to 'a conscious leaching of entertainment techniques into news judgements' (Lloyd, 2004: 132). It may be argued that none of this is particularly new. The interest of the popular press in sensational coverage has a long tradition in British journalism. For instance, Stephenson argues that:

> the journalistic values of today's popular press – and the reaction of politicians and the 'chattering classes' to them – are part of an historical continuum. Sex, lies, and the invasion of the privacy of individuals have certainly been an important part of the staple diet of popular British newspapers since popular British newspapers have existed. (Stephenson, 1998: 19)

In response to this criticism Franklin argues that the situation is worse than before. First, the balance in favour of entertainment in news media content has rarely, if ever, been so apparent. Second, there has been a decline in media attention to news and especially certain kinds of news, such as foreign news and investigative journalism. Finally, he argues, this decline in news coverage and ascendancy of entertainment is evident across all news media (Franklin, 1997: 6). Other commentators agree, arguing that tabloid news values have increasingly penetrated into the broadsheet sector (Bromley, 1998).

In similar vein, Sparks argues that while the large amount of space devoted to entertainment-oriented content in the mass circulation, popular press is not a particularly new phenomenon, 'within the total output of the press, including newspapers and magazines, the historical trend is towards an erosion of those products concerned primarily with issues of the public sphere' (Sparks, 1991: 68). With the rise in magazines aimed at particular occupational and leisure niches on the one hand and the decline in the circulations of general information newspapers on the other, more journalists are 'directly concerned with entertainment or specialized information provision rather than the general political and social functions which have traditionally been ascribed to them' (ibid.: 69).

Barnett also points to some changes in media structures and functioning which may be having the effect of 'degrading public discourse' in contemporary Britain. Media competition in itself he rejects as a satisfactory explanation. Rather, he points to four principal causes (Barnett, 1998: 82–6). These are the shift in regulatory culture in broadcasting and the general relaxation of regulatory regimes; more consumerist decision-making as media seek to brand themselves and target specific audiences; the increased power of advertisers to determine the nature of editorial content and the growing influence of the public relations industry in general; and, finally, the speed with which journalists have to work and the volume they have to produce to service proliferating media outlets. The particular news values of media proprietors and the role of government patronage are two additional factors that may be exacerbating any drift towards tabloidization and the erosion of public culture.

The fourth and final element of Blumler and Gurevitch's critique is that there is a widespread projection of an image of the 'turned-off' citizen. 'Media commentary on politics is increasingly suffused with references to the public's disenchantment with their leaders and institutions' (Blumler and Gurevitch, 1995: 212). According to proponents of the 'media malaise' theory, media coverage has had a harmful effect on the conduct of democratic politics, with audiences growing increasingly disenchanted and cynical about politicians and the political process, and turning away from political participation. While scepticism on the part of voters may be a healthy and even desirable attribute of informed citizenship, cynicism is not. Public levels of trust in politicians (and also journalists) are low. In addition, voter turnout has been on the decline, with a particularly high level of electoral abstentionism evident at the 2001 general election.

Crisis, what crisis?

In opposition to this 'crisis of public communication' thesis are those commentators who argue for an alternative, more optimistic evaluation of the contemporary public sphere and its contribution to the political process. For McNair, for instance, the 'public sphere has become, from the viewpoint of the individual, a communicative space of infinite size' (McNair, 2000: 40). He argues not only that the quantity of political information in mass circulation expanded hugely in the late twentieth century with politics firmly at the heart of the contemporary news agenda (ibid.: 46), but also that political journalism has become steadily more rigorous and effective in its criticism of elites, more accessible to the public and more thorough in its coverage of the political process. In particular, McNair criticizes the applicability of the 'dumbing down' thesis with regard to the press by pointing to an increase in the overall circulation of the elite broadsheets and the expansion in the resources devoted by elite newspapers to political journalism. He believes that market forces do not always degrade the content of political journalism, but rather can improve it and move it upmarket.

In his examination of the debate on the alleged 'tabloidization' of the media, Barnett argues that, with regard to both the press and broadcasting, there is no concrete evidence that we are witnessing 'a process of displacement in which more emphasis is placed on entertainment, showbusiness, scandal and prurience at the expense of more serious, challenging material like current affairs, policy issues, the arts, or foreign affairs' (Barnett, 1998: 76). Nor does he fully accept that the nature of serious or challenging material is being debased through various packaging and presentational strategies to make it more populist (ibid.: 77). One could just as well argue that tabloid journalism has a long and honourable history of making difficult concepts or stories come alive for people who lack either the ability or inclination to read long-winded articles on complex subjects (ibid.: 77–8).

For McNair process and sleaze journalism do not predominate in British political journalism; there is a considerable amount of policy coverage. Substantive political issues are given due weight. Moreover, inasmuch as process and sleaze journalism are a feature of contemporary media coverage of politics, these can be regarded as largely positive elements in the political public sphere. In any case, policy and process journalism should not be regarded as separate discourses (McNair, 2000: 50). Instead, process journalism may well provide audiences with important contextual information for the understanding and evaluation of public policy-making and thus make an important contribution to voters' overall political knowledge.

McNair sometimes accepts the existence of many of the trends criticized by the 'crisis' commentators. For instance, he admits that contemporary political journalism is more focused than before on performance aspects of political communication, on the mechanics of news management and on interpretation and commentary (ibid.: 171). However, he parts company with them by arguing that these trends do not form part of a narrative of decline. Instead, McNair praises much commentary and columnist journalism, is positive about the contribution of political interviews to media coverage of politics and welcomes public access broadcast programming. In addition, he condemns the critique of spin as too one-sided, sweeping and ahistorical, arguing that political spin is not new, not all-powerful and can be actually helpful for journalists seeking out the line for a news story. Spin can be functional to the work of journalists, helping them make sense of an issue in an era of information overload and rolling deadlines.

Brants also takes issue with the proponents of the crisis in public communication thesis. With regard to television he argues that the evidence for the 'infotaining' of political communication in selected European countries, including Britain, is not convincing (Brants, 1998). Television news programmes have not been pushed to the margins of schedules, and while 'we might see a slight tendency towards a popularization of news, there is little evidence that politicians and politics are dramatically more personalized and sensationalized than before' (ibid.: 323). In any case, Brants is less fearful of the inter-mingling of information and entertainment in political communication than some other commentators, whether this translates into political informative elements in entertainment programmes (such as chat shows) or entertainment characteristics in traditionally informative programmes (such as current affairs) (ibid.: 327). He argues that it is not just formally labelled informational programmes such as news that can be regarded as legitimate outlets for civic communication. For example, a chat show may be more informative about the qualities of a candidate than a news or current affairs programme is about issues and policies. In any event, in an era of reduced ideological competition between political parties, Brants argues that personal characteristics of politicians are neither unimportant nor irrational elements in voter choices and evaluations of politics.

Brants accepts that there may be conditions under which the info-taining of politics on television might be undesirable; for example, if it were to become the dominant form in which politics is portrayed, if it allowed politicians to avoid the professional scrutiny of political journalists, or if it led to a distorted image of politics. However, he argues that none of these conditions seems to be unconditionally the case (ibid.: 329). McQuail too contends that while new genres and formats may not match the standard of information value of old media, they may still serve a valuable purpose alongside more tradi-tional media forms that have not in fact disappeared (McQuail, 2000: 106). Hargreaves agrees with this assessment: (Hargreaves, 2003: 136–7): 'News has always been conveyed in a wide range of styles, and with a wide range of content. We only have a problem with tabloidization if it drives out other types of journalism and diminishes diversity.'

Traditional criteria for what constitutes quality political journalism may be too restrictive in their emphasis on 'rational' and 'serious' political issues. Interestingly, even Blumler agrees that 'the notion that only programmes formally labelled as "informational" should be regarded as legitimate outlets for civic communication is unsustain-able' (Blumler, 1999: 243). Brants argues that if audiences are not wholly rational, then why should political communication treat them as if they were? 'The fear of losing the citizen and trading him or her for the consumer is based on a distinction which seems to miss the point in the television age. In political communication, the affect of the supposed consumer should be taken as seriously as the cognitive of the acclaimed citizen.' (Brants, 1998: 332). It should certainly be remembered that there has never existed a halcyon era in which well-informed voters made a rational choice on the basis of perfect infor-mation and a comprehensive understanding of the issues at stake. Before the age of mediatized politics there is little evidence of a better informed or more rational electorate.

Finally, with regard to the specific charge that the media turn citi-zens off politics, two responses have been put forward. The first is that far from having a malign impact on audiences, the media exert a posi-tive influence in informing and educating citizens. Because of a 'virtuous circle', attention to the news media gradually reinforces civic engagement, just as civic engagement prompts attention to the news (Norris, 2000b). The second response is that the media are not particularly powerful independent actors in influencing attitudes and behaviour. For Newton, the media cannot be held primarily responsible for any decline in public trust or electoral participation, because they are 'generally a weak force in politics and government' (Newton, 2006: 210). Newton argues that many of the claims regarding the power of the media do not stand up to investigation, in part because those members of the public most susceptible to media influence are least likely to use the media for soliciting information, and in part because those who do take an interest in media coverage of an issue of which they have firsthand experience are more likely 'to trust their own judgements rather then the media's' (ibid.: 226).

In addition, it might be noted that while some communication scholars make much of the media's contribution to depressing electoral participation, election experts tend to emphasize other, non-media variables. For instance, in a chapter specifically entitled 'Turnout: Why People Vote (or Don't)', Denver makes no reference whatsoever to any possible impact of the media as an explanatory factor. The main reasons, he argues, 'for the lower turnouts seen in elections at all levels since 1997 are structural and political' (Denver, 2003: 46), including the first-past-the-post electoral system, a decline in party identification among voters and a narrowing in the ideological gap between the main parties.

The debate assessed

The debate about media performance in Britain is significant, because it is linked to issues of citizen empowerment and institutional legitimacy. It is also a debate which, far from being confined to a small band of academic researchers, concerns all the actors involved in the process of political communication: politicians, media personnel and voters. It is important, therefore, to try to disentangle some of the different elements involved in the controversy.

First, the critique presented by Blumler and Gurevitch is wide-ranging, embracing a variety of features which they assert to be characteristic of contemporary political communication. While it is clearly possible to accept their critique as a whole, one might instead argue that only some (or even none) of these features are to be found – in which case their critique may be significantly weakened. Moreover, it is also possible to agree about the existence of certain features but to evaluate their contribution to public communication from a different perspective. For instance, one could regard some of the features of their 'crisis model' – such as the professionalization of political advocacy – not as negative but rather as neutral or even positive. Blumler himself accepts the need to be open-minded about developments in 'infotainment', arguing that 'paternalistic discourse is no longer an option. Communicators who wish to inform and empower their auditors must . . . adapt more closely than in the past to what ordinary people find interesting, engaging, relevant and accessible' (Blumler, 1999: 243–4).

Second, one should bear in mind that many of the key concepts in the 'crisis of public communication' debate may be difficult to operationalize with any precision. There is, for example, no universal agreement on what type of media content can be classified under the heading of 'infotainment' or how one might prove or disprove any alleged trend towards 'tabloidization' in the news media (Sparks and Tulloch, 2000: 1–40). This definitional problem is not helped by the fact that several terms, such as 'dumbing-down', have a strongly negative connotation which make them unsuitable as labels for scientific categorization of media content.

Third, hard empirical research data are not always available. In the absence, for example, of detailed longitudinal analyses of media content, it is impossible to be precise about the extent of any alleged changes in the media's coverage of politics over a specific time period. It is not even always clear what constitutes 'coverage of politics': a narrow definition might include only items covered by political correspondents and columnists, while a wider definition would extend to embrace social and cultural issues and events with broad political significance.

Moreover, even where content studies have been carried out (McLachlan and Golding, 2000: 75–89), there are 'hidden definitional risks in an apparently simple process of counting minutes or column inches' (Barnett, 1998: 80). For instance, if one were to find that, in terms of column inches, there was *both* more 'high quality' *and* more 'low quality' political journalism in Britain's newspapers than in the past because of the increased press coverage of politics as a whole, of what would this be evidence? Moreover, in addition to the evaluation of quantitative data there is the need for qualitative assessments of media content, format, language and style, all of which are likely to change over time in keeping with wider changes in social norms. For instance, a journalist's interview style which might be widely regarded as hostile in one era may be seen as wholly acceptable thirty years later.

Finally, and perhaps most importantly, the multi-faceted debate about the 'crisis in public communication' is not primarily about contrasting definitions of contested concepts or divergent assessments of media change. Rather at the heart of this controversy lies a normative clash about the political communication role the media should fulfil in an information-rich society and mass democratic polity. In other words, what is at stake is not what constitutes 'infotainment' in media content or how much the political coverage of the media has changed over time, but rather the contribution of the media to a democratically healthy society. This is a debate about the possibility and desirability of reasoned and informed discussion about political matters so as to help produce what Schudson calls the informed, rather than merely the informational, citizen (Schudson, 1995: 169). In short, 'while attempts at quantification – for example of levels of foreign news coverage, or the number of peak-time current affairs programmes devoted to policy issues – may allow for some tentative conclusions, they will always be predicated on some subjective assessment of what constitutes a healthy journalistic culture in a thriving democracy' (Barnett, 1998: 88).

The media and the public sphere

How then should the media contribute to the functioning of a representative democracy? Where should the media stand in relation to civil society, the market and the state? These normative questions came to the fore in the last decade of the twentieth century, in part because of growing concern about the structures and functioning of the media in established democratic societies, such as the growth of corporate media power, and in part because of the transition to liberal democratic politics of previously authoritarian and one-party states, including the countries of the former Soviet bloc.

One of the most influential normative approaches to the democratic role of the media is based on the concept of the public sphere. Situating the media within the public sphere can be contrasted with two undesirable but historically prevalent conditions of market domination and political control. Located between the private sphere and civil society, the public sphere is an institutional framework and set of practices that encourage wide and inclusive public debate about issues of social and political importance. The domain of the public sphere refers to the conceptual 'space' that exists in a society outside the immediate circle of private life and the walls of enclosed institutions and organizations pursuing their own (albeit sometimes public) goals. In this space, the possibility exists for public association and debate leading to the formation of public opinion and political movements and parties that can hold private interests accountable. The media are now probably the key institution of the public sphere, and its 'quality' will depend on the quality of media. (McQuail, 2000: 502)

The concept of public sphere derives from the work of Habermas, in particular his study *The Structural Transformation of the Public Sphere* ([1962] 1989). In this work Habermas argued that the coffee houses of late seventeenth and early eighteenth century Europe acted as a bourgeois public sphere, allowing for the interchange of views among elites and opinion formers. However, 'the institutionalised dialogue of the salons and coffee houses was to give way as communication became increasingly organised through large commercial concerns' (Stevenson, 1995: 49). For Habermas, the mediation of public communication with its emphasis on commercialism and commodification has weakened the application of the public sphere in contemporary advanced societies:

> The cultural transformation and processes outlined above, if we follow Habermas, have led to the refeudalisation of the public sphere. Whereas once publicity meant the exposure of domination through the use of reason, the public sphere is now subsumed into a stage managed political theatre. Contemporary media cultures are characterised by the progressive privatisation of the citizenry and the trivialisation and glamorisation of questions of public concern and interest. The hijacking of communicative questions by monopolistic concerns seemingly converts citizens into consumers and politicians into media stars protected from rational questioning. (Ibid.: 50)

Habermas's empirical analysis has been subject to criticism. For example, the historical accuracy of his account of the bourgeois public sphere has been questioned (Garnham, 1992), as has his alleged concentration on the production and content of cultural forms at the expense of the ability of the audience to read texts differently (Stevenson, 1995: 56–8). He has also been accused of being too pessimistic regarding the possible existence of public sphere elements in contemporary society, such as through public service broadcasting values and institutions (ibid.: 60–1).

In any event, as outlined by Habermas, the concept of the public sphere does not provide a working model or blueprint for the role of the media in contemporary democracy. Nonetheless, the essential principles associated with the concept have been used by various academic commentators as normative guidelines for framing discussion of an ideal-type relationship between the media and politics in advanced liberal democratic societies (Boyd-Barrett and Newbold, 1995; Curran, 1996; Wheeler, 1997).

One of the main contributors to this debate in Britain is Curran, who has argued for a fundamental rethinking of the informational role of the media and proposed reforms accordingly. For Curran the media ought to perform three main functions in a democratic society (Curran, 1996: 103–4). First, the 'public dialogue staged by the media should give the public *access* to a diversity of values and perspectives in entertainment as well as public affairs coverage.' A second 'democratic function of the media system is to act as an agency of representation. It should be organized in a way that enables diverse social groups and organizations to *express* alternative viewpoints.' The 'third democratic function of the media is to assist the realization of the objectives of society through agreement or compromise between opposed groups. The media should contribute to this process by facilitating democratic procedures for resolving conflict and defining collectively agreed aims.'

To facilitate the effective performance of these functions, Curran supports a complex, multi-layered media system, consisting of several different elements. At the heart of this system are what he calls the 'core media'. These are public service organizations, either in public ownership or publicly regulated commercial organizations (ibid.: 106). Revolving round the core public service media are other, complementary media sectors. These include a civic media sector, embracing media linked to collective organizations but aimed, in principle at least, at a general audience; subcultural media, such as magazines for gays and lesbians; organizational media, which serve as channels of communciation between members of a group; a professional media sector, promoting independent truth-seeking journalism; a private enterprise sector; and a social market sector, supporting innovatory forms of media organization through a public funding agency and tough anti-monopoly measures.

Another influential contributor to the normative debate on the media and democracy is Keane. Keane is critical of Habermas's failure 'to analyse the ways in which twentieth-century struggles to nurture public life can take advantage of new media developments' (Keane, 1991: 36). He challenges this pessimism, arguing for 'a radically new public service model which would facilitate a genuine commonwealth of forms of life, tastes and opinions' (ibid.: xi). For Keane, simple conceptions of liberty of the press need to be abandoned in favour of a more complex and differentiated notion of freedom of communication (ibid.: 43). In particular, he rejects the association between the ideal of freedom of communication and unlimited freedom of the market:

> In short, it must be concluded that there is a structural contradiction between freedom of communication and unlimited freedom of the market, and that the market liberal ideology of freedom of individual choice in the marketplace of opinions is in fact a justification of the privileging of corporate speech and of giving more choice to investors than to citizens. (Ibid.: 89)

Instead, Keane advocates a new model of public service communications, 'which resolves the flaws of market liberalism, and which, consequently, is more genuinely open and pluralistic, and therefore accessible to citizens of all persuasions' (Keane, 1992: 118).

What would a redefined, broadened and more accessible and accountable public service model look like in practice? One priority would the exposure and repeal of the censorial methods of contemporary state power (Keane, 1991: 127). A second priority would be the development of a plurality of *non-state* media of communication which would both function as permanent thorns in the side of political power (helping thereby to minimize political censorship) and serve as the primary means of communication for citizens living, working, loving, quarrelling and tolerating others within a genuinely pluralist society (ibid.: 150). The decommodification and deconcentration of existing media would be accompanied by the development of media in neither state nor commercial hands (ibid.: 158). 'In practical terms, the maximization of freedom and equality of communication requires efforts to "de-concentrate" and publicly regulate privately owned media and to restrict the scope and intensity of corporate speech' (Keane, 1992: 120).

Keane therefore proposes 'the development of a dense network or "heterarchy" of communications media which are controlled neither by the state nor by commercial markets. Publicly funded, non-profit and legally guaranteed media institutions of civil society, some of them run voluntarily and held directly accountable to their audiences through democratic procedures, are an essential ingredient of a revised public service model' (ibid.: 121). Examples he gives include the BBC, community radio, cooperative publishers and political newspapers.

While the critique of market and state power in media matters may be cogent, Keane admits that 'more detailed consideration must be given to the financial, legal and political feasibility of these kinds of decommodifying strategies' (Keane, 1991: 157), accepting that 'no model legislation or budget or detailed political strategy has been provided' (ibid.: 182). 'It is difficult to be precise about which market-regulating and market-suspending strategies can maximize freedom of communication, since their actual shape and effectiveness will vary from context to context, and from time to time' (Keane, 1992: 119).

The proposals put forward by Curran and Keane are attempts to reformulate the relationship between the media and society with an emphasis on the importance of the empowerment of citizens and not just the satisfaction of consumers. Their emphasis on the centrality of public service elements in their ideal media blueprints is based on a critique of the inability of market mechanisms on their own to deliver the desired range and quality of information necessary for a healthy functioning democracy. While their proposals may seem idealistic in an era where so much of the media is dominated by profit-seeking commercial companies operating across national boundaries, one of the strengths of their arguments lies in the capacity to make us aware of the possibilities for ameliorative change.

Such change can come about in different ways. For instance, there are the possibilities opened up by new technology. For some commentators the internet has the capacity radically to alter the ways in which citizens connect with the political process. Coleman, for instance, emphasizes that the 'internet could be a new medium for horizontal communications and interactions and thereby new relations between citizens' (Coleman, 2004: 91). More particularly, the internet could help to hold governments to account, contribute to the process of consultation on policy options, aid political mobilization and recruit-ment, facilitate transactions between citizens and governments (local, devolved and national), and strengthen representation 'by creating more direct channels of engagement, consultation and discursive interaction between representatives and represented' (ibid.: 91). As part of this blueprint, Coleman calls for the creation of a 'civic commons' whereby 'an area of the internet [is] given over to a new public service framework, designed to enable and organise consulta-tion and deliberation between citizens and political institutions over issues of public policy' (ibid.: 96).

While examples from the United States and other countries testify to the success of online deliberative forums in subnational communities, there is as yet insufficient case study evidence from Britain to come to any hard and fast conclusions. Apart from the technical issue of domestic access to the internet – still not all households have a broadband connection – there are three questions that need to be addressed (see Chadwick, 2006: 83–113, for an up-to-date overview of the e-democracy debate). The first is the level of public interest in e-democracy. The second concerns the skills required to participate effectively in deliberative discussion, which are in part linked to citizens' levels of educational attainment. The third is the 'missing link between e-democratic activity in civil society and policy making that takes place in formal institutional spheres' (ibid.: 113). The resolution of the last issue may well determine whether a high public level of interest in online deliberation can be generated and sustained.

A focus on the democratizing possibilities of the internet should not lead us to forget the established news media of press and broadcasting. At the level of employment practices, for instance, there is an increasing awareness among media managers and news editors of the need to ensure a workforce whose gender and ethnic composition reflects the diversity of British society. In addition, an emphasis on ethics and codes of behaviour is now a more integral part of journalists' formal professional training. While these initiatives do not resolve all issues of public confidence in the media, they at least show some media organizations are taking their social responsibilities seriously.

At the same time, established media need to consider their contribution to keeping the public not just informed about politics, but also politically engaged. One initiative which has received support is the further development of public access programmes such as BBC television's *Question Time* where politicians are asked questions by members of the audience (Livingstone and Lunt, 1994). These programmes not only allow an albeit limited form of interactive discussion, but compel the politician to engage with 'ordinary' voters. The results can be compelling viewing. For instance, when Blair appeared on various audience participation programmes in early 2003 to make the case for British involvement in military intervention in Iraq, he was subjected to some very hostile questioning from members of the public and at times the Prime Minister looked visibly shaken by the experience. The strength of his own convictions and of the audience's views were clearly in evidence. It is argued by supporters that such programming can contribute to the mobilization of citizens as well as to an increase in their cognitive resources.

A third avenue for ameliorative change is through public policy initiatives regarding media structures and behaviour. Media policies should recognize that 'in the cultural industries the unfettered pursuit of profit is unlikely to produce the opportunities for knowledge and understanding that an informed, effective, participatory democracy requires' (Barnett, 1998: 89). This normative judgement recognizes that media policy is not just about how to deal with the impact of technological change or how to manage competition to promote consumer welfare: it is also about values and, in particular, about the socio-political contribution of the media to the fostering of citizenship. In this context key policy issues in the future will include the social accountability of the media and inequalities of public access to information.

Of course, in practice these three sources of potential reform – developments in new technology, mainstream media practices and public policy initiatives – are inter-related. For instance, established news media such as the BBC are closely involved in the exploitation of new technology, while public policy may encourage or inhibit both 'old' and 'new' media in their attempts to foster public engagement. Or, to put it another way, technology may open up deliberative possibilities which the media, 'old' and 'new', will seek to exploit within a regulatory context shaped by public policy.

Conclusion

One does not have to be a cultural pessimist to argue that some aspects of media performance may be open to criticism in terms of their contribution to the creation of a healthy public sphere in contemporary Britain. A case for both structural and behavioural reform can certainly be made with the objective of improving the media's contribution to democratic interchange. Yet at the same time it is important not to single out the media and make them the scapegoat for all the perceived ills – real and imaginary – of contemporary society and politics.

Such a 'media malaise' perspective would be a mistake for three reasons. First, the media frequently play a positive role in the performance of functions such as information provision and watchdog. Instances of media excess and abuse of power need to be offset against examples of responsible, informative journalism so that a balanced assessment can be made. Second, a media-centric analysis focuses attention away from the input of other political communication actors such as government and parties, in particular their public relations, news management and 'spinning' activities. It must be remembered that the functioning of a healthy public sphere is not simply the responsibility of the news media alone. The other actors involved in political communication also need to change some of their practices. Finally – and here we leave a media perspective behind entirely – inasmuch as there is evidence of political cynicism towards the political process in contemporary Britain, it is essential to factor in non-media variables, including the public's personal experience of service delivery, their evaluation of governmental policy decisions and their assessment of the behaviour of leading politicians. Politics is not just about communication – even in the age of mediatized politics.

References

Aarts, K. and Semetko, H. (2000) 'The Divided Electorate: Effects of the Campaign and Media Use on Political Involvement', paper presented at the ECPR joint sessions of workshops, University of Copenhagen.

Abramson, J., Arterton, C. and Orren, G. R. (1988) *The Electronic Commonwealth*, Cambridge, MA: Harvard University Press.

Ainsworth, L. and Weston, D. (1995) 'Newspapers and UK Media Ownership Controls', *Tolley's Journal of Media Law and Practice*, 16/1: 2–9.

Aitken, I. (1991) 'A Trumpet Call from Number Ten', *British Journalism Review*, 2/4: 53–6.

Allen, R. (1998) 'This is not Television . . .', in J. Steemers (ed.), *Changing Channels: The Prospects for Television in a Digital World*, Luton: University of Luton Press.

Altheide, D. L. and Snow, R. P. (1979) *Media Logic*, London: Sage.

Altman, W., Thomas, D. and Sawers, D. (1962) *TV: From Monopoly to Competition – and Back?*, London: Institute of Economic Affairs.

Anderson, A. (1997) *Media, Culture and the Environment*, London: UCL Press.

Anderson, P. J. and Weymouth, A. (1999) *Insulting the Public? The British Press and the European Union*, London: Longman.

Annan Report (1977) *Report of the Committee on the Future of Broadcasting*, Cm 6753, London: HMSO.

Baisnée, O. (2002) 'Can Political Journalism Exist at the EU level?', in R. Kuhn and E. Neveu (eds), *Political Journalism: New Challenges, New Practices*, London: Routledge.

Ballinger, C. (2002) 'The Local Battle, the Cyber Battle', in D. Butler and D. Kavanagh (eds), *The British General Election of 2001*, Basingstoke: Palgrave.

Barnett, S. (1998) 'Dumbed Down or Reaching Out: Is it Tabloidisation wot done it?', in J. Seaton (ed.), *Politics and the Media: Harlots and Prerogatives at the Turn of the Millennium*, Oxford: Blackwell Publishers.

Barnett, S. (2001) 'Half-baked Plans for Broadcasting', *British Journalism Review*, 12/1: 64–8.

Barnett, S. (2004) 'Which End of the Telescope? From Market Failure to Cultural Value', in D. Tambini and J. Cowling (eds), *From Public Service Broadcasting to Public Service Communications*, London: Institute for Public Policy Research.

Barnett, S. and Curry, A. (1994) *The Battle for the BBC*, London: Aurum Press.

Barnett, S. and Gaber, I. (2001) *Westminster Tales: The Twenty-first-century Crisis in Political Journalism*, London: Continuum.

Bartle, J. (2005) 'The Press, Television and the Internet', *Parliamentary Affairs*, 58/4: 699–711.

Barwise, P. (2004) 'What are the Real Threats to Public Service Broadcasting?', in D. Tambini and J. Cowling (eds), *From Public Service Broadcasting to Public Service Communications*, London: Institute for Public Policy Research.

BBC (2005) *Review of the BBC's Royal Charter: BBC response to 'A Strong BBC, Independent of Government'*, London: BBC.

Bennie, L. G. (1998) 'Brent Spar, Atlantic Oil and Greenpeace', *Parliamentary Affairs*, 51/3: 397–410.

Bergg, D. (2004) 'Taking a Horse to Water? Delivering Public Service Broadcasting in a Digital Universe', in D. Tambini and J. Cowling (eds), *From Public Service Broadcasting to Public Service Communications*, London: Institute for Public Policy Research.

Berry, D. (2005) 'News Shouldn't be a Free Ride', *British Journalism Review*, 16/2: 55–9.

Beveridge Report (1951) *Report of the Broadcasting Committee, 1949*, Cm 8116, London: HMSO.

Bevins, A. (1990) 'The Crippling of the Scribes', *British Journalism Review*, 1/2: 13–17.

Birkinshaw, P. and Parkin, A. (1999) 'Freedom of Information', in R. Blackburn and R. Plant (eds), *Constitutional Reform: The Labour Government's Constitutional Reform Agenda*, London: Longman.

Blanchard, S. and Morley, D. (eds) (1982) *What's this Channel Four?*, London: Comedia.

Blumler, J. G. (ed.) (1992) *Television and the Public Interest*, London: Sage.

Blumler, J. G. (1999) 'Political Communication Systems All Change: A Response to Kees Brants', *European Journal of Communication*, 14: 241–9.

Blumler, J. G. and Gurevitch, M. (1995) *The Crisis of Public Communication*, London: Routledge.

Blumler, J. G. and Gurevitch, M. (2001) '"Americanization" Reconsidered: UK–US Campaign Communication Comparisons Across Time', in W. L. Bennett and R. M. Entman (eds), *Mediated Politics*, Cambridge: Cambridge University Press.

Blumler, J. G., Kavanagh, D. and Nossiter, T. J. (1996) 'Modern Communications versus Traditional Politics in Britain: Unstable Marriage of Convenience', in D. L. Swanson and P. Mancini (eds), *Politics, Media, and Modern Democracy*, Westport, CT: Praeger.

Blumler, J. G. and McQuail, D. (1968) *Television in Politics*, London: Faber.

Bolton, R. (1990) *Death on the Rock and Other Stories*, London: W. H. Allen.

Boorstin, D. J. (1961) *The Image*, New York: Athenaeum.

Boyd-Barrett, O. (1980) *The International News Agencies*, London: Constable.

Boyd-Barrett, O. (1995) 'The Political Economy Approach', in O. Boyd-Barrett and C. Newbold (eds), *Approaches to Media*, London: Arnold.

Boyd-Barrett, O. (1999) 'Trends in World Communication', *Global Dialogue*, 1/1: 56–69.

Boyd-Barrett, O. and Newbold, C. (eds) (1995), *Approaches to Media*, London: Arnold.

Brants, K. (1998) 'Who's Afraid of Infotainment?', *European Journal of Communication*, 13: 315–35.

Briggs, A, (1961) *The Birth of Broadcasting*, Oxford: Oxford University Press.

Brittan, S. (1987) 'The Fight for Freedom in Broadcasting', *The Political Quarterly*, 58: 3–23.

Brittan, S. (1989) 'The Case for the Consumer Market', in C. Veljanovski (ed.), *Freedom in Broadcasting*, London: Institute of Economic Affairs.

Broadcasting Research Unit (1985) *The Public Service Idea in British Broadcasting*, London: Broadcasting Research Unit.

Bromley, M. (1998) 'The "Tabloiding" of Britain: "Quality" Newspapers in the 1990s', in H. Stephenson and M. Bromley (eds) *Sex, Lies and Democracy*, London: Longman.

Budge, I. and Farlie, D. (1983) *Explaining and Predicting Elections*, London: Allen & Unwin.

Burrell, I. (2004) 'Watching with Tessa', *The Independent (Review)*, 2 March.

Butler, D. and Kavanagh, D. (1992) *The British General Election of 1992*, Basingstoke: Macmillan.

Butler, D. and Kavanagh, D. (1997) *The British General Election of 1997*, Basingstoke: Macmillan.

Butler, D. and Kavanagh, D. (2002) *The British General Election of 2001*, Basingstoke: Palgrave.

Calcutt Report (1990) *Report of the Committee on Privacy and Related Matters*, Cm 1102, London: HMSO.

Calcutt Report (1993) *Review of Press Self-Regulation*, Cm 2135, London: HMSO.

Campbell, V. (2004) *Information Age Journalism*, London: Arnold.

Chadwick, A. (2006) *Internet Politics*, Oxford: Oxford University Press.

Chippindale, P. and Franks, S. (1991) *Dished! The Rise and Fall of British Satellite Broadcasting*, London: Simon & Schuster.

Chippindale, P. and Horrie, C. (1988) *Disaster! The Rise and Fall of 'News on Sunday'*, London: Sphere.

Cloonan, M. (1998) 'Privacy and Media Intrusion in a Democratic Society: Britain and the Calcutt Reports', *Democratization*, 5/2: 62–84.

Cockerell, M. (1988) *Live from Number 10: The Inside Story of Prime Ministers and Television*, London: Faber & Faber.

Cockerell, M., Hennessy, P. and Walker, D. (1984) *Sources Close to the Prime Minister*, London: Macmillan.

Cohen, N. (2000) *Cruel Britannia*, London: Verso.

Coleman, S. (2001) 'Online Campaigning', *Parliamentary Affairs*, 54: 679–88.

Coleman, S. (2004) 'From Service to Commons: Re-inventing a Space for Public Communication', in D. Tambini and J. Cowling (eds), *From Public Service Broadcasting to Public Service Communications*, London: Institute for Public Policy Research.

Collins, R. (1993) *Audiovisual and Broadcasting Policy in the European Community*, London: University of North London Press.

Collins, R. (1994) *Broadcasting and Audio-Visual Policy in the European Single Market*, London: John Libbey.

Collins, R. (2004) 'Public Service Broadcasting: Too Much of a Good Thing?', in D. Tambini and J. Cowling (eds), *From Public Service Broadcasting to Public Service Communications*, London: Institute for Public Policy Research.

Collins, R. and Murroni, C. (1996) *New Media, New Policies*, Cambridge: Polity Press.

Commission of the European Communities (1992) *Pluralism and Media Concentration in the Internal Market – An Assessment of the Need for Community Action*, COM 92 480 final, Brussels: European Commission.

Commission of the European Communities (1994) *Follow-up to the Consultation Process relating to the Green Paper on 'Pluralism and Media Concentration in the Internal Market – An Assessment of the Need for Community Action'*, COM 94 353 final, Brussels: European Commission.

Congdon, T. (1995) 'The Multimedia Revolution and the Open Society', in T. Congdon, A. Graham, D. Green and B. Robinson, *The Cross Media Revolution: Ownership and Control*, London: John Libbey.

Corfield, I. (1999) 'Broadcasting and the Socially Excluded', in A. Graham *et al.*, *Public Purposes in Broadcasting: Funding the BBC*, Luton: University of Luton Press.

Corner, J., Harvey, S. and Lury, K. (1994) 'Culture, Quality and Choice: the Re-regulation of TV 1989–91', in S. Hood (ed.), *Behind the Screens: the Structure of British Broadcasting in the 1990s*, London: Lawrence & Wishart.

Cottle, S. (2003) 'News, Public Relations and Power: Mapping the Field', in S. Cottle (ed.), *News, Public Relations and Power*, London: Sage.

Cowling, J. (2004) 'From Princes to Paupers: The Future for Advertising-funded Public Service Television', in D. Tambini and J. Cowling (eds), *From Public Service Broadcasting to Public Service Communications*, London: Institute for Public Policy Research.

Crewe, I. (2005) 'The Opinion Polls: The Election They Got (Almost) Right', *Parliamentary Affairs*, 58/4: 684–98.

Cuilenburg, J. van and Slaa, P. (1993) 'From Media Policy towards a National Communications Policy: Broadening the Scope', *European Journal of Communication*, 8: 149–76.

Curran, J. (1996, 2nd edition) 'Mass Media and Democracy Revisited', in J. Curran and M. Gurevitch (eds), *Mass Media and Society*, London: Arnold.

Curran, J., Gaber, I. and Petley, J. (2005) *Culture Wars: The Media and the British Left*, Edinburgh: Edinburgh University Press.

Curran, J. and Seaton, J. (1991, 4th edition) *Power without Responsibility*, London: Routledge.

Curran, J. and Seaton, J. (1997, 5th edition) *Power without Responsibility*, London: Routledge.

Currie, D. and Siner, M. (1999) 'The BBC: Balancing Public and Commercial Purpose', in A. Graham *et al.*, *Public Purposes in Broadcasting: Funding the BBC*, Luton: University of Luton Press.

Curtice, J. (1997) 'Is the *Sun* Shining on Tony Blair? The Electoral Influence of British Newspapers', *Harvard International Journal of Press/Politics*, 2/2: 9–26.

Curtice, J. and Semetko, H. (1994) 'Does it Matter What the Papers Say?', in A. Heath, R. Jowell and J. Curtice with B. Taylor (eds), *Labour's Last Chance: The 1992 Election and Beyond*, Aldershot: Dartmouth.

Curtis, L. and Jempson, M. (1993) *Interference on the Airwaves*, London: Campaign for Press and Broadcasting Freedom.

Davidson, A. (1992) *Under the Hammer*, London: Heinemann.

Davies, G. (2004) *The BBC and Public Value*, London: Social Market Foundation.

Davis, A. (2002) *Public Relations Democracy: Public Relations, Politics and the Mass Media in Britain*, Manchester: Manchester University Press.

DCMS (2005) *Review of the BBC's Royal Charter: A Strong BBC, Independent of Government*, PP789, London.

De Bens, E. and Østbye, H. (1998) 'The European Newspaper Market', in D. McQuail and K. Siune (eds), *Media Policy: Convergence, Concentration and Commerce*, London: Sage.

Deacon, D. (1996) 'The Voluntary Sector in a Changing Communication Environment: A Case Study of Non-official News Sources', *European Journal of Communication*, 11/2: 173–99.

Deacon, D. (2004) 'Politicians, Privacy and Media Intrusion in Britain', *Parliamentary Affairs*, 57/1: 9–23.

Deacon, D. and Golding, P. (1994) *Taxation and Representation: The Media, Political Communication and the Poll Tax*, London: John Libbey.

Deacon, D., Golding, P. and Billig, M. (1998) 'Between Fear and Loathing: National Press Coverage of the 1997 British General Election', in D.

288   *References*

Denver, J. Fisher, P. Cowley and C. Pattie (eds), *British Elections and Parties Review, Volume 8, The 1997 General Election*, London: Frank Cass.

Deacon, D., Golding, P. and Billig, M. (2001) 'Press and Broadcasting: "Real Issues" and Real Coverage', *Parliamentary Affairs*, 54: 666–78.

Dearing, J. W. and Rogers, E. M. (1996) *Agenda-setting*, Thousand Oaks, CA: Sage.

Denver, D. (1994, 2nd edition) *Elections and Voting Behaviour in Britain*, London: Harvester Wheatsheaf.

Denver, D. (2003) *Elections and Voters in Britain*, Basingstoke: Palgrave Macmillan.

Department of National Heritage (1992) *The Future of the BBC*, Cm 2098, London: HMSO.

Department of National Heritage (1994) *The Future of the BBC*, Cm 2621, London: HMSO.

Department of National Heritage (1995a) *Media Ownership*, Cm 2872, London: HMSO.

Department of National Heritage (1995b) *Privacy and Media Intrusion*, Cm 2918, London: HMSO.

Doig, A. (2005) '45 Minutes of Infamy? Hutton, Blair and the Invasion of Iraq', *Parliamentary Affairs*, 58/1: 109–23.

Doornaert, M. and Omdal, S. E. (1989) *Press Freedom under attack in Britain*, Brussels: International Federation of Journalists.

Downing, J. (1986) 'Government Secrecy and the Media in the United States and Britain', in P. Golding, G. Murdock and P. Schlesinger (eds), *Communicating Politics*, Leicester: Leicester University Press.

Downs, A. (1972) 'Up and Down with Ecology: The Issue Attention Cycle', *Public Interest*, 28: 38–50.

Doyle, G. (1999) 'Convergence: "A Unique Opportunity to Evolve in Previously Unthought-of-ways" or a Hoax?', in C. Marsden and S. Verhulst (eds), *Convergence in European Digital TV Regulation*, London: Blackstone.

Doyle, G. (2002) *Media Ownership*, London: Sage.

DTI/DCMS (1998) *Regulating Communications: Approaching Convergence in the Information Age*, Cm 4022, London: HMSO.

DTI/DCMS (2000) *A New Future for Communications*, Cm 5010, London: HMSO.

DTI/DCMS (2002) *The Draft Communications Bill*, Cm 5508, London: HMSO.

Dyer, C. (2000) 'Four Threats to the Public's Right to Know', *The Guardian*, 22 May.

Dyke, G. (2004) *Inside Story*, London, HarperCollins.

Eldridge, J. (ed.) (1993) *Getting the Message: News, Truth and Power*, London: Routledge.

Ericson, R. V., Baranek, P. M. and Chan, J. B. L. (1989) *Negotiating Control: A Study of News Sources*, Milton Keynes: Open University Press.

Esser, F., Reinemann, C. and Fan, D. (2000) 'Spin Doctoring in British and German Election Campaigns', *European Journal of Communication*, 15/2: 209–39.

Ewing, K. D. and Gearty, C.A. (1990) *Freedom Under Thatcher*, Oxford: Clarendon Press.

Evans, H. (1983) *Good Times, Bad Times*, London: Weidenfeld & Nicolson.

Fairbairn, C. (2004) 'Commentary: Why Broadcasting is still Special', in A. Peacock, *Public Service Broadcasting without the BBC?*, London: Institute of Economic Affairs.

Fairclough, N. (2000) *New Labour, New Language?*, London: Routledge.

Fairweather, B. and Rogerson, S. (2003) 'Internet Voting – Well at Least It's Modern', *Representation*, 39/3, 182–95.

Feintuck, M. (1999) *Media Regulation, Public Interest and the Law*, Edinburgh: Edinburgh University Press.

Finlayson, A. (2002) 'Elements of the Blairite Image of Leadership', *Parliamentary Affairs*, 55: 586–99.

Fishman, M. (1980) *Manufacturing the News*, Austin: University of Texas Press.

Foley, M. (2000) *The British Presidency*, Manchester: Manchester University Press.

Foley, M. (2002) *John Major, Tony Blair and a Conflict of Leadership*, Manchester: Manchester University Press.

Fowler, R. (1991) *Language in the News*, London: Routledge.

Franklin, B. (1994) *Packaging Politics*, London: Edward Arnold.

Franklin, B. (1995) 'Taming An Unruly Leviathan: Regulating Tabloid Journalism', paper presented to the conference on *The Press in Europe – Past, Present and Future*, City University: London.

Franklin, B. (1997) *Newszak and News Media*, London: Arnold.

Franklin, B. (2001a) *British Television Policy: A Reader*, London: Routledge.

Franklin, B. (2001b) 'The Hand of History: New Labour, News Management and Governance', in S. Ludlam and M. J. Smith (eds) *New Labour in Government*, Basingstoke: Macmillan.

Franklin, B. and Murphy, D. (1991) *What News? The Market, Politics and the Local Press*, London: Routledge.

Gaber, I. (2000) 'Lies, Damn Lies . . . and Political Spin', *British Journalism Review*, 11/1: 60–70.

Gaber, I. (2002) 'A History of the Concept of Public Service Broadcasting', in P. Collins (ed.), *Culture or Anarchy? The Future of Public Service Broadcasting*, London: Social Market Foundation.

Gaber, I. (2003) 'Going from Bad to Worse: Why Phillis (and the Government) have got it Wrong', paper presented at the conference 'Can Vote, Won't Vote: Are the Media to Blame for Political Disengagement', Goldsmiths College London, 6 November.

Galtung, J. and Ruge, M. H. (1965) 'The Structure of Foreign News', *Journal of International Peace Research*, 1: 64–90.

Gamble, A. (1988) *The Free Economy and the Strong State: the Politics of Thatcherism*, Basingstoke: Macmillan.

Gandy, O. (1982) *Beyond Agenda Setting: Information Subsidies and Public Policy*, Norwood, NJ: Ablex.

Gans, H. J. (1980) *Deciding What's News*, Constable: London.

Garnham, N. (1980) *Structures of Television*, London: British Film Institute.

Garnham, N. (1992) 'The Media and the Public Sphere', in C. Calhoun (ed.), *Habermas and the Public Sphere*, Cambridge, MA: MIT Press.

Gavin, N. and Sanders, D. (2003) 'The Press and Its Influence on British Political Attitudes under New Labour', *Political Studies*, 51: 573–91.

Gibbons, T. (1998a, 2nd edition) *Regulating the Media*, London: Sweet & Maxwell.

Gibbons, T. (1998b) 'De/Re-Regulating the System: The British Experience', in J. Steemers (ed.), *Changing Channels: The Prospects for Television in a Digital World*, Luton: University of Luton Press.

Gibbons, T. (1999) 'Concentrations of Ownership and Control in a Converging Media Industry', in C. Marsden and S. Verhulst (eds), *Convergence in European Digital TV Regulation*, London: Blackstone.

Gibson, R. and Römmele, A. (2005) 'Truth and Consequence in Web Campaigning: Is There an Academic Digital Divide?', *European Political Science*, 4/3: 273–87.

Gibson, R. and Ward, S. (1998) 'UK Political Parties and the Internet: "Politics as Usual" in the New Media?', *Press/Politics*, 3/3: 14–38.

Gibson, R., Ward, S. and Lusoli, W. (2003) 'The Internet and Political Campaigning: The New Medium Comes of Age?', *Representation*, 39/3, 166–80.

Gilmour, I. (1992) *Dancing with Dogma*, London: Simon & Schuster.

Glasgow University Media Group (1976) *Bad News*, London: Routledge & Kegan Paul.

Glasgow University Media Group (1980) *More Bad News*, London: Routledge & Kegan Paul.

Glasgow University Media Group (1982) *Really Bad News*, London: Writers and Readers.

Glasgow University Media Group (1985) *War and Peace News*, Milton Keynes: Open University Press.

Glees, A. (2005) 'Evidence-Based Policy or Policy-Based Evidence? Hutton and the Government's Use of Secret Intelligence', *Parliamentary Affairs*, 58/1: 138–55.

Goddard, P., Scammell, M. and Semetko, H. (1998) 'Too Much of a Good Thing? Television in the 1997 Election Campaign', in I. Crewe, B. Gosschalk and J. Bartle (eds), *Political Communications: Why Labour Won the General Election of 1997*, London: Frank Cass.

Goldberg, D., Prosser, T. and Verhulst, S. (1998) *EC Media Law and Policy*, London: Longman.

Golding, P., Billig, M., Deacon, D. and Middleton, S. (1992) 'Two Shows for the Price of One', *British Journalism Review*, 3/2: 6–10.

Golding, P. and Elliott, P. (1979) *Making the News*, London: Longman.

Golding, P. and Murdock, G. (1991) 'Culture, Communications, and Political Economy', in J. Curran and M. Gurevitch (eds) *Mass Media and Society*, London: Edward Arnold.

Goodman, G. (1990) 'A Moment for Truth', *British Journalism Review*, 2/2: 3–5.

Goodwin, P. (1998) *Television under the Tories: Broadcasting Policy 1979–1997*, London: BFI.

Graham, A. (1999) 'Broadcasting Policy in the Multimedia Age', in A. Graham, *Public Purposes in Broadcasting: Funding the BBC*, Luton: University of Luton Press.

Graham, A. and Davies, G. (1997) *Broadcasting, Society and Policy in the Multimedia Age*, Luton: University of Luton Press.

Grant, W. (1989) *Pressure Groups, Politics and Democracy in Britain*, Hemel Hempstead: Philip Allan.

Green, D. (1995) 'Preserving Plurality in a Digital World', in T. Congdon, A. Graham, D. Green and B. Robinson, *The Cross Media Revolution: Ownership and Control*, London: John Libbey.

Greenslade, R. (2004) *Press Gang: How Newspapers Make Profits From Propaganda*, London: Pan Books.

Gunter, B., Svennevig, M. and Wober, M. (1986) *Television Coverage of the 1983 General Election*, Aldershot: Gower.

Habermas, J. ([1962] 1989) *The Structural Transformation of the Public Sphere*, Polity: Cambridge.

Hagerty, B. (2000) 'Cap'n Spin *Does* Lose his Rag', *British Journalism Review*, 11/2: 7–20.

Hall, S. (1992) 'Encoding/decoding', in S. Hall, D. Hobson, A. Lowe and P. Willis (eds) *Culture, Media, Language*, London: Routledge.

Hall, S., Critcher, C., Jefferson, T., Clarke, J. and Roberts, B. (1978) *Policing the Crisis*, London: Macmillan.

Hallin, D. C. (1986) *The 'Uncensored War'*, Oxford: Oxford University Press.

Hallin, D. C. and Mancini, P. (2004) *Comparing Media Systems*, Cambridge: Cambridge University Press.

Hansen, A. (1993) 'Greenpeace and Press Coverage of Environmental Issues', in A. Hansen (ed.), *The Mass Media and Environmental Issues*, Leicester: Leicester University Press.

Harcourt, A. (2005) *The European Union and the Regulation of Media Markets*, Manchester: Manchester University Press.

Harding, L., Leigh, D. and Pallister, D. (1997) *The Liar*, Harmondsworth: Penguin.

Hargreaves. I. (2003) *Journalism: Truth or Dare?*, Oxford: Oxford University Press.

Harris, R. (1983) *Gotcha! The Media, the Government and the Falklands Crisis*, London: Faber & Faber.

Harris, R. (1990) *Good and Faithful Servant*, London: Faber & Faber.

Harrison, J. (2000) *Terrestrial TV News in Britain*, Manchester: Manchester University Press.

Harrison, M. (1985) *TV News: Whose Bias?*, Hermitage: Policy Journals.

Harrison, M. (1992) 'Politics on the Air', in D. Butler and D. Kavanagh, *The British General Election of 1992*, Basingstoke: Macmillan.

Harrison, M. (1997) 'Politics on the Air', in D. Butler and D. Kavanagh, *The British General Election of 1997*, Basingstoke: Macmillan.

Harrison, M. (2002) 'Politics on the Air', in D. Butler and D. Kavanagh, *The British General Election of 2001*, Basingstoke: Palgrave.

Harrison, M. (2005) 'On Air', in D. Kavanagh and D. Butler, *The British General Election of 2005*, Basingstoke: Palgrave.

Harrop, M. and Scammell, M. (1992) 'A Tabloid War', in D. Butler and D. Kavanagh, *The British General Election of 1992*, Basingstoke: Macmillan.

Hearst, S. (1992) 'Broadcasting Regulation in Britain', in J. G. Blumler (ed.), *Television and the Public Interest*, London: Sage.

Heffernan, R. and Marqusee, M. (1992) *Defeat from the Jaws of Victory*, London: Verso.

Held, D. and McGrew, A. (eds) (2000) *The Global Transformations Reader*, Cambridge: Polity.

Hennessy, P. (2000) *The Prime Minister*, London: Allen Lane.

Herman, E. S. (1986) 'Gatekeeper versus Propaganda Models: A Critical American Perspective', in P. Golding, G. Murdock and P. Schlesinger (eds), *Communicating Politics*, Leicester: Leicester University Press.

Herman, E. S. and Chomsky, N. (1988) *Manufacturing Consent*, New York: Pantheon Books.

Herman, E. S. and McChesney, R. W. (1997) *The Global Media*, London: Cassell.

Hetherington, A. (1985) *News, Newspapers and Television*, London: Macmillan.

Hetherington, A. (1989) *News in the Regions*, Basingstoke: Macmillan.

Hirsch, F. and Gordon, D. (1975) *Newspaper Money*, London: Hutchinson.

Hollingsworth, M. (1986) *The Press and Political Dissent*, London: Pluto Press.

Hollins, T. (1984) *Beyond Broadcasting into the Cable Age*, London: British Film Institute.

Home Office (1988) *Broadcasting in the '90s: Competition, Choice and Quality*, Cm 517, London: HMSO.

House of Commons Culture, Media and Sport Committee (2003) *Privacy and Media Intrusion*, HC 458-1, London: The Stationery Office.

House of Commons Select Committee on Public Administration (1998) *The Government Information and Communication Service*, HC 770, London: The Stationery Office.

http://www.e-envoy.gov.uk

http://www.number-10.gov.uk

http://www.ofcom.org.uk/consultations/current/psb/meaning/

http://www.the-hutton-inquiry.org.uk

http://www.ukonline.gov.uk

Hughes, C. and Wintour, P. (1990) *Labour Rebuilt*, London: Fourth Estate.

Humphreys, J. (2005) 'The Iraq Dossier and the Meaning of Spin', *Parliamentary Affairs*, 58/1: 156–70.

Humphreys, P. and Lang, M. (1998) 'Digital Television between the Economy and Pluralism', in J. Steemers (ed.), *Changing Channels: The Prospects for Television in a Digital World*, Luton: University of Luton Press.

Hutchison, D. (1999) *Media Policy*, Oxford: Blackwell.

Hutton, Lord (2004) *Report of the Inquiry into the Circumstances Surrounding the Death of Dr David Kelly C.M.G. by Lord Hutton*, HC 247, London: The Stationery Office.

Index on Censorship (1993) 22/8–9, September–October.

Ingham, B. (1991) *Kill the Messenger*, London: Fontana.

International Institute of Communications (1996) *Media Ownership and Control in the Age of Convergence*, London: International Institute of Communications.

Iosifidis, P., Steemers, J. and Wheeler, M. (2005) *European Television Industries*, London: British Film Institute.

Isaacs, J. (1989) *Storm over 4*, London: Weidenfeld & Nicolson.

Jay, P. (1994) 'The Economy 1990–94', in D. Kavanagh and A. Seldon (eds), *The Major Effect*, London: Macmillan.

Johnson, J. (1998) 'Rupert's Grip?', *British Journalism Review*, 9/1: 13–19.

Johnson, J. (1999) 'Second Most Powerful Man in Britain?', *British Journalism Review*, 10/4: 67–71.

Jones, N. (1986) *Strikes and the Media: Communication and Conflict*, Oxford: Blackwell.

Jones, N. (1995) *Soundbites & Spin Doctors*, London: Cassell.

Jones, N. (1999) *Sultans of Spin*, London: Victor Gollancz.

Jones, N. (2002) *The Control Freaks*, London: Politico's.

Katz, Y. (2000) 'The Diminishing Role of Governments in Cable Policy', *European Journal of Political Research*, 38: 285–302.

Kavanagh, D. (1995) *Election Campaigning: The New Marketing of Politics*, Oxford: Blackwell.

Kavanagh, D. and Butler, D. (2005) *The British General Election of 2005*, Basingstoke: Palgrave.

Kavanagh, D. and Morris, P. (1989) *Consensus Politics from Attlee to Thatcher*, Oxford: Basil Blackwell.

Kavanagh, D. and Seldon, A. (2000) *The Powers Behind the Prime Minister*, London: HarperCollins.

Kaye, R. P. (2005) ' "OfGov": A Commissioner for Government Conduct?', *Parliamentary Affairs*, 58/1: 171–88.

Keane, J. (1991) *The Media and Democracy*, Cambridge: Polity.

Keane, J. (1992) 'Democracy and the Media – Without Foundations', in D. Held (ed.), *Political Studies*, Special Issue: Prospects for Democracy, 116–29.

Kellner, P. (1992) 'Defeat – of the pollsters', *British Journalism Review*, 3/3: 5–11.

King, A. (1998) 'Thatcherism and the Emergence of Sky Television', *Media, Culture & Society*, 20: 277–93.

King, A. (ed.) (2002) *Leaders' Personalities and the Outcomes of Democratic Elections*, Oxford: Oxford University Press.

Klein, N. (2000) *No Logo*, London: Flamingo.

Koss, S. (1990) *The Rise and Fall of the Political Press in Britain*, London: Fontana.

Lambert, S. (1982) *Channel Four*, London: British Film Institute.

Leam, D. (2002) 'The Regulatory Framework for Public Service Broadcasting in the UK', in P. Collins (ed.), *Culture or Anarchy? The Future of Public Service Broadcasting*, London: Social Market Foundation.

Leapman, M. (1999) 'A Decade of Withered Hopes', *British Journalism Review*, 10/4: 18–25.

Lees-Marshment, J. (2001) *Political Marketing and British Political Parties: The Party's Just Begun*, Manchester: Manchester University Press.

Le Grand, J. and New, B. (1999) 'Broadcasting and Public Purposes in the New Millennium', in A. Graham *et al.*, *Public Purposes in Broadcasting: Funding the BBC*, Luton: University of Luton Press.

Lewis, J. and Brookes, R. (2004) 'Reporting the War on British Television', in D. Miller (ed.) *Tell Me Lies: Propaganda and Media Distortion in the Attack on Iraq*, London: Pluto Press.

Levy, D. (1999) *Europe's Digital Revolution*, London: Routledge.

Lichtenberg, J. (2000) 'In Defence of Objectivity Revisited', in J. Curran and M. Gurevitch (eds) *Mass Media and Society*, London: Edward Arnold.

Lipsey, D. (2002) 'In Defence of Public Service Broadcasting', in P. Collins (ed.), *Culture or Anarchy? The Future of Public Service Broadcasting*, London: Social Market Foundation.

Livingstone, S. and Lunt, P. (1994) *Talk on Television*, London: Routledge.

Lloyd, J. (2004) *What the Media Are Doing to Our Politics*, London: Constable.

MacArthur, B. (2000) 'Watch out Tony, the Worm is Turning', *The Times*, 28 January.

McCombs, M. E. and Shaw, D. L. (1972) 'The Agenda-setting Function of Mass Media', *Public Opinion Quarterly*, 36: 176–84.

McCurry, M. (1996) 'The Background on Background', *Harvard International Journal of Press/Politics*, 1/4: 4–9.

McGinniss, J. (1969) *The Selling of the President 1968*, New York: Simon & Schuster.

MacInnes, J. (1992) 'The Press in Scotland', *Scottish Affairs*, 1: 137–49.

McIntyre, I. (1993) *The Expense of Glory*, London: HarperCollins.

McKie, D. (1998) 'Swingers, Clingers, Waverers, Quaverers: The Tabloid Press in the 1997 General Election', in I. Crewe, B. Gosschalk and J. Bartle (eds), *Political Communications: Why Labour Won the General Election of 1997*, London: Frank Cass.

McLachlan, S. and Golding, P. (2000) 'Tabloidization in the British Press: A Quantitative Investigation into Changes in British Newspapers, 1952–1997', in C. Sparks and J. Tulloch (eds), *Tabloid Tales*, Lanham, Maryland: Rowman & Littlefield.

McLaughlin, G. and Miller, D. (1996) 'The Media Politics of the Irish Peace Process', *Harvard International Journal of Press/Politics*, 1/4: 116–34.

McLeod, R. (1998) 'Calf Exports at Brightlingsea', *Parliamentary Affairs*, 51: 345–57.

McNair, B. (1996, 2nd edition) *News and Journalism in the UK*, London: Routledge.

McNair, B. (2000) *Journalism and Democracy*, London: Routledge.

McNair, B. (2003, 3rd edition) *An Introduction to Political Communication*, London: Routledge.

McQuail, D. (1992) *Media Performance*, London: Sage.

McQuail, D. (1995) 'Western European Media: The Mixed Model under Threat', in J. Downing, A. Mohammadi and A. Sreberny-Mohammadi (eds), *Questioning the Media*, London: Sage.

McQuail, D. (2000, 4th edition) *McQuail's Mass Communication Theory*, London: Sage.

Manning, P. (1998) *Spinning for Labour: Trade Unions and the New Media Environment*, Aldershot: Ashgate.

Manning, P. (1999) 'Categories of Knowledge and Information Flows: Reasons for the Decline of the British Labour and Industrial Correspondents' Group', *Media, Culture and Society*, 21: 313–36.

Manning, P. (2001) *News and News Sources: A Critical Introduction*, London: Sage.

Marr, A. (2004) *My Trade: A Short History of British Journalism*, London: Macmillan.

Meech, P. (1990) 'The British Media: Structures in Transition', *Innovation*, 3/2: 227–51.

Meier, W. A. and Trappel, J. (1998) 'Media Concentration and the Public Interest', in D. McQuail and K. Siune (eds), *Media Policy: Convergence, Concentration and Commerce*, London: Sage.

Michalis, M. (1999) 'European Union Broadcasting and Telecoms: Towards a Convergent Regulatory Regime?', *European Journal of Communication*, 14/2: 147–71.

Miller, D. (1993) 'Official Sources and "Primary Definition": The Case of Northern Ireland', *Media, Culture and Society*, 15: 385–406.

Miller, D. (1994) *Don't Mention the War: Northern Ireland, Propaganda and the Media*, London: Pluto Press.

Miller, W. (1991) *Media and Voters*, Oxford: Oxford University Press.

Morgan, D. (1991) 'Media-Government Relations: The Right to Manage Information versus The Right to Know', *Parliamentary Affairs*, 44/4: 531–40.

Morrison, D. (1992) *Television and the Gulf War*, London, John Libbey.

Morrison, D. and Tumber, H. (1988) *Journalists at War*, London: Sage.

Murdock, G. (2000) 'Digital Futures: European Television in the Age of Convergence', in J. Wieten, G. Murdock and P. Dahlgren (eds), *Television Across Europe*, London: Sage.

Murschetz, P. (1998) 'State Support for the Daily Press in Europe: A Critical Appraisal', *European Journal of Communication*, 13/3: 291–313.

National Heritage Select Committee (1993) *Privacy and Media Intrusion*, Ref. 294-I, London: HMSO.

Needham, C. (2005) 'Brand Leaders: Clinton, Blair and the Limitations of the Permanent Campaign', *Political Studies*, 53: 343–61.

Negrine, R. (ed.) (1988) *Satellite Broadcasting: The Politics and Implications of the New Media*, London: Routledge.

Negrine, R. (1989, 1st edition) *Politics and the Mass Media in Britain*, London: Routledge.

Negrine, R. (1990) 'British Television in an Age of Change', in K. Dyson and P. Humphreys (eds), *The Political Economy of Communications*, London: Routledge.

Negrine, R. (1994, 2nd edition) *Politics and the Mass Media in Britain*, London: Routledge.

Negrine, R. (1996) *The Communication of Politics*, London: Sage.

Negrine, R. (1998) *Television and the Press since 1945*, Manchester: Manchester University Press.

Negrine, R. and Papathanassopoulos, S. (1990) *The Internationalisation of Television*, London: Pinter.

Negrine, R. and Papathanassopoulos, S. (1996) ' "The Americanization" of Political Communication', *Harvard International Journal of Press/ Politics*, 1/2: 45–62.

Neil, A. (1997) *Full Disclosure*, London: Pan.

Neil Review (2004) *The BBC's Journalism after Hutton*, http://www.bbc.co.uk/info/policies

Newton, K. (1993) 'Caring and Competence: The Long, Long Campaign', in A. King, I. Crewe, D. Denver, K. Newton, P. Norton, D. Sanders and P. Seyd, *Britain at the Polls 1992*, Chatham, NJ: Chatham House Publishers.

Newton, K. (2001) 'The Transformation of Governance?', in B. Axford and R. Huggins (eds), *New Media and Politics*, London: Sage.

Newton, K. (2006) 'May the Weak Force be with You: The Power of the Mass Media in Modern Politics', *European Journal of Political Research*, 45: 209–34.

Newton, K. and Brynin, M. (2001) 'The National Press and Party Voting in the UK', *Political Studies*, 49: 265–84.

Norris, P. (1998) 'The Battle for the Campaign Agenda', in A. King, D. Denver, I McLean, P. Norris, P. Norton, D. Sanders and P. Seyd, *New Labour Triumphs: Britain at the Polls*, Chatham, NJ: Chatham House Publishers.

Norris, P. (2000a) 'The Internet in Europe: A New North–South Divide?', *Harvard International Journal of Press/Politics*, 5/1: 1–12.

Norris, P. (2000b) *A Virtuous Circle: Political Communications in Postindustrial Societies*, Cambridge: Cambridge University Press.

Norris, P., Curtice, J., Sanders, D., Scammell, M. and Semetko, H. (1999) *On Message: Communicating the Campaign*, London: Sage.

O'Malley, T. (1994) *Closedown? The BBC and Government Broadcasting Policy 1979–92*, London: Pluto.

O'Malley, T. (2001) 'The Decline of Public Service Broadcasting in the UK 1979–2000', in M. Bromley (ed.), *No News is Bad News*, Harlow: Longman.

O'Malley, T. and Soley, C. (2000) *Regulating the Press*, London: Pluto.

O'Shaughnessy, N. J. (2004) *Politics and Propaganda*, Manchester: Manchester University Press.

Oborne, P. (1999) *Alastair Campbell: New Labour and the Rise of the Media Class*, London: Aurum.

Oborne, P. and Walters, S. (2004) *Alastair Campbell*, London: Aurum.

Ofcom (2003) *Ofcom Review of Public Service Broadcasting*, London: Ofcom.

Ofcom (2005) *Viewers and Voters: Attitudes to Television Coverage of the 2005 General Election*, London: Ofcom.

Østergaard, B. S. (1998) 'Convergence: Legislative Dilemmas', in D. McQuail and K. Siune (eds), *Media Policy: Convergence, Concentration and Commerce*, London: Sage.

Palmer, J. (2000) *Spinning into Control: News Values and Source Strategies*, London: Leicester University Press.

Parsons, D. W. (1989) *The Power of the Financial Press*, Aldershot: Edward Elgar.

Peacock, A. (1989) 'The Future of Public Service Broadcasting', in C. Veljanovski (ed.), *Freedom in Broadcasting*, London: Institute of Economic Affairs.

Peacock, A. (1997) 'The Political Economy of Public Service Broadcasting', in A. Peacock, *The Political Economy of Economic Freedom*, Cheltenham: Edward Elgar.

Peacock, A. (2004) *Public Service Broadcasting without the BBC?*, London: Institute of Economic Affairs.

Peacock Report (1986) *Report of the Committee on Financing the BBC*, Cm 9824, London: HMSO.

Peak, S. (ed.) (1993) *The Media Guide 1994*, London: Fourth Estate.

Peak, S. and Fisher, P. (eds) (1995) *The Media Guide 1996*, London: Fourth Estate.

Peak, S. and Fisher, P. (eds) (2000) *The Guardian Media Guide 2001*, London: HarperCollins.

Phillis, B. (2004), *An Independent Review of Government Communications*, London: The Stationery Office. http://www.gcreview.gov.uk

Philo, G. (1987) 'Whose news?', *Media, Culture and Society*, 9: 397–406.

Philo, G. (1990) *Seeing and Believing*, London: Routledge.

Phythian, M. (2005) 'Hutton and Scott: A Tale of Two Inquiries', *Parliamentary Affairs*, 58/1: 124–37.

Pilkington Report (1962) *Report of the Committee on Broadcasting, 1960*, Cm 1753, London: HMSO.

Pimlott, B. (1992) *Harold Wilson*, London: HarperCollins.

Pratten, S. and Deakin, S. (2004) 'Commentary: The Scope of Public Service Broadcasting', in A. Peacock, *Public Service Broadcasting without the BBC?*, London: Institute of Economic Affairs.

Ramsden, J. (2006) *Don't Mention the War: The British and the Germans since 1890*, London: Little, Brown.

Rawnsley, A. (2000) *Servants of the People*, London: Hamish Hamilton.

Reith, J. (1949) *Into The Wind*, London: Hodder & Stoughton.

Riddell, P. (1992) 'Media Manipulation Much Exaggerated', *British Journalism Review*, 3/2: 11–16.

Riddell, P. (1998) 'Members and Millbank: the Media and Parliament', in J. Seaton (ed.), *Politics and the Media: Harlots and Prerogatives at the Turn of the Millennium*, Oxford: Blackwell.

Robinson, B. (1995) 'Market Share as a Measure of Media Concentration', in T. Congdon, A. Graham, D. Green and B. Robinson, *The Cross Media Revolution: Ownership and Control*, London: John Libbey.

Rogers, H. (1989) '*Spycatcher*: My Country Wright or Armstrong?', in N. Buchan and T. Sumner (eds), *Glasnost in Britain?*, Basingstoke: Macmillan.

Roschko, B. (1975) *Newsmaking*, Chicago: University of Chicago Press.

Rossiter, A. (2005) *News Broadcasting in the Digital Age*, London: Social Market Foundation.

Roth, A. (1999) 'The Lobby's "Dying Gasps"?', *British Journalism Review*, 10/3: 21–5.

Royal Commission on the Press 1947–1949 (1949) Cm 7700, London: HMSO.

Royal Commission on the Press (1977) Cm 6810, London: HMSO.

Rusbridger, A. (1997) *The Freedom of the Press, and Other Platitudes*, James Cameron Memorial Lecture, London: *The Guardian*.

Sabato, L. J. (1991) *Feeding Frenzy: How Attack Journalism Has Transformed American Politics*, New York: Free Press.

Sales, R. (1986) 'An Introduction to Broadcasting History', in D. Punter (ed.), *Introduction to Contemporary Cultural Studies*, London: Longman.

Sambrook, R, (2004), 'Tragedy in the Fog of War', *British Journalism Review*, 15/3: 7–13.

Scammell, M. (1995) *Designer Politics*, London: Macmillan.

Scammell, M. (1999) 'Political Marketing: Lessons for Political Science', *Political Studies*, 47/4: 718–39.

Scammell, M. (2001) 'The Media and Media Management', in A. Seldon (ed.), *The Blair Effect: The Blair Government 1997–2001*, London: Little, Brown.

Scammell, M. (2003) 'Towards a New Marketing of Politics?', in J. Corner and D. Pels (eds), *Media and the Restyling of Politics*, London: Sage.

Scammell, M. and Harrop, M. (1997) 'The Press', in D. Butler and D. Kavanagh, *The British General Election of 1997*, Basingstoke: Macmillan.

Scammell, M. and Harrop, M. (2002) 'The Press Disarmed', in D. Butler and D. Kavanagh, *The British General Election of 2001*, Basingstoke: Palgrave.

Scammell, M. and Harrop, M. (2005) 'The Press: Still for Labour, Despite Blair', in D. Kavanagh and D. Butler, *The British General Election of 2005*, Basingstoke: Palgrave.

Scannell, P. (1990) 'Public Service Broadcasting: The History of a Concept', in A. Goodwin and G. Whannel (eds), *Understanding Television*, London: Routledge.

Schlesinger, P. (1978) *Putting 'Reality' Together*, London: Constable.

Schlesinger, P. (1987) *Putting 'Reality' Together*, London: Methuen.

Schlesinger, P. (1990) 'Rethinking the Sociology of Journalism: Source Strategies and the Limits of Media-Centrism', in M. Ferguson (ed.) *Public Communication: The New Imperatives*, London: Sage.

Schlesinger, P. (1998) 'Scottish Devolution and the Media', in J. Seaton (ed.), *Politics and the Media: Harlots and Prerogatives at the Turn of the Millennium*, Oxford: Blackwell.

Schlesinger, P., Murdock, G. and Elliott, P. (1983) *Televising 'Terrorism'*, London: Comedia.

Schlesinger, P. and Tumber, H. (1994) *Reporting Crime*, Oxford: Clarendon Press.

Schudson, M. (1991) 'The Sociology of News Production Revisited', in J. Curran and M. Gurevitch (eds), *Mass Media and Society*, London: Edward Arnold.

Schudson, M. (1995) *The Power of News*, Cambridge, MA: Harvard University Press.

Schudson, M. (2000) 'The Sociology of New Production Revisited (Again)', in J. Curran and M. Gurevitch (eds) *Mass Media and Society*, London: Edward Arnold.

Scott, R. (1998) 'My Father Drowned. The Guardian's Independence was his Bequest', *The Guardian*, 24 November.

Seaton, J. (1994) 'Broadcasting in the Age of Market Ideology: Is it Possible to Underestimate the Public Taste?', *The Political Quarterly*, 65/1: 29–38.

Seldon, A. (1997) *Major: A Political Life*, London: Weidenfeld & Nicolson.

Semetko, H., Scammell, M. and Goddard, P. (1997) 'Television', in P. Norris and N. Gavin (eds), *Britain Votes 1997*, Oxford: Oxford University Press.

Semetko, H., de Vreese, C. H. and Peter, J. (2000) 'Europeanised Politics – Europeanised Media? European Integration and Political Communication', *West European Politics*, 3/4: 121–41.

Seymour-Ure, C. (1974) *The Political Impact of Mass Media*, London: Constable.

Seymour-Ure, C. (1992) 'Press Partisanship: Into the 1990s', in D. Kavanagh (ed.) *Electoral Politics*, Oxford: Clarendon Press.

Seymour-Ure, C. (1994) 'Mass Media', in D. Kavanagh and A. Seldon (eds), *The Major Effect*, London: Macmillan.

Seymour-Ure, C. (1996, 2nd edition) *The British Press and Broadcasting since 1945*, Oxford: Blackwell.

Seymour-Ure, C. (1997) 'Newspapers: Editorial Opinion in the National Press', in P. Norris and N. Gavin (eds), *Britain Votes 1997*, Oxford: Oxford University Press.

Seymour-Ure, C. (1998) 'Are the Broadsheets becoming Unhinged?', in J. Seaton (ed.), *Politics and the Media: Harlots and Prerogatives at the Turn of the Millennium*, Oxford: Blackwell.

Seymour-Ure, C. (2003) *Prime Ministers and the Media*, Oxford: Blackwell.

Shah, S. (2004) 'Planet Murdoch', *The Independent (Media Weekly)*, 18 October.

Shaw, E. (1994) *The Labour Party since 1979: Crisis and Transformation*, London: Routledge.

Silcock, R. (2001) 'What is e-Government?', *Parliamentary Affairs*, 54: 88–101.

Skogerbø, E. (1997) 'The Press Subsidy System in Norway', *European Journal of Communication*, 12/1: 99–118.

Smith, P. (1999) 'Political Communication in the UK: A Study of Pressure Group Behaviour', *Politics*, 19/1: 21–7.

Snoddy, R. (1992) *The Good, the Bad and the Unacceptable*, London: Faber & Faber.

Sparks, C. (1991) 'Goodbye Hildy Johnson: The Vanishing "Serious Press"', in P. Dahlgren and C. Sparks (eds), *Communication and Citizenship*, London: Routledge.

Sparks, C. (1995) 'Concentration and Market Entry in the UK National Daily Press', *European Journal of Communication*, 10/2: 179–206.

Sparks, C. and Tulloch, J. (eds) (2000) *Tabloid Tales*, Lanham, MD.: Rowman & Littlefield.

Stanyer, J. (2001) *The Creation of Political News*, Brighton: Sussex Academic Press.

Steemers, J. (1998) 'On the Threshold of the "Digital Age": Prospects for Public Service Broadcasting', in J. Steemers (ed.), *Changing Channels: The Prospects for Television in a Digital World*, Luton: University of Luton Press.

Steemers, J. (2004) *Selling Television*, London: British Film Institute.

Stephenson, H. (1994) *Media Freedom and Media Regulation*, London: Association of British Editors, the Guild of Editors and the International Press Institute.

Stephenson, H. (1998) 'Tickle the Public: Consumerism Rules', in H. Stephenson and M. Bromley (eds) *Sex, Lies and Democracy*, London: Longman.

Stephenson, H. and Bromley, M. (eds) (1998) *Sex, Lies and Democracy*, London: Longman.

Stevenson, N. (1995) *Understanding Media Cultures*, London: Sage.

Street, J. (2001) *Mass Media, Politics and Democracy*, Basingstoke: Palgrave.

Swanson, D. L. and Mancini, P. (eds) (1996) *Politics, Media, and Modern Democracy*, Westport, CT: Praeger.

Tait, R. (1998) 'The Debate that Never Happened: Television and the Party Leaders, 1997', in I. Crewe, B. Gosschalk and J. Bartle (eds), *Political Communications: Why Labour Won the General Election of 1997*, London: Frank Cass.

Tambini, D. (2004) 'The Passing of Paternalism: Public Service Television and Increasing Channel Choice', in D. Tambini and J. Cowling (eds), *From Public Service Broadcasting to Public Service Communications*, London: Institute for Public Policy Research.

Taylor, P. (1992) *War and the Media*, Manchester: Manchester University Press.

Thatcher, M. (1993) *The Downing Street Years*, London: HarperCollins.

Thompson, K. (1998) *Moral Panics*, London: Routledge.

Thomson, S., Stancich, L. and Dickson, L. (1998) 'Gun Control and Snowdrop', *Parliamentary Affairs*, 51: 329–44.

Thornton, P. (1987) *The Civil Liberties of the Zircon Affair*, London: National Council for Civil Liberties.

Tivey, L. (1973) *Nationalization in British Industry*, London: Jonathan Cape.

Tongue, C. (1999) 'Culture or Monoculture? The European Audiovisual Challenge', in C. Marsden and S. Verhulst (eds), *Convergence in European Digital TV Regulation*, London: Blackstone.

Tracey, M. (1998) *The Decline and Fall of Public Service Broadcasting*, Oxford: Oxford University Press.

Trenaman, J. and McQuail, D. (1961) *Television and the Political Image*, London: Methuen.

Truetzschler, W. (1998) 'The Internet: A New Mass Medium?', in D. McQuail and K. Siune (eds), *Media Policy: Convergence, Concentration and Commerce*, London: Sage.

Tuchman, G. (1972) 'Objectivity as Strategic Ritual: An Examination of Newsmen's Notions of Objectivity', *American Journal of Sociology*, 77/4: 660–79.

Tuchman, G. (1978) *Making News*, New York: Free Press.

Tumber, H. (1993) '"Selling Scandal": Business and the Media', *Media, Culture & Society*, 15/3: 345–61.

Tumber, H. (ed.) (1999) *News: A Reader*, Oxford: Oxford University Press.

Tumber, H. (2001) '10pm and All That: The Battle over UK TV news', in M. Bromley (ed.), *No News is Bad News*, Harlow: Longman.

Tumber, H. and Palmer, J. (2004) *Media at War: The Iraq Crisis*, London: Sage.

Tunstall, J. (1970) *The Westminster Lobby Correspondents*, London: Routledge & Kegan Paul.

Tunstall, J. (1971) *Journalists at Work*, London: Constable.

Tunstall, J. (1984) 'Media Policy Dilemmas and Indecisions', *Parliamentary Affairs*, 37/3: 310–26.

Tunstall, J. (1996) *Newspaper Power*, Oxford: Clarendon Press.

Tunstall, J. and Machin, D. (1999) *The Anglo-American Media Connection*, Oxford: Oxford University Press.

Ward, S. and Lusoli, W. (2003) 'Dinosaurs in Cyberspace? British Trade Unions and the Internet', *European Journal of Communication*, 18/2: 147–79.

Waters, M. (1995) *Globalization*, London: Routledge.

Wernick, A. (1991) *Promotional Culture*, London: Sage.

Wheeler, M. (1997) *Politics and the Mass Media*, Oxford: Blackwell.

White, D. M. (1950) 'The Gatekeeper', *Journalism Quarterly*, 27: 383–90.

Whiteley, P. (1997) 'The Conservative Campaign', in P. Norris and N. Gavin (eds), *Britain Votes 1997*, Oxford: Oxford University Press.

Whittam Smith, A. (1989) 'A New "Golden Age"?', *British Journalism Review*, 1/1: 19–21.

Wilkes, G. and Wring, D. (1998) 'The British Press and European Integration: 1948 to 1996', in D. Baker and D. Seawright (eds), *Britain For and Against Europe: British Politics and the Question of European Integration*, Oxford: Clarendon Press.

Williams, G. (2001) 'Outraged Onlookers or Influential Voices? The Role of Lobby and Pressure Groups in the UK and USA', in M. Bromley (ed.), *No News is Bad News*, Harlow: Longman.

Wilson, D. (1984) *Pressure: The A to Z of campaigning in Britain*, London: Heinemann.

Wilson, H. H. (1961) *Pressure Group: The Campaign for Commercial Television*, London: Secker & Warburg.

Windlesham, Lord and Rampton, R. (1989) *The Windlesham/Rampton Report on 'Death on the Rock'*, London: Faber & Faber.

Winseck, D. (1998) 'Pursuing the Holy Grail: Information Highways and Media Reconvergence in Britain and Canada', *European Journal of Communication*, 13: 337–74.

Wlezien, C. and Norris, P. (2005) 'Conclusion: Whether the Campaign Mattered and How', *Parliamentary Affairs*, 58/4: 871–88.

Wring, D. (2005a) *The Politics of Marketing the Labour Party*, Basingstoke: Palgrave Macmillan.

Wring, D. (2005b) 'The Labour Campaign', *Parliamentary Affairs*, 58/4: 712–24.

Index